FISHERMEN

FOR MY MOTHER

FISHERMEN

Sally Festing

DAVID & CHARLES

Newton Abbot   London   North Pomfret (Vt)   Vancouver

ISBN 0 7153 7448 6
Library of Congress Catalog Card Number: 77-89369

Set in 11 on 13pt Baskerville
and printed in Great Britain
by Redwood Burn Limited, Trowbridge & Esher
for David & Charles (Publishers) Limited
Brunel House   Newton Abbot   Devon

Published in the United States of America
by David & Charles Inc
North Pomfret   Vermont 05053   USA

Published in Canada
by Douglas David & Charles Limited
1875 Welch Street   North Vancouver   BC

CONTENTS

A FISHERMAN'S PRAYER

Pray God lead us,
Pray God speed us,
From all evil defend us,
Fish for our nation God send us:
Well to fish and well to haul,
And what He pleases to pay us all.
A fine night to land our nets,
And safe in with the land,
Pray God hear our prayer.

—Anon.

INTRODUCTION

The Lord is my pilot, I shall not drift,
He lighteth me across dark waters,
He steereth me in deep channels,
He keepeth my log,
He guideth me by the Star of Holiness,
Yea for his name's sake.
— *Fishermen's 23rd Psalm*

For generations fishermen have toiled all round the British coast. While their deep-sea brothers have gone to far-off fishing grounds, from the Scottish islands to Land's End, from Iceland to the Wash, the longshoremen in their little boats have worked their lines and shot their nets within sight of their homes. Many methods of catching fish have been employed and many different kinds of fish caught.

Now they have more sophisticated gear and techniques have improved, some of the catches are good. It is still possible to see a trawler unload a feast of shrimps at Wells and a large boat recently joined the whelk fishery there. Inshore fishing is not yet dead but it is a far cry from the days when the town sent 3-4,000 tubs of oysters annually to Norwich and Lynn. Even in the 1870s the inhabitants were talking of a disappearance of fish. Haddock that had been taken by trot lines with lugworm bait was entirely gone. Cod, too, they said, had nearly deserted the coast, while skate, turbot, gurnards, whiting, flounders, dabs and plaice had all diminished in number. There was a time when 'No finer mussels than those which come from the Brancaster "scaups" are to be obtained anywhere along the English coasts', and Blakeney was a noted fishing town with a yearly fish fair.

7

Sheringham had a 'very considerable fishery of cod, skate and whitings' besides crabs and lobsters, Stiffkey was famous for its 'Stewky blues' and hundreds of men from Palling, Winterton and Caister joined the herring fishing out of Yarmouth harbour.

But the tale is everywhere the same. There are fishermen's quays in Lancashire slowly silting, boats at Lerwick are forced to tie up while foreign vessels fish offshore and Cornish liners wait for mackerel shoals in vain. In some places there is nothing but pile upon pile of shells to bear witness to the past. Although this book concentrates on a small area with its particular features, the pattern is repeated up and down Britain's coasts. Where there were hundreds of boats a century ago, today there are dozens; where there were dozens, only one or two remain. If they are not converted into pleasure yachts they lie rotting in the mud.

Just why is the inshore fisherman leaving the sea? Before he joined up with the forces, typically the navy, in the two world wars, he came from a long line of fishermen who were 'born to the life', never doubting that they would follow in the family tradition. 'In no section of our population is the heredity of occupation so rigidly preserved as among our fishermen', commented the Duke of Edinburgh in 1885. When the fisherman came home things had changed. He had travelled, had seen more and experienced more than the generations before him. He sometimes decided there was an easier life elsewhere. After the First World War sail and oar were rapidly being replaced by motor and mechanisation took some of the back-breaking labour out of his daily life but in the 1920s, though there were still plenty of fish, prices were poor. Yet these are not the only reasons for their dwindling numbers. The downward trend was in full swing fifty years before the First World War.

Inevitably there has been local competition of the small shopkeeper variety and even if each community fished in its own waters which might by gentleman's agreement be rigidly defined, one was bound to be affected by exploitation in neighbouring grounds. But if local rivalry was all they had to face, how happy the case might be!

Just a hundred years ago, when a report for the Home Secretary was prepared, it was found that vast numbers of small fish were being destroyed by trawling. At first, when comparatively small vessels towed moderately small trawls, there was room and fish enough for everyone, but bigger craft were built to work larger trawls, their numbers increased and they started operating close to the coast. Considerable friction arose when they poached on the longshoreman's ground. Firstly they were after his fish, but equally important, their heavy beams dragged over the sea bed, destroying the lines of the hook fishermen. Although the Sea Fisheries Act of 1868 helped to regulate them, inshore fishermen obtained no real protection from unscrupulous and selfish foreign boats. Foreign trawlers with small-meshed nets have consistently scoured British coastal waters catching fish of any size to feed the insatiable demands of their fishmeal factories, and more and more hook boats have been driven from their rightful grounds.

Nor has Britain a history of concern for preserving the fish in her waters for the benefit of her own fishermen. In 1818 R. Fraser, who reviewed the domestic fisheries of Great Britain and Ireland, drew attention to the comment of a Mr Andrew Yarranton:

> So prodigiously rich is the fishing trade, and so plainly the right of the King of England, that with good reason is our negligence taken notice of by all Europe, and our prudence questioned by it, that we keep so little a share of it to ourselves as we do, and let our neighbours grow great and haughty by the peaceable and full enjoyment of that considerable trade. It was a most unlucky piece of goodness that some of our former princes ever suffered a foreign buss to visit the English coasts.'

Perhaps the fate of the North Sea herring is the best illustration of lack of regard for conservation. James Bertram, author of several books about the sea, wrote in 1885:

The idea of a slowly but surely diminishing supply of fish is no doubt alarming . . . it has never sufficiently been brought home to the public mind that it is possible to reduce the breeding stock of our best kinds of sea fish to such an extent as may render it difficult to repopulate those exhausted ocean colonies which in years gone by yielded, as we have often been told, such miraculous draughts.

About this time, when ripples of the problem first came to public attention, international legislation might have saved the situation. Unfortunately, it was a period of intense exploitation.

There are other claimants for water which fishermen have called their own since the Magna Carta spoke of 'the freedom of the seas'. Commercial users for instance; gas installations affect fishing because they occupy sea bed. Then, concomitant with the steady rise in population, recreation has increased and will continue to do so. Already launching quays and jetties are jammed up with sea anglers, skin-divers pinch the longshoreman's lobsters, while water-skiers, yachts, and speed boats all compete with him for sea space. There is increasing traffic in toxic waste materials, more dumping at sea, local pollution, and the invasion of summer visitors to sea-side houses pushes up the price of the fisherman's potential home.

Some problems are specific to Norfolk. Throughout history the flat sea-worn coasts of the east have fought against an ever-encroaching ocean. There are records of great chunks of land with corn still growing on them floating away from a shore that at one count lost seventeen yards within the space of five years. Yet how capricious the sea is! Norfolk's northern shores collect material moved down by wave action so that at Blakeney, Cley and Wells, the situation is just the reverse.

Although I have known this stretch for more than twenty-five years even a casual visitor returning two or three successive seasons will notice the changes that take place along its shores. Sandbanks move and water channels change course, creeks which could be comfortably sailed up one summer have silted up the next, and pools that were fit for diving level disconcertingly below the waist. What were tiny embryo dunes, no more than ripples 'on the ribbed sea sand', may be whiskered with couch and marram. It is just such changes which have, over the years, led to so fine a complex of sandflats, marshes and dunes. But, if moss green vegetation, ochre sands, steel grey water and thin blue skies make a splendid sight, they also pose a problem, for this land that is being reclaimed for agriculture is contributing to the silting up of local harbours. So the day may come when all the boats are forced to move away, when mussel lays are entirely smothered and harbours are only accessible at high tide. Perhaps coastal protection, reinforced since the 1953 floods has accelerated the natural course of events.

In the past the fisherman was largely self-sufficient. He barked and tarred his ropes and sails, made his pots and sometimes twisted his ropes while his wife mended nets and knitted his 'gansey'. Now they cannot easily get raw materials, and even if it lasts a lot longer the price of his gear has risen. Fuel alone has doubled in price in the past year, while bait is expensive and difficult to obtain. We have come a long way from the days when two men could go into partnership, buying a fully equipped crab boat for £20. There are other pressures, more invidious ones. Will Common Market agreements to some extent indicate common fishing policies? Does that mean our British fisherman with minority interests, must accept other nations working right up to his coasts? Against such giant legislation, how can he protect himself? One might answer that historically the fisherman has done very little to safeguard his own interests. Sometimes moreover, he has been his own worst enemy. Either he was sceptical of scientific evidence, lazy and careless, and ruined the very beds that offered him a living, or his happy-go-lucky attitude led him to break regulations designed to protect his own future. Fishermen have been notoriously slow to unite, join co-operatives or societies affiliated to big producer organisations competing on twentieth century lines. For the fisherman is foremost as individualist, self-reliant and self-contained. Since too many leaders do not make a good team, it seems as if his character has worked against him.

Individually, fishermen are as varied as the men in any occupation but hardships, scanty remuneration, exposure to danger and the most unremitting labour have bred a sturdy, persevering race, full of resource, essentially non-conformist, recognisably anti-authoritarian, blunt, uncompromising and genuinely sincere. In 1893, when an enquiry was made into the fishermen's objections to setting up the Eastern Sea Fisheries, the Inspector of Fisheries summed up their feelings in the expression 'they want no interference'.

At one time the populations of coastal communities from the Wash right round the Norfolk bulge to the Thames estuary lived largely on or from the sea. Life in them was close-knit and parochial, and each village had its own identity. It was a rough life they led but there were many whose principles were strict enough. The spirit of sacrifice showed itself time and again in rescue operations and as the majority of them were religious, when the Salvation Army began its work, many flocked to it. Large families brought together under constant threat of sudden bereavements shared one another's prolonged sorrows and brief joys. There is no mistaking that they live as they are, without any attempt at pretension or disguise. Life for them must be taken as it comes with all its paradoxes. And not least of their attractions is a readiness to experience realities. Often it is the trivial, the chance remark that reveals this attitude, an unconscious yearning to plummet back to the fount of things. They feel, sometimes without the means to express themselves, that counterfeit happenings tend to drive out spontaneous enjoyment of what is real, what finally matters.

Spanning the coast from Hunstanton to the edge of Great Yarmouth, this work is not concerned with a single community but a brotherhood that transcends the boundaries of

town and village. Wherever the hard black line of the road
that dips and dodges along the coast meets the wavering line
of the sea it passes through a chain of little coastal places
once filled with fishing people. They all wear slops and thigh
boots, all are torn relentlessly by the wind off the North Sea.
On this road perhaps better than anywhere on the coast can
be seen the effects of heavy east winds which bend and twist
hedgerow trees into fantastic shapes.

A ragged coast fringed by salt marsh runs east from
Brancaster. Sometimes marram-covered dunes and shingle
ridges protect tidal mud flats and saltings lying on their
landward side. Between Stiffkey and Blakeney the marshland
widens before giving way to a line of cliffs extending from
Happisburgh to Weybourne. They reach their maximum
height just north of Mundesley where long silver beaches
separated from the land by man-made sea walls stretch to the
south of Yarmouth. The sea defences are by no means
impregnable. Periodically villages lying behind the saltings
have been inundated by scouring tides or in places, entirely
lost to the sea.

The North Sea is unpredictable and the coast is treacherous.
Bars or sandbanks running across harbour mouths have
increased the difficulties of navigation and the open, un-
protected beaches are notoriously dangerous. Not only is it
difficult to push off boats against an oncoming wind but it
requires masterly precision to land them up the steep slope of
the shelving beaches. On one occasion two Cromer boats were
dashed to pieces as they set off and seven men in them were
drowned in a sudden gale within 50 yards of the shore they
had just left. More recently, the fishermen remember occasions when the wind blew so hard as fast as water rushed into
the boats, it was blown out again. Sudden squalls whip up the
sea to a fury and the lifeboats have always made a fair
proportion of their rescues to the local fishing fleet. Haisboro'
Sands, Winterton Ness, Devil's Throat. These are names
dreaded by seafarers. Norfolk, it is said, asks for trouble by

sticking its neck out into the North Sea. And gets it! After bad storms the shore might be littered with wrecks and often the toll of life was formidable. To counter the danger fifteen lifeboats were at one time stationed around the shores.

Mussels, cockles and winkles lie in the North Norfolk harbours whereas the best commercial whelks are found in the open sea, usually on a mixture of mud, sand and shells. Wells has been for many years the most important supplier to the market in Great Britain with Brancaster not far behind. Crabs and lobsters, more plentiful on a rugged sea bottom, occupy fifteen miles of coast from Salthouse to Mundesley, extending about two miles offshore. Despite the relatively limited area of the fishery, it is an important one. The flamboyant days of herring fishing at Yarmouth are over, but the few fishermen still working between Cromer and Caister remember when herring came up in bucketfuls, when white fish and pilchards were plentiful too.

The tide is turning. What were substantial communities have split up and dispersed. Yet old customs, beliefs, feelings and language linger. When I realised just how fast they were slipping away, it seemed imperative to record something of the spirit that remains. George Ewart Evans said, 'Occasionally a body of factual knowledge does exist only in the memories of men and women, and it would be lost, or greatly attenuated, were it not taken down before they died.' Perhaps a little of this has been tapped as well.

1

EARLY DAYS

Ready am I to go, and my eagerness with sails full
set awaits the wind

— *Gibran*

Little Em'ly's father was a fisherman, her mother was a
fisherman's daughter and her Uncle Ben a fisherman. Where
her father's grave was, wrote Dickens, no one knew, except
that it was somewhere in the depths of the sea.

There are passages in *David Copperfield* to remind us of
life along the shore in the early nineteenth century. Of days
when mingled smells of fish, pitch, tar and oakum wrapped
the air around gasworks, rope-walks, boat-builders' yards,
riggers' lofts and smiths' forges at the edge of the sand. To
Master Davy, from his exalted position on Ham's shoulders,
they were unforgettable sights and smells.

All round Britain little industries were once part of the
coastal scene and right up until today, from Norfolk villages
huddling behind the dunes, men have launched crab boats
from open beaches or sailed cobles and smacks from creeks
and harbours. They have dredged for oysters, set pots for
crabs, lobsters or whelks, raked cockles and, in season, gone
musseling, trawling for shrimps and flatfish, long-lining for
cod, seine-netting for sea trout and drift-netting for mackerel
and herring.

James Bertram (1883) found the life of fishing people 'of
the same complexion wherever they live'. But the men
employed in these fisheries are disappearing. Each year the
average age rises, for as the older ones retire their places are
no longer being filled. The fisherman's son packs his bags
and moves inland. But who will beat the Salvation Army

drum, who will man the lifeboats, who answer to the strange nicknames, 'Lettuce', 'Cod' or 'Squinter'? We are losing more than just his expertise and intimate local knowledge; we are losing the fisherman's way of life.

Along the East Anglian coast there used to be prolific beds of oysters and other shellfish which the Romans caught in winter, packed in snow and ice and put in cloth bags to send to Rome. Perhaps the Danes prized them too, for it is to Danish raids, followed by large-scale invasion and settlement, that East Anglia owes its Scandinavian influence. There are certainly traces of Scandinavian blood among the fishermen, although names like Emery and Johnson are of Norman origin. So probably the Anglo-Saxon element predominates.

From earliest times the sea has been inevitably bound up with the history of the string of tiny East Coast havens, playing a dual rôle of provider and adversary. It offered subsistence in the form of fish, trade in days when the sea was a major means of communication with the outside world, and two-fold peril — from the fury of the sea itself and, time and again, from the threat of invasion.

While Great Yarmouth and King's Lynn, outstanding in age and prestige, are historically the most prominent Norfolk ports, there has always been trading along the ninety miles that separates them, particularly from the northern harbours where it flourished from the Middle Ages right into the early twentieth century. Now relegated to pleasure sailing, Blakeney was once a port surpassing King's Lynn and Yarmouth in importance. Even little places like Brancaster and Holkham invited significant local traffic and by the fourteenth century journeys to Iceland were common. The huge fleet of Edward III included a couple of ships and thirty-eight mariners from Blakeney, as well as many from Lynn and Yarmouth. In fact, the important position Britain once held must to some extent be attributed to her fishermen, who were the first seamen and manned the King's navy.

For centuries England produced the finest wool in Europe.

16

From Norfolk it went to France and Flanders to be woven into cloth, some of which was sold back again. As a result, Blakeney and Cley were bustling with wool exports when Liverpool and Southampton were scarcely known. In fact it was this trade using North Norfolk ports, that earned her town's prosperous churches by the fourteenth and fifteenth centuries. One of the earliest accounts of shipping at Wells tells of a cloth-laden vessel from Calais bound for Boston anchoring off the coast at Holkham where it met a decidedly uncivil reception. Residents attacked the ship, carried off its cargo and wounded the men in charge — 'Some to death, and some by mutilating them'. Scores of similar episodes give a fair idea of lawlessness and violence on the North Sea, which was, of course, rife with piracy.

Fishing boats along the Norfolk coast were often arrested by King's commission to provide transport until local men petitioned Parliament, objecting tactfully. Not only did they suffer, but so indirectly did the entire country. Could they not pursue their business quietly as they were mere fishermen, ignorant about navigation. King Richard II agreed that as fishing vessels were not really suitable for transporting warlike stores, they should be left alone unless the case was urgent.

From Domesday times these little communities probably raided other parts of the coast and were in turn raided themselves. On top of that they were vulnerable to foreign invasion. First they were warned to guard against landing from the Spanish Armada; when war was declared between England and Holland, it was the Dutch, and later the French. They managed to turn the situation to their own advantage by wheedling ammunition out of the authorities, on condition it should be used for defence, and not embezzled.

During 1693 200 ships foundered in what was then called 'Cromer Bay'. A year earlier a single storm at Winterton Ness caused the loss of 200 ships and the lives of more than a thousand men, while as late as 1866 nearly a thousand boats were lost on the east coast within six months. Sandbanks lying offshore are lethal and trade routes were crowded with ships in the age of sail, some of them far from seaworthy. In response, a community of sturdy lifeboatmen and beachmen grew up to serve the shipping. The beachmen organized themselves into companies, each with its own regulations, a fast open boat or yawl for salvaging, a gig for light work and a look-out tower on shore for spying wrecks. Until quite recently these three great strands — fishing, salvaging and the lifeboats — have been woven into the fabric of the coastal communities.

In the nineteenth century Norfolk had its share in the whale fishery off Greenland and Davis' Straits and both Sheringham and Cromer were involved in deep-sea fishing in luggers, or the 'great boats' as they called them — sailing drifters crewed by about a dozen men that went crabbing or herring and mackerel fishing off the Yorkshire coast. Apparently they brought back live crabs from Yorkshire to replenish the local stock where light brown crabs are still referred to as 'Yorkshiremen'. Because there is a dearth of records we do not know so much about small-boat fishing. There is the odd newspaper report of fishermen banding together to supply the London market 'in a more regular manner' and accounts appear of indictments for bringing ashore undersized fish, but it was not until 1875, when Frank Buckland, inspector of salmon fisheries, made a comprehensive survey of the Norfolk fisheries for the government that we have any definite idea of what was going on. The Yarmouth herring industry, celebrated for 800 years, was still in full swing. Dutch and Frenchmen came in hordes to join in the six weeks' huge free fare. Sea trout were present in abundance along the coast although skate fishing had declined to such an extent that whereas twenty years earlier each coble averaged twenty skate a day from Christmas to March, the fishery was so bad no lines had been laid. Shrimps, mullet and flatfish too, were all scarce in the north coast harbours. Presumably because the volume of fish caught was insignificant, the inspector did not deal in any detail with smaller villages but he made thorough surveys at Wells, Cromer and Sheringham.

At Wells things were on the decline. Railway competition had reduced shipping and the fishing industry had almost ceased. Compared with thirty-two fishing vessels working there in 1844, only two cobles carried on line-fishing and that with little success. Walter Rye's advice to 'Try the celebrated Burnham oysters which now run Whitstables hard in price' was superfluous — they had all disappeared. Exploitation, particularly by trawlers, was the main cause but the authorities were obviously not happy about haphazard inshore fishing methods. No consideration was being given to restocking and crabs were being sold far too small. Buckland found there was scarcely any legislation and although fishing was the principal industry and consequently of immense importance to the people, beds had been allowed to decline. 'If some remedy is not speedily applied', he concluded, 'their extinction is feared'.

Decreases in crab and lobster populations were due, Buckland decided, chiefly to the destruction of small crabs called 'toggs' or 'short crabs' and the slaughter of crabs and lobsters in spawn or 'berry'. It seemed that although the Cromer men returned toggs to the sea, sometimes as many as 800 a day, the Sheringham people did not. Little crabs were also smashed up to use as bait for lobsters, butt and other fish. Merchants of long experience at Sheringham estimated that at least 28,000 undersized crabs worth barely a farthing each, brought in and sold in the course of a day, accounted for the loss of about three-quarters of a million in a month, apart from those destroyed at sea or on the shore. They agreed that they could formerly take more good-sized crabs in a day than they were receiving in a week. In consequence, an order defining minimum sizes for crabs and lobsters and prohibiting the killing of those in berry was renewed in more stringent terms.

There are only scraps of information about the fishermen's

lives before the early 1800s. A contemporary account of Sheringham refers to its inhabitants as a remarkably handsome set of fishermen who 'marry almost before they have done growing, girls of their own village', rearing 'rough and ready families in a state of chronic starvation'. At best they were 'insolently independent', and in their own calling 'fearless enough'. Drowning was so common it was not difficult to find women who had lost fathers and husbands, sons and grandsons one after another in the same way.

As one local man said, 'Most of the fishermen hadn't two pennies to rub together', and if fishing was bad during the winter certainly the pantry was often bare. 'My grandmother was widowed early', he told me. 'She would walk four miles to West Beckham where the board of guardians met once a month, they'd give her a ticket to get flour or so many yards of calico. Even my mother, she walked to Cromer where Barclays would give out tickets for lunch and perhaps a pair of shoes.' Things might have been desperate had not landowning families helped through bad patches. Perhaps most remembered were the Upchers of Sheringham Hall who did more than run second-hand clothing stalls, give the town its first lifeboat, lend money to the fishermen to buy boats and start Bible classes and Sunday schools, they concerned themselves with the fishermen's daily trials.

When Emma Piggot, born Upcher, died, six fishermen and six Upper Sheringham men who had known her all their lives bore her down the village street to the church, passing the pebble houses she had often visited when wild March winds rushed round the corners of narrow alleys, forcing tottering old women, wandering home with bits of driftwood, to draw their shawls tighter. Fortunately, some of Mrs Piggot's intimate recollections about the fishermen went into a journal that has been preserved.

An entry written between 1861 and 1863 tells of a plan arranged between a clergyman (Mr S) and sixteen leading religious fishermen to hold prayer meetings every afternoon for a week, after which they would divide into four parties, each visiting a certain number of houses until the entire village had been covered.

The service began by singing a verse of a hymn. Mr S said a few words, three men offered up a prayer one after another, then the voices all burst out in another wild hymn unknown to us, to which the fishermen beat time with their feet. They all stood or knelt with their backs turned to us, and now and then their voices rang through the room.

The following spring, generally a very bad time for fishing, saw miraculous draughts of cod.

Religious fervour based on strict Puritan and Methodist influence was not restricted to East Anglia. In 1896 a group of Lowestoft drifters putting in at Newlyn harbour so infuriated the Cornish fishermen by refusing to observe the Sabbath that riots ran rife and only the presence of armed troops finally restored order.

Something of each element flourishes today. John Henry Loose, an earnest Brancaster fisherman, affirms, 'Religion is important to us. It's important in all aspects of life', while Alf Large from the same village honestly admits, 'We work Sundays. We go to church down the road called Barclay's Bank'.

Another entry in Emma Piggot's diary records a sudden storm, the inevitable accident with a young man called Bishop lost overboard. There is a harrowing footnote to the episode. 'Since these words were written Robert Priest Bishop has been again in sore trial, two more sons and his son-in-law being drowned by the upsetting of a boat.'

Small wonder the fishermen who are left retain a doggedness, a buoyancy. Laddy Lane from Overy insists his authority over the mussel lays. 'If I want anything I'll take it and they can come after me if they want and do what they like but I'm their daddy as long as I live in that creek and nobody's going to stop me.' While 'The Professor' from Wells says, 'A challenge, that's all my life has been'.

Of 250 small boats and twenty luggers working off Sheringham beach towards the middle of the nineteenth century, Buckland calculated there were only about 100 crab boats left in 1875, in fact there were still just too many working the same grounds. Besides, a fierce independence instilled by competition was being undermined to some extent by fish merchants acting as middle men. So, for a variety of reasons, the fishermen decided to pack their bags and try their luck up and down the coast. Crab boats were loaded up with household goods and went off under oar and sail anywhere between the Thames estuary and the Yorkshire coast. North they colonised Wells, Brancaster, Mablethorpe, Grimsby, Bridlington and Whitby, and south they dispersed to Overstrand, Mundesley, Happisburgh and Palling, as far as Harwich, Brightlingsea and Whitstable. In all these places Sheringham fishing names were heard: Cooper, Farrow, Pegg, and Craske, West, Cox, Grimes, Grice, Bishop, Little and Johnson. Which brings the story within the scope of men's memories.

Percy Feek's reflection that 'It weren't no life for the women' acknowledges the slog, the responsibilities they bore. Yet this was compensated for to some extent by rich relationships and community interest. Myrtle West's open gusto for all that went on around her assures us:

> Now my mother's father, Cooper — they used to call him 'Old Filaloo' — was coxswain of the first Institution lifeboat, the *Duncan*. I was only fourteen when he died, it was the 19th of April and there was snow up that Sheringham road nearly as high as these picture rails. They dug out the middle so we could get through to the cemetery. There was once a wreck in the part where the Sheringham lifeboat should have gone but the Cromer boat got there first, so my grandfather Cooper had to go and be reprimanded. He went to his second coxswain and said 'Come on, we've got to be reprimanded. I don't know if that's something you eat or hang on the wall but we'd better go'.

Sheringham began its existence with a nucleus of fishermen.

22

Shopkeepers, net makers and rope twisters moved in to support them and created a community. But everyone was wrapped up to some extent in the fishing. In a good season the whole town prospered, in a bad one all felt the pinch.

Concomitant with the fishermen's migrations came another big change — the building of the railway. Now their cottages were open to visitors during the summer and since the businessman's family stayed on holiday from May until September, his servants mingled with fishing people. Some married, bringing new blood into the district.

During the First World War, troops were billeted in private houses all along the coast. Scottish, Welsh and Liverpool regiments hobnobbed with fishing families and, probably for the first time, the little towns and villages realised how the rest of the world lived. Though they remained largely rigid in their customs, correspondence was maintained after the war and some local girls were eventually whisked away. Twenty years later the pattern was repeated, only this time the anti-aircraft range at Weybourne kept fishermen off their whelk grounds and disturbed titled visitors with all-night firing. When they decided to move on, Sheringham's hotels closed, camps and caravans changed the holiday pattern to shorter visits, coach trips faded because visitors had their own cars and the fisherman's immediate market disappeared.

Meanwhile fishing had steadily declined — a trend that has continued, especially in the south. Walter Chaney from Hemsby still catches what is going. 'I like fishing', he said, 'but if I'm catching no fish there's just nothing to it'. While Philip Green of Stiffkey echoes sentiments many of them feel: 'The inshore fisherman is just dying slowly on his feet. Very slowly but surely, all the time. Like the musseling we once had at Blakeney. Now what is there? Nothing! There's a barren waste. Just a barren waste'.

2

CRABS AND LOBSTERS

I must down to the seas again, for the call of the
running tide
Is a wild call and a clear call that may not be
denied;
And all I ask is a windy day with the white clouds
flying,
And the flung spray and the blown spume, and the
sea-gulls crying.
—Masefield, *Sea-Fever*

Although Upper and Lower Sheringham became separate
parishes at the turn of this century, the church of All Saints
served as parish church for both until 1953. Now it presides
over only Upper Sheringham, a cluster of pebble houses
nestling in a hollow with the Cromer/Holt ridge on the south,
Oakwood Hill on the west, Morely Hill on the east, and
Skelding Hill to the north. Yet the size of its churchyard
indicates that it once served a much larger area. Forays into
an undergrowth of nettles and brambles are rewarded by
revealing more and more graves, some almost lost beneath a
leafy tangle. For it is here on the tombstones that the story of
the fishing families from this windswept north Norfolk town is
told in succinct and poignant words.

To the memory of Cutler Craske, aged 49
and of his youngest son
Nathaniel aged 13 who
perished at sea in the hurricane
29th November 1836
within sight of home
My Father, My Brother, God's holy word hath laid

In loving memory of
John Bayfield Grimes
son of John and Zalindia Grimes
who drowned at sea July 29th 1886
aged 26 years

One summers' noonday when all was fair
And the sunbeams sailed around,
A little boat o'er water blue
To its island home was bound

We watched it coming to the shore
It was surely drawing near
But swift as the tide the summons came
Which caused us many a tear

In loving memory of
Joshua Henry West Long
the beloved husband of
Sophia Long
who was drowned at sea
July 18th 1909
aged 36 years

I am resting so sweet in Jesus now
I sail the wide sea no more
The tempests may sweep o'er the wild stormy deep
I am safe while the storms come no more

In loving memory of
our dear mother
Lucy Anne Cooper
who died 28th December 1917
aged 77 years

White is the robe and bright the crown
The ransomed spirit wears;
Oh who would wish to call her back
To share our griefs and cares?

There are so many others:
'Robert Henry Grimes, died 9th June, 1904. The Lord drew me out of many waters.' 'Robert Thomas West, aged 39, drowned at sea 31st July 1909.' 'Joseph, beloved husband of Ann Cooper, aged 29, drowned at sea October 29th 1880.' 'William, eldest son of John and Harriet Grimes, aged 22 years, drowned at sea June 2nd 1855.'

The sparse, white mid-fourteenth century church with a carved loft and rood screen holds an air of sincere rebellion. During the fifteenth century the aisles were rebuilt with tall perpendicular windows; three on the south, where the women traditionally sat, are stained to reduce the sun's glare. The ends of the pews, again fifteenth century, are ornamented with vigorous, almost primitive carvings: a sleek mother cat with a kitten in its mouth, a chrysom child in a shroud, and, at the back of the church, a mermaid, on a bench where generations of fishermen have prayed whilst their youngsters drove penknives into the seat. They scratched, of course, ships.

The chancel is dominated by an elaborate neo-classical memorial signed by John Bacon and Samuel Manning. A woman lies in utter desolation on a broken column, a scrap of foliage trailing from her hand. The column represents the abruptly terminated life of Abbot Upcher who bought Sheringham estate and manorial rights and built Sheringham Hall but did not survive to inhabit it, the grieving woman is his widow, the Hon Charlotte, who survived him by thirty-eight years.

Ever since the mid-nineteenth century, when the railway opened up north Norfolk to cheap and rapid transport, holidaymakers have flocked to its seaside towns and villages. Yet these places' long and important maritime histories are little suspected by those who lie on the beach, join sailing clubs or swim in the chilly sea. If they wander from Sheringham's tinselled amusement arcades they may come across a slipway lined with ropes, crabpots and a piece or two of old bait blessed with a good stink. Sometimes a knot of fishermen stand at the top, sheltering as they have always done in the lee of the boathouse, arguing amongst themselves while they watch for a break in the weather. On the beach below lie a handful of brightly painted close-ribbed crab boats — all that remain of more than two hundred small craft and a fleet of forty fishing luggers that flaunted their sails to follow the herring at Yarmouth, Scarborough and up the Yorkshire coast.

Summer and winter, every day, eighty-year-old Jimmy 'Paris' West potters down the short length of road from a spruce little house in Cliff Road to explore his bit of beach and watch the gulls. There are only three 'old-uns' left in Sheringham. He is one of them. 'Got to make sure the sea is still there', he remarks typically. While quiet courage, humour and a resilient spirit keep Jimmy 'Paris' from retiring completely into his memories, like others of his generation he recalls a rich slice of Sheringham fishing life. The extraordinary vividness is his own.

Whether or not they accepted its implications, all the old fishermen were affected by folklore. It is not surprising. Where lives were laced by chance, superstition ran rife.

Jimmy 'Paris' deliberates:

I never was superstitious although I sometimes used to have a twinge about it because my relations were. They were always against anything with four legs. If you talked about rabbits or horses, oooh! they'd carry on awful, especially if you mentioned them in the mornings before you went to sea. They reckoned it was a superstition to put in the gold ear-rings. I had them when I was twelve. All fishermen used to wear them, and the girls, too. But I don't think it did my eyesight any good. Personally I didn't take no notice er that. Every Saturday we would have a proper clean up and scrub out the boats at high-water time. They'd be on their sides, more or less half over, and we'd throw buckets of sea water up the high side. All the water come down this side, then you scooped it out with hand cups. That's a metal bowl with a wooden handle for baling out water. When we had engines they thought it was bad luck if the boards got

27

turned the wrong way up after they'd been scrubbed. We got a
good hiding if we did that. Good Lord, it was murder! We
wouldn't have a woman near the boat and if two nuns came
walking along the front together that meant a two-reef breeze,
three of them, you got a three-reef breeze. That was a good bit
of wind. But if you saw a clergyman come down the quay there
wouldn't be no trip.

Superstition was by no means confined to Sheringham. We
hear later of a Brancaster man who wore a gold chain to
ward off the Devil and an Overy man with a firm belief in
evil spirits. Each community evolved its own variations.
Harold Emery, a Sheringham boat-builder, brings some of
these comments up to date.

> Father would never put a boat down in the stocks to start on
> a Friday. He'd say 'We'll leave that till Monday'. And the
> fishermen now would never launch on a Friday. They all went
> to sea with a bit of coal in the boat, most of them do now — at
> least the old fishermen, these proper fishermen's sons.

'I am a Shannock' is more than a simple statement of
identity. It is a claim with infinite connotations, carrying
strong, proud echoes that travel back and back in the town of
their birth. But life in the town today is more uniform, more
egalitarian than it was in Jimmy 'Paris' West's young days:

> I'm a Shannock because I live here and I was born here.
> When I was a kid we lived in two old cottages in the High
> Street. The big folk would come and stay at the Sheringham
> hotels for six weeks with their chauffeurs in livery, and
> nursemaids. They had balls at 'The Grand' with men in top
> hats and I remember nannies walking along the prom with
> huge prams. They used bathing machines down on the beach
> and the women wore more to go swimming than you wear now
> just walking down the road. Sometimes we'd collect pails of
> water for people to ease their feet in and one day a couple of
> visitors were asking us what we were doing, so we told them.
> Next time they come back the tide was out so they must have
> thought we done a good trade. There were rowing races in the
> regattas, two-oars and four-oars. They can't row today, they
> don't shiver the oar. When you're rowing against the wind you

put the oar in flat-ways and when you bring it up you turn it. We called it shivering. But they haven't got time for it now.

Laura Upcher was sister to the old squire. I'd go up and clean her knives and boots and shoes before I went to school. I got half-a-crown a week, a golden half-quid every month. It seemed a lot when I was ten or twelve. I carried it home to my mother because my father died when I was about two. I had two brothers and two sisters. When that was rough weather some of the fishermen used to go up in the woods on the Upcher estate and set young trees or chop wood. The Upchers were good friends to the fishermen. They gave us the first lifeboat, the *Augusta,* then the *Henry Ramey Upcher,* and they took an interest in everybody. I don't say they threw their money about, nothing like that, but I know what they did do because I went there myself. In wintertime if it was bad weather these small boats couldn't get out to sea. Well if that had been rough for two or three weeks they would set up a soup kitchen on the front. There was a great barn building where they'd come twice a week with the pork and the peas and two big old coppers to make pea soup; at twelve o'clock you'd go and get a jugful. Of course Upcher owned nearly all the cottages; ours belonged to him and we payed £6 rent a year. We used to go up behind the baker's shop to pump fresh water and carry it in buckets to the houses and cottages, then we had dry closets outside for lavatories. Once a week they came round and emptied them last thing at night. We'd lie in bed listening to them rattling about. Upcher owned nearly all of Sheringham, so other fishermen lived in his houses, too.

A Sheringham man from a fishing family told me about the lingering, almost feudal relationship between the Upcher family and the fishermen:

He always called us by our first names. I remember when he last saw my mother, she must have been in her eighties and he hadn't seen her since she was a girl but he remembered her as little Annie West. When fishing was bad he would tap on the door and say 'How's things?'. He once appeared when a fisherman was just back, washing off the sweat and filth in the bathroom. So his wife went to the door, saw the old squire and said 'Don't worry Jack, it's only the Squire'. He was so much welcomed, and his wife was always called the 'Squire's Lady'. The present Mr Upcher is president of Sheringham RNLI. Not many years ago they were asking 'Is the young squire away?'. They still called him that.

Walking down one of Sheringham's narrow streets on a summer's afternoon a hundred years ago one might have seen a small fleet of fishing luggers at anchor in front of the town. These vessels, R.W. Malster tells us, very similar to the Yarmouth herring luggers, were owned in Cromer, Sheringham and neighbouring villages. During the 1860s the fleet consisted of nearly forty but only the 'old-uns' remember them, for within ten years it had shrunk to about thirty, two of them converted to dandy rig—a gaff mainsail on a short foremast and a lug mizzen. By the 1890s it numbered only eleven. They were largely the products of Yarmouth boat-yards, and most were owned in Sheringham.

These 'great boats', as they were known, followed the herring up the coast and engaged in the home fishing from Yarmouth with the Yarmouth drifters. They also spent part of the year lining for cod or went to the Yorkshire coast for crabs, taking a couple of crab boats on deck to work the pots.

Luggers and dandies were too big to be hauled up the beach like the crab boats and hovellers. They only returned home two or three times a year to land equipment before lying up in Yarmouth or Blakeney haven, or to load new gear, which was ferried out as they lay at anchor. Jimmy 'Paris' says:

> I was about ten years old when the great boats last came in here. They were lovely smacks! After the herring they used to fish off Grimsby for crabs and long-line with whelks, then they'd go down to the Dogger. But all of a sudden the cod would go, they wouldn't get one and the trawlers would come over the same place and fill the decks full. The cod start spawning in March and the trawlers would take all the spawn and destroy the fishing. That's what they're doing even up to today. Everything's scarce, fish and fishermen. It's dying out. Science with all its expert knowledge has given them trawl nets and echo-sounders to find the fish, they've got a wireless on board to tell their chums where they are and the fish h'aint got no chance. They found this with whitebait and herring. If you

get all the big ones there's not going to be any left to spawn and that's what's carrying on in this North Sea. In the First World War all the trawlers were mine-sweeping so there was a good period until the fish were cleaned up. Then just after the last war there were tons of fish but now they're cleaned up again. Every year it gets worse and worse, yet they continue with the trawlers night and day, Sundays and weekdays. The big ones can go out in practically any weather. I know the North Sea is a big place but that's over-fished. The twelve-mile limit's no good because the fish don't always breed inshore. Then they've only got a few police boats and it's the easiest thing in the world for the trawlers to come inside the limit. Crabs and lobsters seem good this year. They should be increasing because cod live off crabs when they're in soft condition. So now there's no more cod the crabs should be more plentiful.

Then there's this pollution. It comes out of the Humber and the rivers. You can hardly catch anything with a rod. There's no dabs, no nuth'un. If there are going to be any fish left we'll have to make a close season. I can remember fifty or sixty boats at Sheringham and upwards of 300 fishermen. Now there are fewer than twenty. It's too risky, too expensive and there's not enough money in it. In twenty years there'll be no one left except after-tea fishermen and unless they ban fishing on the breeding grounds there will be nothing for *them* to catch.

'Shrimp' Davies, a Cromer fisherman, realises that even the sophistication of their own methods has helped to deplete the stock of fish.

Herrings have almost finished now. They would come back but they're trawled and caught with seine nets. In the days of the old drift nets that hung in the water like a curtain, the mesh was about an inch wide so small herring escaped and probably the big ones didn't get caught at all. Just the right-sized ones, what we call the 'longshore herring' would be meshed in. Like when we had to haul the crabs by hand the way Jimmy 'Paris' did and I did as a young man up until a few years ago, we'd get blisters on each finger when we started the job, then blisters on top of those blisters. And when you started the next morning the underneath one would bust so they were raw. We used to wear mittens but that didn't stop it. It wasn't only that but if there's too much tide and you're hand hauling,

31

you had to keep your engine running and stem the tide, keep your head to it. So you had to steer the boat and haul the pots at the same time. Now they nearly all have mechanical haulers near the stern. They can also stem the tide but they start downtide and steam down, it makes life much easier. If the hauler breaks down now there aren't more than two boats that can hand haul. But if less people went out it would help to conserve the crabs.

Nevertheless, it is the trawlers, they all know, which are the real culprits.

Last winter there was no long-lining at all from Cromer. There was a little at Sheringham but not much. There were no fish. There is no doubt about it, that's the trawlers. The twelve-mile limit only affects foreign boats, so the British ones come in at three miles. Even they didn't get many last winter, I think they had them all the year before! They trawl up our lines. You can swear at them but you can't do anything much.

Quite apart from the vicissitudes of fishing, life in Jimmy 'Paris' West's time had its ups and downs. One wonders indeed if only the toughest have survived to pass on the tale:

My father died when I was two from a strained heart he got going to sea. Two of my uncles were lost mackerel fishing and soon after I left school my brothers, Ernest and Teddy, were lost crabbing off Weybourne. Everything I touched has been wrong but I seemed to have a charm of my own. I used to caddy at Sheringham golf club when Ben Johnson played there, earned 8d a round caddying and sometimes there was the tuppence tip. I played it myself for years. But somebody passed the other day in his car, said 'Coo, Mr Upcher would turn in his grave to see them playing on Sunday'. I was exempt from the war because I was sole supporter of the family. Between the wars I had a third share in a boat and things were looking up a bit but if we had a spare shilling we had to take care of it in case of rough weather. There were plenty of crabs but no money. They made thirty shillings a long hundred, that's 240, and the herring were 1s 3d a hundred, that's 132. Then sometimes you couldn't sell them at all.

Perhaps his memories of the sea ring loudest and clearest of all.

That first mile off the coast is the worst and the first half mile is treacherous. To get clear of the shore, the breakers where they hit over the beach is everybody's fear and that's what we have to go through each day when we're doing our job. That was the reason the lifeboat had to come off so many times. We wouldn't be completely all right at sea but we'd be a lot safer than we were near the shore, so we had assistance to get home when that come on rough. Sometimes they'd give us lifejackets to put on and come in along with us. We never did carry them in the boats. Never used to think about them. But nine times out of ten people were drowned within the last 200 yards. I've even known one or two steam boats to sink out there.

Years ago there was no way of sending news. It's so easy now that they can speak to the shore and say they're at Sheringham Shoals or they're in difficulties, but we had nothing of that sort. There were several morse lamps and flags, but signalling, that was hopeless. My chum, Henry Little, he'd be up on the thwart as high as he could, I'd grab him to hold him steady and another one grab me. Then when we dropped this side of the swell they couldn't see. He'd be wobbling about trying to save himself, he wouldn't get no letters out half the time. It was all right in fine weather but you wouldn't need them then, not as a rule. Honest truth that was ridiculous.

Because there were too many boats working the same grounds some had to go further afield in search of a catch. They were often caught in storms and had to be escorted home. We are told 'Get the old lifeboat off!' was a frequent shout on the cliff top, and time and again the crew launched in swirling seas.

I've been rescued myself seven times. On my first sea trip the old *Henry Upcher* had to come to our assistance and the last time I lost everything I had. Came ashore with just my slop on. It was February and we were about two miles at sea off Blakeney when we heard the swell come in. We was hoping that was a steam boat, then a few specks of snow arrived and I knew there was a lot of wind not far from us. We decided we'd beach her at Cley if that was possible, but when we got there the water was hitting the bottom of the beach and shooting up over the top. As we dropped on the swell we missed the land minutes of time and when we went up on the top we could see for miles. Well, we knew a lifeboat would be after us but we weren't thinking about lifeboats then—all we wanted was to keep clear of the swell. We got up here as far as the old ship at Weybourne where the breakers were going right inland over the beach, huge things. We had an old four horsepower engine at the time and we managed to keep afloat. Kept a-coming, kept a-coming. My mate, 'Teapot' West, never hardly spoke much. I said, 'They'll be off after us, Bob', shouting because the gale come south-east along. There wasn't much wind, just the gale. So I said 'Is she going all right?' He never spoke. It kept a-coming, kept a-coming. 'I see they're off after us', but it was the swell I thought was the lifeboat. Still he never spoke.

Then we saw the Cromer lifeboat was coming down this way for us. I was worried about Teddy 'Fiddy's' brother, Robert, who took off and I hadn't seen him since. I said, 'What about Robert, poor fellow? What's up with him?' That put the wind up me because it seemed as if I'd been on the big sea and it had broke, his boat was on the back part being drawn away, being drawn in, and it was all foam ahead of them. I thought they were gone. They tell me it was a miracle they got ashore. Then another boat come up with my chum Henry, 'Sparrow' Hardingham and Jack Craske. I got the lifejacket in one hand and threw it to Henry Little, then made him put it on because they had made up their minds they were going to try and get through the last two or three hundred yards to land. In the meantime they clawed me aboard the lifeboat and I decided what I was going to do because I expected something to happen. I don't know how things kept atop at all because they weren't in a motor boat, only the rowing lifeboat. And my God, she took one! I turned round, I could see two oars, the blades of two oars coming up out of the surf. So I took the whole coil of rope, I should think there was a good hundred-weight, off my boat, picked it up and put it overboard, casting her adrift. I couldn't hang on to it while people were in the water you see, and we went after Sparrow in the lifeboat. First of all he come up under one of the men's oars but we couldn't get at him, when he showed up again it was on my side.

Jack Craske was hanging on to the mast, Henry had my lifejacket and sat upright in the water but poor old Sparrow, he hadn't one. Anyway, when he came up it wasn't panic but everything was flustered. I was lucky to lean over the top, that's a long way down to the water, but when he came up on the swell I grabbed hold of his slop, just with the end of my fingers. He was facing the other way. I said 'For God's sake someone come and help, I can't hang on much longer', but the people either side couldn't get near him because the boat was so high. Well there come an enormous swell and I pulled so he came aboard still the wrong way round. Honest truth he was black. I said 'this man's going to die, don't nobody know what to do?' Then I got hold of him, turned him over on the thwart and pressed into his side until it belched out of him. It seemed pints come out and last of all he groaned. All this time they'd been rowing for the shore and when we got there the doctor was down to meet him. They did a little on the beach and he was all right but the other, poor Jack who was on the mast, was gone. The Cromer lifeboat came for him but he either slipped or banged his head on something. The second coxswain jumped over into the water and grabbed him. They gave him artificial respiration and took him to Cromer, but he died.

If this incident is indelibly printed in the pages of Sheringham's history, so is the victorious occasion that Jimmy 'Paris' turns to next:

I enjoy the sea. It's a friend to me even though it's done some terrible things. There were plenty of times I didn't think I'd make it, but you're too busy at the time to worry. I volunteered for the lifeboats myself when I was nineteen. One day I was with a chap called 'Pints', Smith was his name, 'Pints' we called him and we'd gone to Yarmouth to buy some net ropes. They're bottom ropes off the herring nets we used to haul the crab pots with. We looked all round Yarmouth until at last we got some when that started to snow. I thought we'd better get our ropes to the station and while we tied the labels on them for the train it snowed and blowed. Then we went into Yarmouth to have a feed. We kept going to see if it was time for the train, having bites here and bites there, and by the time we were in the High Street sharing the food out it was coming into a proper blizzard.

At Sheringham that evening it was still snowing so we said we'd go to the pictures. I had a pair of short dock-wailers on, leather boots they used to work in the dock with years ago, rather like sea boots only they come just below your knee. 'Pints', by Jove, only had a pair of shoes. It was a funny thing because we sat at the pictures and there was a gale on the film. There was an old sailing ship going for'ard then sinking, and all of a sudden the maroons went off. You could hear them for miles. There were three young fishermen there and I said 'Good Lord! The mortars have gone'. They said 'Can't you see, on the pictures'. But they hadn't settled down a minute when there come the manager. 'Come on boys, she's gone!' I said 'I told you so', and we went straight out. We found our way across the golflinks—the lifeboat was kept a mile and a half from Sheringham then—and we were falling in bunkers because they were all levelled over with the snow. It was now getting feet deep and 'Pints', poor boy, only had his shoes on. Well when we reached the lifeboat shed it was blowing a living gale. Between the squalls the full moon lit up brilliant, only for a little while, perhaps a quarter of an hour, then that would all blacken out again. The snow was terrific but we put on the jackets and strapped everything down. We pulled them extra tight that night. I always remember my uncle, Obadiah Cooper, he was a religious man and a good seaman, coxswain of the boat. He said, 'D'you know boys, that's a rough night'. Then he got in the boat and said 'Now I want you to know there's a message from Cromer, unable to launch, and we've now got a message from Wells, unable to launch. So it's up to you. Please yourself what you're going to do.' Well we didn't go on about it, we said we'd go.

There was a big acetylene light stuck in the cliff to show you the sea and we got the boat out on the hill. There was a thick rope, 200 yards long, kept at sea the whole time with an anchor on it which come up to a post as the lifeboat shed, and you'd pull it aboard for'ard and aft by lizzards—you see the rope went through this big eye and was attached to the lifeboat at each end. You've got this carriage on top of the big hill, all stones, and you've got to get it right to the edge of the water. There's no chance of rowing; you couldn't hold an oar in your hand, the wind or the sea would break on to it. Well, we stood at the top of this hill and they said 'Let go!'. I was up for'ard and when they let her go the bows went straight under, for a minute I thought I had all the North Sea to myself. It felt minutes although it could only have been seconds while the water was bubbling in my mouth and ears. Last of all she lifted out. They said 'Go at her boys!', then you'd all go at this rope, pulling. And when a big one came they'd cry 'Hang on!'. So you'd hang on. Then again 'Go at her boys!' and you'd go again. 'Hang on!' Coo! She was a beautiful boat, the *J.C. Madge*. At last we got out there as far as the anchor and the next job was to get the mast up. That was tricky in this rough weather. Well we got it up and hooked on the smallest scrap of sail we had. The canvas in those old sails was like mahogany, stiff, and if it happened to catch you, that would knock the skin off. Anyway we got the sail up, too. She would never turn over but the job was to keep in her. When a big 'un come you had to hang on.

We got on our way towards Wells. Between the squalls the moon shone like a flood of light but it blew terrific. Of course we were going with the wind, everything was in our favour. They said, 'You young 'uns keep a look-out, see if you can see the lights'. This was one of my first trips and we hadn't gone far when I said, 'There she be, look!'. But I was pointing to the Wells lifeboat showing a great flare to guide us. Away we went for Blakeney Overfalls, that's a sandbank off Blakeney where there's an old bell buoy. Whenever the swell went, the sound was like going out into a graveyard but we didn't hear it that night. At last I could see rockets coming out of the sky as plain as ever I saw in my life but this time I dussn't speak. Some of the others saw them and shouted out. When we reached her, it was the *Uller*, a Norwegian steamship. 'She's sunk', they said. 'She's on the sand, she's sunk.' There was a tricky sort of scud going, she was down for'ard and half the propeller was out at the back. Anyway we made out that she wasn't sunk and we got alongside somehow, which wasn't easy. When she settled, it was the second coxswain's duty to go aboard with another deck hand or one of the crew. 'I ain't going aboard, she's sunk' they said, but eventually they did go on and told us the boat had hit a sandbank, drifted for eighteen hours, then hit another sandbank and got inside it in deep water so we reckoned it was just inside the Blakeney Overfalls. They'd got all their bags ready to put aboard the lifeboat, ready to leave ship, but now that our two were aboard, although he knew it was impossible to reach Yarmouth, their captain said if we'd stand-by as long as his pumps held he would keep afloat. He had half-steam on his engine and half-steam on his pumps and wanted to try and save the ship.

We said we'd stand-by, though we didn't know our exact position and we couldn't tell him to get under way when he might go over the sand again. We were going to wait until daylight but just before that the old hands among us practically knew where we were. They decided to steam up this deep water to try and find the bell buoy, so we told the captain to steam up a mile if he could. That was a devil of a job. She was going for'ard with her snout down in the gale but finally she made it and when we turned round the bell buoy to get on the way, everything was free for us. Because the propeller was half out of the water they couldn't steer properly and when she'd take a long yaw, the towing rope bulges slack and she come forward too fast. So they put up two balls, like plates on a swivel, to indicate 'Not under control'. Other ships would then keep clear. We were going free now, heading for the Humber at Grimsby. That's fifty-three miles or more but we were doing a lot more than we should with the big yaws. Unfortunately we passed another ship throwing distress signals but there were two more steam boats not far from her so we reckoned they'd go after her. When we got to Grimsby we heard she was lost. Well we got inside the Humber. I suppose the *Uller* had some communications because we spoke to a big government ship. They asked us what lifeboat we were and we told them. Then the pilot boat came but they wouldn't go on her at first because it was still blowing a little gale. 'How long is it going to be before she sinks?' they said. We told them where we'd come from and what we'd done until at last they went aboard. They said they couldn't do anything for her at Grimsby so our two who were aboard transferred back into the lifeboat and the pilot boat took her on to Hull. Then we crossed the Humber for Grimsby. Well she had just a little bit of sail and on that smooth water that was like being on ice, like one skid, that was marvellous.

When we got out of the lifeboat two or three of us were like clods, we'd been thrown about so much that when we stood still we went down. It was forty-eight hours after the launch. There were a lot of Sheringham people fishing at Grimsby and when we got there they opened a big tea shop and took us to their homes. Cor, I could have eaten leather! When they were ordering teas, I said, 'I want two here'. They said 'Why two?' 'When this lot's gone, I'll have another.' Well I slept with one of them that night. The oiled slops used to be dressed in tar stuff, they stuck to us and we had to slit our clothes with a knife to get them off.

Next morning we were called out to go to Spurn Point. A ship had gone ashore and they called us to stand-by in case they wanted us, but they were all right. The Salvation Army band was playing down at the lifeboat shed, there were flags flying and cigarettes and 'baccer. We was living in clover. A French steam boat that was going that way towed us back to Sheringham, so it wasn't so bad coming home.

A stone's throw from Jimmy 'Paris' West's home, 'I Dunno', a green wooden bench sits at the meeting of five narrow roads. A zealous road sweeper wheels across his green bin and brushes up past Teddy West's old shop, then a little police car swivels round in the centre and shoots off. A couple holding hands pass on their way to the town centre. Beyond a picturesque pebble dwelling, a short road with more terraced pebble cottages up one side and some rather bare stone houses on the other runs down to an orange bingo hall, straight ahead is the sea. But before you reach the end, raised steeply above the road stands an unpretentious house where budgies twitch about their cage inside a polythene entrance porch. It is the home of Mr and Mrs Pegg. Jo Pegg is a slight, long-faced, 75-year old with a high boyish voice and a stringy sense of survival. A solidly entrenched Salvationist whose whole life has been spent amongst fishermen. Not, except for a brief spell, himself a fisherman, yet inescapably one of the community, his relations and companions are all fishing people. It is the domestic scene he remembers particularly well.

There were eleven of us born and bred in Wyndham Street. Father went to sea at seven as a cabin boy and his father was a whale catcher. Later on he went gardening because he got a better living. Laid nearly all the greens on the golf links. Then all of a sudden he went to sea again. He probably missed it because all his brothers went to sea. Mother was a Londoner. With no public assistance I don't know how she ever managed but we never did want. She always had something for us to eat, such as it was. She could make a dinner that was really tasty from all these pieces and one thing and another. Pea soup with pig's trotters and shortcake once a week on Saturday. She died when she was sixty and it worry me as much as anything to think that if she was here now we could do something for her. Of course she used to make a lot. She had a little sewing machine and if I got the backside out of me trousers, which boys do going down the cliffs, she'd go and get one of the girl's skirts and I'd have a pair for Sunday. No end of people used to come and say, 'Flo, could you cut these out for my husband?' She wouldn't say 'no' to them.

At Christmastime we always had a tree and always there was stuff on it. I'd go up to my uncle's who lived in the same yard as we did. He was a fisherman and he'd give us these great white boot stockings to hang up. The tree, there'd be something on it you could eat. Little ice watches and birds in their cages, then there was sugar mice. Always blamed me; used to come down in the morning and several had their heads bitten off. It wasn't a big house. There was two bedrooms but Mum had it parted off with thick curtains to make it four. There was only two of us boys at first, the others was all girls so they had to move around a bit to make room. But we was never in bed long enough to want much sleeping and the girls went into service soon as they left school. The baker used to come Monday nights down Wyndham Street, and he always had what he called 'day-olds' which you brought for about a penny each. Think Mother used to take a dozen. Course she never did go out much herself. We had a donkey and carriage we let out to visitors and she'd go down the allotments if we couldn't and bring that home as well as any feller. Digging. She was only a little woman really but she ran about for other people.

Played football for Upper Sheringham, never played for Sheringham. I was up early as a schoolboy, keeping pigs and taking the milk round, and I used to hawk the country with crabs. We all pinched apples and what we could get. We'd meet at nights and Oh! there was some lovely fruit around! A chap grew a lot of strawberries, real good 'uns. We nipped in over the fence one time when he appeared. I was off but my pal got fastened on the netting and the owner got a-hold of him while he was trying to get out. He clipped a great lump out of my pal's hair so his father would know and he wouldn't go back no more. We'd be up early picking mushrooms. I remember one morning I got up on the recreation ground and it was still dark. I was waiting for it to get light so I could see the blessed things. Well later I went to school and about eleven o'clock, of course, I was nodding off. The master suddenly wiped everything off the board, 'Pegg, what was on that board?' I didn't know. But we got our own back. We opened his desk where he kept his stick and covered his gloves with that thick white glue we always used to have in pots. The headmaster was a fine old chap but his wife, she was a terror. I've seen her get that excited her hair would come right over. She'd lay a boy across the desk and wham with a stick. They used to come and see if your boots was clean — very strict with us because we didn't have the best of boots them days. Had the little slippers; you could buy them cheaper'n anything. When we heard the mortars go off, we'd be out of those desks and down there. Schoolmaster used to come along the promenade hunting for us and we'd get underneath the boats 'cos you can get right under them. Especially the small 'uns. We didn't break windows or that sort of thing. We only wanted something for our stomachs and we got it. We'd sit outside watching the Salvation Army, munching.

We were brought up with the Bible. I've got my fifty-year badge with the Salvation Army. It have been my life. Father was a bandsman. Played the monster bass and one of his brothers, 'Go-Father' Pegg, a chapel preacher, used to walk miles preaching. My two brothers sang in the Songster's Brigade, went travelling round singing in their sea gear, and one sister followed Mum in the Church Army. I started in the junior section when I was seven and later I played the cornet. For years I was sergeant major. I'm still in the band and now I have the job of welcoming people at the door. I always wanted that job. When the fishermen finished fishing here they'd go lining at Grimsby. That's where they first started the corps, then came home and opened one here — July 18, 1896. The net loft in the old boathouse was the old Salvation Hall before the new one was built in Cremer Street. We played at all sorts of things. Each year at the children's sanatorium, and the funerals then was very respectful. When we played the 'Dead March' in *Saul* that was a tricky piece. I had to play the drum because that was a difficult part. Brum, brum after every bar.

If, three-quarters of a century ago, there was some choice of occupation for a fisherman's son who was obviously not fitted for the sea, it was extremely limited. In fact, it boiled down to little more than living on his wits. Part of the reason was poor education. 'Why worry about books?' was the prevailing attitude. Girls, by nature more conscientious, took greater pains. Which was fortunate since their future roles as book-keeper and family accountant demanded literacy. Sometimes they even tried to teach their husbands how to read and write and classes for illiterate adults were run through the influence of the Upchers. But the whole social structure tended to keep the fisherman where he was. Since the relatively well-off could afford to send their children to a grammar school, only the exceptionally bright from the fishing community ever got through. It was not until the education system changed and grammar school places could be won on merit that they first had an opportunity to better themselves. And they took it.

But things had not changed in Jo Pegg's day.

After I left school I did odd jobs, anything for a living. I worked gardening for a Member of Parliament, a fine gentleman too. Then I had two or three tries at fishing but never did make a go of it. I was cab driving, with a horse and cab, but there was nothing much to do here. So I went with the Exide Battery people. My first job was in London. There was seven or eight men in this here battery room, erecting big batteries for storage for London trams and that sort of thing. We'd be cleaning positive and negative plates ready to go into big boxes for big cells. We unloaded them, ooh! they was some weight, and the foreman, he'd be at the burner, sitting on top of the cells burning the plates on as we was cleaning 'em. There'd be as many as two hundred in this here room. I watched the other fellers and I ain't long picking up anything, you know. But my hands shook when I took me first week's wages because I wasn't getting above thirty shillings here in Sheringham, thirty shillings was big wages. Well I got five pound. Anyway I played with Salvationists all over the country. I always carried my instrument with me and my uniform. At Hull there was a concertina band, all girls. My wife and her sister was in it and that's where we met.

About ten years ago I was foreman of the stone-picking down here. We had a station then. Lorries come down on the beach about three times a day and the men loaded them up

42

from little rubber buckets. It went to Stoke-on-Trent to be
ground down into a white powder for pottery and some to
cement workers, but years ago it went for building. In the
1880's there would be forty or fifty children picking the stones
and carrying them to boats waiting on the sands for the tide.
Ships used to come from Boston for them. Sometimes they
would anchor and the stones was ferried out to them by
fishermen. Even the last time it was mostly fishermen done it in
their spare time. The stones all had to be graded — 1½ -2
inches, 2-3 inches or 3-4 inches. But some people said it was
taking away the sea defence. That's rubbish! These stones come
in on the tide from Cromer and back. They all come down
from the west. You see the white rock on the beach — what we
call marl. The sea keeps pounding away at that so large chunks
fall off. They break up and get ground down rubbing against
each other, then rounded with the water.

When social functions were limited, the annual town
regatta was the highlight of the year. There are sports and
carnivals today, of course, but the old ones, where fishermen
competed against each other in gigantic family rivalries, are
remembered with affection. Jimmy 'Paris' mentioned them,
so did many others. Jo Pegg was in his element at a
ceremony.

Regattas and carnivals, I've been in them as long as I can
remember. There would be crab-boat racing at the annual
regatta between the fishermen and the fire brigade, and the
Ramey Upcher, the fishermen's lifeboat, would be anchored
off beach at high water with a greasy pole. On the end was a
box with a pig in it. 'Fatty' Pegg, he was an uncle, used to win
it every year. I took children for rides in a little go-cart with a
nanny goat when I was ten or twelve. Once had an old lady
weighed fourteen stone. I didn't take her for a ride, it was just
for a photo. She was a cook and it was her footman I think
who bet her ten shillings she wouldn't get in that little cart. He
paid me. We propped a bit of wood back and front and it took
the weight. It was worth it you see for the ten shillings.

Just how do the fishermen fit into the larger communities
in which they live? 'They are in it by virtue of living there',
said a Sheringham man aptly, 'but not of it. They are

separated by the nature of their work. Engines may have made them less dependent on tides but they still can't keep ordinary working hours. They're off in the morning when everyone is asleep and sometimes late back. They can't be town councillors. As some of them got on and became merchants, they moved onto the local council, but we've only had the odd one who actually went to sea.'

Partly, I suspect, because the fisherman feels an amateur except in his own business, and partly because his working hours handicapped him, he has preferred to elect representatives to voice his opinions and protect his interests. Jo Pegg has long been a mouthpiece for the fishing community.

I've been on voluntary committees all me life. On Sheringham council since 1937, well over thirty years. The Plowlet was money left to the poor of Sheringham and that was mostly fishing people. We put up a notice to find out who is entitled to it. They've got to be seventy-year-old and worthy. That's one of the main reasons I stay on the council. Because I know all these old people. I am one of the trustees and I take it round to them and feel I'm doing something. There are only two or three of us now who are local on the council. The rest are new-comers to the town.

Bob Rushmer also represents the fishing people. 'Secretary, North Norfolk Fishermen's Assocn' reads the sign beside the door of his neat semi-detached house just south of Sheringham. Mr Rushmer is a cautious, unassuming, quiet-voiced person — almost one of the fishermen, to his chagrin, not quite. He notes, like Jimmy 'Paris' West before him, that fishing is in the doldrums.

Sheringham fishing is reduced to the lowest I've ever known it. There have been fishermen here from time immemorial so this is just one of the unfortunate changes in history. It's difficult to explain how it has come about. The easiest answer is to say they're are not many sons who have followed their fathers. Take Henry 'Joyful', the lifeboat coxswain. He's got two sons neither of whom has gone to sea. They're both university boys and they're putting their skills into another kind of life. Teaching and that sort of thing. Mind you, I think the rewards ashore are more certain, that influences them, coupled with the expense of going to sea. If anyone wants to go in on their own there's the tremendous cost of boat and gear.

Compare this with the views of 'Shrimp' Davies from neighbouring Cromer and George Cox of Mundesley to get a wider picture. First 'Shrimp':

Fishing is declining because at one time there were almost a hundred from Cromer going to sea. It has declined because it was such a precarious and hard living; there's no doubt about it. If the weather was bad during the winter months they had absolutely nothing coming in, and they didn't earn a lot of money in the summer. Years ago there was no industry in the area so they had to work on the land or be fishermen. They chose to be fishermen if father was one. But when the school-leaving age rose to fourteen in local council schools and you had a chance to win a scholarship and go to grammar school, many of them tried and many did get on, of course. And got out. I don't think things were much better at Cromer than at Sheringham. When the railways came and hotels were being built lots of chaps got jobs as labourers, went in for brick-laying, plastering and that sort of thing. We had the railway first and Cromer was a pleasure resort before Sheringham.

It was the same with farm labourers. Think how many of them over the years have left the land for pretty well the same reason — because they can earn more in industry. There's another reason, too. Father and son in our family drowned in 1918 so no more of that family went to sea. It's safer now than it has ever been but no matter what size boat or ship you've got, if the weather is bad an accident can happen.

Then George Cox:

I don't know how long these youngsters can stick the pace. I've heard that some of their wives aren't going to leave it to their husbands. They can earn money in a good season crabbing but not enough to tide them through the winter. The season is getting shorter and shorter, so more of them will turn away to get another job. A man can say what he likes but if his wife is going to put her foot down you knuckle under. If you have commitments you must ensure you have sufficient pounds a week coming in. So if these boys get a decent job during the winter they might not be able to go back crabbing. And over

45

the next years there will be a decline in boats even if it doesn't exactly end. It's going to be a hard job for people outside the coastal fringe to get a Cromer crab unless they travel for it. We used to deliver from Mundesley right the way to Lowestoft. Well now, with the increased price of petrol, the majority at Cromer are selling what they catch themselves, cutting the other man out. This will stop the crabs going inland and once the fish merchants can't get them when they want them I'm afraid they will finish with them altogether.

And now back to Mr Rushmer:

For the first time ever there's no fishing on the East Beach. No one can go out from there alone because they've got to have help getting the boats up and down. They've got to rely on one another to a certain extent whether they like it or not. And this is one of the reasons we've reached such a small number of boats. If I go back to my last year as fishery officer, in 1972, there were about twenty full-time and about fifteen part-time crab boats in the north Norfolk district from Hunstanton to Great Yarmouth. Of course the part-timers do make a contribution to the catch. But if Jimmy 'Paris' sounded light-hearted when he said we shall soon only have afternoon fishermen, it could well be true. The financial risks are so great compared with the rewards in industry. If you have any education I'm certain your future is more secure on land.

At one time, we know, there was little alternative to following one's father's occupation. Then seaside resorts boomed, house-building required young men and industry generally offered more choice. Yet perhaps the old life, with all its physical insecurities, was simpler because these great decisions never arose. After hanging on for years, desperately trying to eke a living from the sea, George Cox admits, 'If I could still get a good living all the year round from fishing I wouldn't have gone where I am now with the gas people.' While the frustration of Bob Rushmer's own choice in no way lightened the burden of helping his son:

My eldest boy who works for a building firm in Sheringham had an opportunity of going to sea. He really thought he would, only when we came to basics it meant he'd have to lay out £1,000 to participate in crab fishing alone. When we put what he might earn — perhaps six, seven or eight hundred pounds from May until the end of October — the risk was too great because at the end of all that he wouldn't have a boat. You need at least £3,500 to buy the class of motor boat that's down on the beach today. He asked for my advice and I've never felt in such a spot in my life. Well, we tried taking it apart piece by piece, being a bit mercenary and ignoring his love of the sea. He eventually said, 'This isn't any good for me, much as I'd like to go'. He's got a wife and two children, a new bungalow and a motorcar, and while one could argue that most fishermen have cars because it's part of their trade, he had such an enormous expense to meet that he felt the risk was rather too great. Now my younger son David has got a degree in economics and he's in an oil company's head office in London. He never had any liking to go to sea. He only thinks about water when he has to wash his face.

The situation is neatly summed up in an Eastern Sea Fisheries Report for 1962:

> From an economic point of view the picture of a reasonably static rate of landings and values is discouraging because there is no doubt that each year costs are rising while the average rates of earnings are not increasing to compensate, and as a result fishermen in this part of the world are getting progressively less and less return on the fishing effort and capital employed therein. It is not encouraging to the older men to remain on largely static earnings while shore employment wages increase from time to time. The younger men just do not stand for it, and the result is that the intake of full-time younger men is very small indeed.

The reasons for Mr Rushmer himself not going to sea were basically similar, only the emphasis has changed.

> Although my father was a fisherman, I didn't go to sea. Not because I didn't want to, because I did. Parental pressure was part of the reason. About 1920, when I was thirteen and longing to go, the fishing was bad. Whelks were only 1s 3d a wash — that's a Sheringham measure equal to about a third of a hundredweight. It was really bad up until 1926, and parents didn't want their sons going fishing. I didn't go to grammar school. I was that thick I wondered why I needed a grammar school to learn how to haul crab pots. If only my headmaster could have told me I could go there and learn navigation and

that sort of thing, I would have looked at it in an entirely different way. Of course I was sorry later, but at the time I couldn't see farther than Sheringham.

I've regretted not going to sea even to the present day because I felt my life was fishing. In a sense, that I was fishery officer for twenty-one years seemed to help, although it never made up for what I feel I've missed.

Not so long ago a considerable proportion of the population in fishing towns and villages were involved indirectly, if not directly, in fishing operations. Gear now comes from far and wide but once it was manufactured locally. Blacksmiths made whelk pots, net makers made fish nets and rope spinners made the tows. There were boat-builders, tanning-yard workers, and fish merchants all tied up with the sea. One fish merchant in particular played a large part in the Sheringham scene, as Mr Rushmer testifies.

Beach auctions used to be held when they were cod lining. The cod were brought ashore and laid out on the west gangway. I can remember one day in particular when it was full from top to bottom, you just couldn't walk in between various catches. All cod. And the merchants would come down, Charlie Holsey, probably Benny Brown or Dick Bishop and Harry Johnson, about four buyers at that time who bid one against the other for the fish. Either the boat owner or one of the crew stood at the foot of his fish, looking to see when they were giving the nods and winks as they do at auctions and he would say 'Now have you all done at such and such a price? Have you all done for the first time? Have you all done for the second? They're going at £25.' He'd have two pebbles from the beach in his hand. Smack! That was as good as a lawyer's letter. A signature to the sale. I can remember a boat having £110 worth of fish, which was a lot of money in those days.

They used to moor crabs in boxes on Saturday morning. My father would nick them to dislocate the pincer joint so that they couldn't attack each other. Then they would go out as usual on a Monday morning and bring in the new catch, which they'd have in addition to the Saturday one. Sometimes wholesalers would only take the new ones so the fishermen had to keep them even longer. There were local merchants who took all the catches but 75 per cent of the men send off their own today. Jimmy 'Paris' was one of the first to break away and send his own off.

To some extent the fishermen were in the hands of wholesalers, which was why Harry Johnson was important locally. In fact, he became the leading fish merchant, almost exercising a monopoly over them. He amassed a tremendous amount of money and ended up owning a couple of hotels in Sheringham, as well as having interests in some in London. Everything he touched turned to gold. Although his father was a fisherman and he probably went to sea as a boy, he started as a clerk at Sheringham railway station. Then he joined the fishing as owner of five whelk coppers. The whelks would be bought directly from the fishermen and he boiled them and sent them away — at a profit, mind. They called him 'Knicker-bockers' because he always wore them even when he was down on the front. He was bright all right. He had all his buttons and probably somebody else's as well! He introduced petrol engines into the boats and his men serviced them when they went wrong, so to a certain extent the fishermen were obliged to give him their catches. He supplied them with petrol, too. He was king pin, supplied the lot. I think he stimulated the community, he was on a lot of committees, but he was always one step ahead of everyone else. They resented it.

In Bob Rushmer's father's time fishing was more varied, less specialised, than it is today. Almost every boat followed the same broad plan. They whelked through the winter from the end of November until March, then caught crabs and lobsters until the end of September when they went drift-netting for mackerel in May and long-lining for skate in both May and September when they come into spawn. Those were the last great days of herring drifting at Yarmouth, where it has now died out completely. The main fishing today is for crabs, whelks and long-lining and subsidiary, and drift-netting has gradually deteriorated over the past fifty years until it's virtually been abandoned.

Were there always two broad types of fishing people, the principled and the rip-roaring? Certainly not all were true to the popular pattern of hard-swearing, hard-drinking old reprobates.

For instance, the Sheringham fishermen who settled in Grimsby helped to build the Citadel in Duncombe Street — they sawed the wood and carved the pulpit and pews themselves, and at one period the Grimsby lifeboat crew was almost solidly Salvationist and Shannock. It was this sort of background the Rushmers came from.

All my people were Methodists and I still am. Even today there are fishermen who won't go to sea on a Sunday but they never used to go however bad the catch had been during the week. When I was young I couldn't whistle on a Sunday and although I lived on that beach the rest of the week, every day before I went to school or as soon as I was out, I was there helping my father or someone else, taking a jug of tea down to the boats for my father. But I never went down there on Sunday — never even thought of going. The Salvation Army had a lot of influence on the fishing community in its early days, lots of fishermen were Salvationists. There'd be a few rough ones but, by and large, they were God-fearing race. John 'Teapot' West and Willy Long were Evangelists and the chapel in Station Road was called the Fishermen's Chapel because the preachers and most of the congregation were fishermen. They were very strict, good-living, Bible-reading people. My aunt and uncle lived next door, and she ran the Sunday School while he was very devout Salvationist and their son was the bandmaster. I think it was the hardships they encountered daily and the things you see at sea, well, the landsman has no knowledge of them. It's as the Psalm 107 says:

> They that go down to the sea in
> ships, that do business in great waters;
> These see the works of the Lord
> and his wonders in the deep.
> For he commandeth, and raiseth
> the stormy wind, which lifteth up
> the waves thereof.

But I wouldn't think the Salvation Army has much influence today and although some of them are Methodists, I don't think even that holds the community together any more.

I was elected to the North Norfolk Fisheries the year after I

50

retired so I can continue my interest in fisheries, and I am involved in some of the day-to-day problems, such as action against trawlers going through pots or trawling on local grounds. The three-mile limit is as far as the Eastern Sea Fisheries jurisdiction goes, after that you come under the Ministry. If some of the EEC partners have been fishing in our waters over a long period of time they have preferential treatment but I entirely disagree with this. I think inshore waters round our island should be for British fishermen completely. So an extension of the limits would be a good thing.

The reputation of the Norfolk crab boat is considerable. Yet nearly twenty winters have passed since the doors of the shed on Lifeboat Plain opened to spill another one, or a whelker, out onto the street. From two families once engaged in the business there is only one survivor—Harold Emery, a short, ruddy-complexioned man with thinning hair and a strange shy twist of the mouth when he speaks. An intense and meticulous concern with detail marks him as a craftsman, while his respect for tradition is not confined to his work, it suffuses his whole way of thinking.

My great grandfather, Lewis, started the boat-building in our family roughly a hundred years ago. He was a fisherman and he wanted a new boat, so he tried it hi'self. From then on he kept at it instead of going to sea. He started building crab boats, clinker-built, double-ended, broad-beamed, yes, and tubby. Before that they were using what they called cobles, which wasn't the answer to what they wanted. My grandfather Robert carried on after him, then my father and then me. Both my father and my grandfather were called 'Caller' because they had curly hair.

For a century the crab boat was the backbone of fishing craft on this part of the coast. As Mr Emery indicates, they changed little over the years.

The crab boats were smaller in the sailing days. About 18ft long, 7ft wide and 3ft depth in the middle. You don't get them much below 20ft now and they're a bit wider, 8 to 8½ft. The weight of the engine puts them further down in the water, so we got to 3ft 3in or 3ft 4in depth. The first boat here with a motor was a converted hoveller but the first motor boat was built by my father in 1914 for old Willy Craske and his partners, 'Decky' Love and Long John. She was called the *Welcome Home*. He made a lot of boats for Harry Johnson because he bought the engines as well and the fishermen paid him so much a week to buy them.

They were made with larch planking and oak ribs. Always oak for keel, stem and stern posts, and always oak ribs unless you had a boat for repairs and it was a different shape to what we were used to. Used to have to get some wood called American elm or American oak that would bend easier but it wouldn't last so long. You know the thwarts, the seats — well the knees are the curved pieces which go through the thwarts and are made fast to the side of the boat to hold the whole lot together. They were natural bends in the oak; they grew that shape. The mast would have been spruce and there were half-round iron splines around the washstrake, what you'd call the rim of the boat, to stop it from wearing when the crab pots came over. The early ones, they could lift them off when they went crabbing, then put them back again for whelking but now they're steadfast. The whole boat wasn't boarded in. They had a board for'ard, what they called the fore sheet, for laying the lobsters and gear on and where they hauled in the stern there was the standing, a bit of board what they stood on. The arruck holes, three a side, were cut about 4½ inches square. They're a must for these sort of boats, to slip the oars through. Even the motor boats, when they go off now, if that's rough they always have the oars cocked in case the engine stops. Then they can nip round, get hold of them and straighten the boat out. Early days, they came ashore, they'd lay the boat lengthwise to the beach so it knocked up with the tide. When they came back later, it'd be nearly up to the stones. That would save them hauling up the sand. They'd put the oars through, crook one arm round and carry them the last bit. Three arruck holes each side, that would be six men to a boat could do it easy. Might be just two and old John Craske, who was called 'Strong Arms', he managed by hi'self. He'd get it across his back and put his arms under the thwart. It was before my time but my grandfather used to tell me about it.

There used to be a sailmaker here and one at Wells, cousins called Grimes, and they did all the sailmaking for everybody.

It was just a lug sail and that'd be tanned dark brown. If there wasn't any wind it'd be lashed on to the boat and they'd be using the oars, but if that was windy they'd lower the sail while they were working and haul it up again when they wanted to come home. For ballast they'd take stones off the beach; fill up a bag with stones and put it in the bottom of the boat. There was a long board right along the middle lengthwise to the keel, what they called the parting board, and they'd shift these stones from one side to the other all according to where they wanted 'em. If it was low water they'd empty the bags on the beach but if it was high water I heard my grandfather say they'd put the bags on their backs and take them home until they had enough to build a house with. That's how you see all these houses stone-built. I can just remember them taking the sacks and humping them up the road somewhere. Of course they wouldn't be allowed to do that now.

When I started with my grandfather, the sailing craft then began to go out. But at one time there were more sailing boats than what there was motor boats. Even when the engines come in a lot of people couldn't go to the expense of buying them so they had to keep on with the old sailing craft. When they changed to motors the shape changed a bit, too. They liked the old boats a bit sharp in the bottom, more V-shaped, but now they're fuller and there's more room in them. Mind you, the ordinary person walking along wouldn't notice it. When my grandfather fitted the first engine he designed a different sternpost. Said he lay a-bed thinking it out 'cos that had to be thicker. They had an engineer from Belfast come down to fit the Belfast Barker engine and he wanted my grandfather to patent his invention but he never would do it. If he had a-done we'd be sitting pretty, 'cos all up and down the country, not only in Norfolk and Suffolk, they have this sternpost. I've seen them myself. He once done a big job for 'Go-Father' Pegg. 'Go-Father' went along the coast to Blakeney and bought this here boat that was short and stubby. He wanted it longer, so my grandfather cut it through the middle and put four foot in. Nobody ever saw him do it because he had it covered over with tarpaulin. He sawed right through, got it wedged up and spliced his keel, then spliced all his planks and made it longer. That turned out to be a good job. One of the best boats old 'Go-Father' ever had. They used to think a lot of these here boats. Grandfather made one for the Science Museum right the same in detail, the fittings and everything. I always ask to see it when I go up to London. It's in there now.

My great grandfather had a place round the west end of town where they built the old *Ramey Upcher* lifeboat. It was my grandfather took over the yard we've got now. It used to be the old Salvation Army hall and before that it was a net chamber for the fishermen. He did two crab boats, one behind the other on the top floor and a whelk boat down below. He built two each winter, but with my father we just did one. We launched them out of the big doors and put the engine in down below, otherwise they'd be a bit weighty to get out. My father built the last one 1957. We launched in April and he died in the June. Quick as that. Then I was left on my own. The old sailing boats cost a pound a foot. Crab boats have been built for only £9. They never did charge enough money for their time and their skill. Never. That's why I wasn't too bothered about it myself because I've only got one pair of hands and I took over the deckchairs. I still get overworked in the winter-time. I do a repair job and it comes to more than the boat used to cost.

We didn't work with plans or patterns. No blue prints. Didn't even have an electric drill before the war. I know that because I was at Brookes at Lowestoft then working on the invasion barges and the first thing they shoved into my hand was an electric drill. I didn't know what it was and that was the truth. I'd never seen one before. Mind you a lot of these old boat-builders, they was in the same plight. But when I came back I thought to myself, well I'm going to get one of these. At Brookes we used to have these here moulds, then we used to bend the ribs in and put the planking all round. Ribs are done first in most forms of construction, but that all seemed so strange to me because we always put the planking in first.

Money used to come secondary to the old ones, not first like it is today. They used to build plenty of boats and didn't get much out of them at all. Long as they were happy with their work, that was all right. My father would be there early in the mornings, see if everything was all right. He lived near by and there wasn't a Sunday morning went by without him glancing in the boathouse when the boat was being built. Just to have a glance at it and shut the doors up again. He couldn't resist the temptation. They used to take a pride in their work different from what we do today. I'm the same way myself and I can't get out of it. People think I take a long while to do a job but I just got to see it's right, however long it takes. Of course as you get old you take longer still. But they keep asking me to do the jobs. Even if I do take longer, and my father worked until he was seventy-two. The boat I'm doing—well twenty years ago I would have done it in half the time. You keep jumping in and out and you can't get out so quick. I realise that. I'm sixty-three and it's dawning on me that I just can't work so fast.

You put the ribs in hot, soak them in a steam trunk or trough for about three hours. You have just like an ordinary copper fire and the steam goes up into the trunk when the water boils. It runs along the trunk and into these ribs, so when you get them out you can bend them where you want to. But, like I say, when the boat was ready to bend those in, if you didn't shore it up from underneath, put some shores in, wedges, it would make the boat go out of shape. Once you've got these ribs in that's OK but until that's done it can easily alter in shape. My father and grandfather took a lot of pride in putting these shores up and getting it just right. They were very particular about it, very particular. They used to have this here shape of the boat in their eye all the time, in their mind's eye. It was there in front of them and they knew exactly what they wanted it to be when it was finished.

I started about eleven, the same age as Father started. When I come home from school I used to go down in the workshop, and he done the same. You've got to do that you know, to pick it up. 'Cos it's a trade, even if you're at it for fifty years, you're learning every day. You've got to have a flair for it. And you're learning new ideas, new ways of doing things to make them a bit better. 'Cos it's hard work all the time. And you're picking up little things to make life a bit easier.

Cromer's ugly red-brick Victorian hotels and boarding-houses that shot up in its heyday as a seaside resort lend the town an air of slightly tired jauntiness, of being past its prime. And recent development with rows of modern bunga-lows, their fronts pricked with wallflowers, has scarcely helped. The promenaded front seems to be dominated by neo-Gothic monstrosities and service stations, laced with a surfeit of cafeterias and ice-cream stalls. But in the middle of the town is a fine old church slightly battered by the war, and

Cromer is by no means without character. Coquettish, she is still busy trying to attract visitors.

On one side of the pier there are beach huts and boats belonging to an angling club, on the other, a line of crab boats lie on a strip of warm yellow sand. Somewhere along the bustling promenade, not far from his stack of deckchairs, 'Shrimp' Davies is hiring them out. H.T. Davies, coxswain of the lifeboat, nephew of the celebrated Capt Blogg and himself a decorated lifeboatman, is highly thought of, a central figure in the town. He is tall and broad, deeply tanned, capped and moustached, with a cigarette dangling from his mouth.

Except that the names are different, he tells us, things at Cromer have paralleled what has happened at Sheringham.

> We go crabbing; *if* there's any herring, which has been very scarce the last few years, we go late September, October and November. Then there could be long-lining for cod. We whelk but only in the winter months. Eleven boats belong principally to Davies and Harrison, two of the oldest families; then there are Coxes, Gaffs and so on. They are nearly all full time. Two years ago there were eighteen boats but that included the Overstrand ones that moved here because their beach was bad. They've gone back again. The Davies are a bit like the Wests of Sheringham, hence all the nicknames, I'm 'Shrimp' and there's 'Little Jo' and 'Old Jo' and so on.
>
> Our Davies ancestors apparently walked from Wales, I would think in the early 1800s. I'm told there were notices posted round the town warning local inhabitants that this stranger had been seen in the vicinity and they were advised to keep their doors and windows locked. We don't know whether he had ever been fishing before but eventually he settled, married a local girl and started up here. His son, my great grandfather, became coxswain of the lifeboat and his son after that, and so on all through the years. The family seemed to grow as there were a lot of boys and they were very nearly all fishermen in the first generations.

So deeply ingrained, so universal is the fishing routine on this coast I would have had a similar explanation whoever

I had asked about it. 'Shrimp' himself comments on the fact that it has changed little over the years.

We keep the boats on four-wheeled carriages and they're pushed down by tractor. They manage by launching the boats with only one or two aboard, then after the spare men have helped everybody down they all get into the last boat and transfer into their own when they get out. The flood tides run from north-west to south-east near enough, and the ebb tides run from south-east to north-west. Now on the ebb we start at the south-east and haul the pots before the tide, and on the flood we start at the north-west in order to haul with the tide again. In a three-man boat we work seven shanks, or perhaps eight while others that take two probably work six shanks, about twenty-five pots to a shank. There's an anchor and a buoy on each end with different coloured flags, or perhaps a different shaped buoy so you can tell your own pots and you remember which end of the shank is which from memory. Here at Cromer you see Beeston Church and three woods on the road to Blakeney which look from the sea like hills. As you go out, Beeston Church moves inwards, you start off with what is known as the Black Hill, then the Middle Hill and then the Inner Hill. Once you get the bearings from those two lined up, that tells you how far out you are. Then you get a mark from a house, or say the lighthouse, and where those imaginary lines cross, puts you on a certain spot. We take a compass but remembering comes to be second nature. You keep a plan in your mind of how those shanks lie all the time and once you start you know exactly where to go for the rest. It's an unwritten law that you don't foul another man's pots. You give him what is called 'a berth' but if you want to fish in the same place it's a matter of getting there first. You have your eye open to see who gets a good catch.

The skipper doesn't always haul because you can put the engine into neutral and gather the pots as the tide drifts the boat up. There's about 14 fathoms of rope between each pot, a fathom is 6 feet, so we'll say 50 fathoms near enough and that'll make it 90 feet. You fix up the buoy, the anchor comes off the ground, goes for'ard, then the pots come up. If there are three hands the pot is passed to the second one, who undoes the door, takes out the bait and throws as many little 'uns over as possible, then he passes it to the man in the centre who is known as the baiter-upper. He puts the good ones in the locker, rebaits the pot, closes the door and puts it for'ard. You remove a white-footed crab, that's probably one that moulted last year and hasn't yet hardened off. They mustn't be landed until July 1st. Not only does the fishery stop us landing white-feet but the fishermen volunteered themselves because though the crabs are good to eat, they're not as good a class as the black-toed. We call them 'white-feet' because the two black toes on the end of the claw change to grey or white. That is how you would know one but of course the fisherman can tell from the weight as soon as he takes hold of the pot, by the strength of them or how they cling. We could almost do it blindfold. Then we're not allowed to land any crab under 4½ inches. Everybody has a measure to slip them in. Somewhere about 1875 the Crab and Lobster Fisheries Act put the minimum limit at 4¼ inches, then the fishermen wanted to put it up to 4½ because there were lots of crabs and we thought it would help save glutting the markets as well as improving the quality and breeding. At the same time the lobster size was put up from 8 to 9 inches by request of Cromer and Sheringham fishermen to try and conserve them. Now they're thinking of putting the legitimate size up again but if they stopped trawlers landing small lobsters or berried lobsters they would do much more good. They ought to throw them back the same as we have to. There are different rules for them. In fact there are lots of places where they don't have fishing inspectors, they can land almost what they like.

We put fresh bait in for crabs but for lobsters you need stinking bait; the older the better. So although you catch them from the same pot the crab likes bait fresh and the lobster likes it salted down and left for a couple of days. During the summer months, when a few more lobsters are about, we bait up some shanks especially for lobsters. We get a better price for them but there's not the quantity. We call two crabs a cast but we only talk in casts at the beginning of the season when we're catching just a few. Otherwise we still count in long hundreds.

The most experienced man will sort out the crabs, putting the proper ones in the locker and he'll let somebody else pay the pots over. Say a shank has done well, he chucks the anchor back in about the same place, each pot follows the other one over, then the last anchor and buoy. Vice versa on the ebb tide.

58

When a boat comes ashore it lies athwart the beach. A rope is attached to the stern, the tractor goes down, pulls the boat round, lifts it on the skeet, carriage is put under, hook on and straight up the beach. Someone from the first boat jumps off and fetches the tractor, turns it round, then perhaps there are two or three all arriving at once so they help out. Sheringham has electric winches that pull the boats right up.

When more people dealt with fishing, marketing the catch was the job of wholesalers, now it has become an important part of the fisherman's own work. 'Shrimp' points out a few of the difficulties.

Marketing is a problem. We have tried Billingsgate but the Londoners prefer the big Cornish crab. They're the same species but larger; the reason being that the water is warmer round Devon, so they grow twice as quickly and probably moult twice a year instead of once. Ours wouldn't grow even if we left them but if the water was extra warm they might. You know as well as I do that there's nothing like the Norfolk crab. They're excellent quality. Most of them used to travel by train in what was called a fish brake, a big wooden carriage that took crabs or fish all over the country, but that all finished when the railways packed up. As our crabs don't make the money they should at Billingsgate, most of us transport them ourselves to different places after we've got them ashore.

Here he discusses some of the crafts traditionally part of the fishermen's work.

All the gear is exactly the same as it was when I first went fishing. We buy the rectangular oak frame and the cast-iron weight for the bottom of the crab pot and make the rest. The iron bit we call a music-bottom—because of the shape I suppose, like notes. I think they come from Leicester now though they were once made at Bungay in Suffolk. But we've only had them in latter years. Before that we used any old lumps of iron in a wooden frame, some still do. Most of the frames are made by Emery at Sheringham, then we put in four hoops of wood, the bows or canes. They are actually made of cane now but they used to be hazel. We'd go up in the wood and cut them, hundreds of branches we pinched. I've never been caught myself but some of them were—and summonsed.

59

Mostly they have bow benders today, a piece of wood shaped round which they can bolt on to a bench. They put the cane round the frame and tie the two ends ready to put in the holes. I still take the cane—you need almost three feet—shave down the ends to fit the hole and bend it round my knees to get the right shape before plonking them in. The netting, when that's finished, has two spouts at each side, opposite each other, joined by a tunnel which the crab gets in through. There's a hole in the middle and down he falls. Every fisherman's son is taught to braid nets before he leaves school. I tried to teach my grandson. The real art is to keep the twine tight so that it doesn't slip when you do the knot.

We didn't use a crab pot in Cromer until 1863. Prior to that they used the hoop nets with a net bag attached to a circular metal ring held up by three pieces of rope. The bar, as we call it, was two pieces of string stretched across the mouth of the bag to hold the bait. But they could only work them on the slack part of the tide. Just as the flood was finishing they'd drop them in and if they were easy tides, neap tides, they'd leave them perhaps an hour. After that they had the single pot—what the Sheringham fishermen call a swummer, with tow and corks on it, perhaps the first about a fathom and a half from the pot, then a fathom, then a half fathom, so that four or five corks were floating on top of the water. Here in Cromer it was called a floatum. They started off working about a score of them, the same number as they had hoops, then someone had the bright idea of tying them all together. It was the secretary of the lifeboat, a man called Sandford, who went somewhere on the south coast, saw the crab pot and introduced it here.

Football has long been the fisherman's favourite past-time. Was a dwindling gene pool, diminished by constant inbreeding responsible for the short, stocky size of some of the Norfolk men? A reporter who first met Shannock footballers when he was a boy, remembered the team as particularly tough—'Not tall men, nor elegant players, but very strong and thick-set, looking nearly as broad as they were long'. Apparently the Lowestoft crowd was more than once so incensed by their hard tackling that the Sheringham bus was stoned before it could leave the scene of the match. George

Cox compares his own hobbies with those of his father:

Father only had one hobby as far as I know and that was going to sea, but I think the majority of them played football. He played for Overstrand mainly but I believe some of them gained county honours. Years ago on a Saturday afternoon during the wintertime you'd see a good gathering of supporters and I've seen some nasty rows starting on the line if things hadn't gone right for Cromer. Especially when rival teams were playing, like Cromer against Sheringham. Invariably the fisherman is a decent dart player and some are good on the billiard table, especially from Sheringham. I read very little. I like my game of billiards, snooker and occasionally darts. Sometimes I play bowls. I like going to sea in my spare time and I like live theatre.

'Shrimp' remembers that the fisherman had two other interests. One was his association with the lifeboat, the other, subsidiary earnings from summer visitors.

I left school when I was fourteen and went straight to sea. I'm sixty-one now, so that makes it about forty years ago. Old Billy Craske was eighty-five or eighty-six before he finished. He got to the stage where they had to lift him into the lifeboat before they launched. I joined the lifeboat crew at seventeen — you're not allowed to go before you've gained a bit of experience at sea. I was elected coxswain in 1947 so I'm in my twenty-eighth year now. We've only had about two launchings this year but from 1964 to 1965 we went out about once a month. Not always to local boats, to big ships and weekend sailors during the summer — those that run out of fuel in the middle of nowhere, don't we have some trouble with them! There's a long open coast here with no harbour to get in. It's difficult unless you have local knowledge. Each lifeboat has its own area and we don't encroach on the other's ground space. All fishermen are lifeboat volunteers. Today we have four regular people; coxswain, second coxswain, first and second mechanic. There is a crew of seven, and they always go. Their lifebelts are kept in the lifeboat while the other three are hung beside the boathouse. The first three men there get them out of about twenty volunteers.

From Sheringham to Caister providing deckchairs along the sea front has always been the prerogative of fishermen.

They have also taken out fishing parties and run pleasure trips, while their wives took in summer visitors. 'Shrimp' is king of deckchairs at Cromer:

When Cromer became known as a watering place and a holiday resort, no one was allowed to undress on the beach. The old wooden bathing machines with four big wheels and steps were towed down into the water by horses, and everybody bathed from them. A family by the name of Miller started the business with Rooks, who were fishermen. Then my grandfather, J. H. Davies, acquired both Miller's and Rook's bathing machines. I think he had 101 and he was a great swimmer. At that time women had to bathe on their own and men had a separate section. A man couldn't go into the sea with his wife. Had anybody been drowned that would have harmed grandfather's business and probably been a bad advertisement for the town, so when Princess Elizabeth of Austria, who stayed at the Royal Tux Hotel, went swimming, he used to go in with all his clothes on and swim round outside the women so that if she got into difficulty he'd be there to rescue her. They'd hire out rough towels or a bathing dress for a penny apiece and they had iron chairs with wooden slats, heavy square upright things, until the deckchair was evolved, about 1895. Then things began to improve and he had some box tents made, six by six with a wooden floor and a pointed roof. Lock-up, of course, so they could be let by the week or the fortnight. At that time of day people came for longer holidays. They hired houses for perhaps the whole summer. Father brought down the family and left them for six or eight weeks while he returned to town for business then picked them up later on. When the railways came in the late 1890s the hotels began to grow almost like mushrooms. There were three or four built in one winter to cope with all the visitors because business became pretty good. Now, of course, it's different. Some of the hotels fell to pieces during the war and two or three have caught fire since, so we are all their guests short. We have more day trippers because the motorcar brings them from almost anywhere in East Anglia in two or three hours. Families have been returning for years. There are children on the beach now whose grandfathers used to come.

Henry Blogg and his brother, Jack Davies, worked with Grandfather at the deckchairs and it has been passed on to us since. But we've lost the old bathing machines, now everyone strips on the beach. A day on the bathing machines, when people had early morning dips, started somewhere around seven. Today, with the deckchairs it's nearer nine until the evening. We spend all day there. In the old days we had many more deckchairs but I suppose now we have 1,500-2,000 left. We work in three lots. My wife looks after the west end, I look after centre beach and my sister-in-law does the east beach. It starts in the spring holidays and goes on until the first week in September, when we start clearing up. By the third, everything will have vanished. In Grandfather's time they cost a penny a chair. When I was young it went up to 2d and since then they've risen, like everything else. Now the price is 10p. Of course, we have to pay rent for the beach. Everybody who hires the foreshore has to pay the district council for the season. Then it's so much a site per hut on the beach, as it was for the bathing machines. At one time when Grandfather had his machines on the east and west beaches and the little box canvas huts, he paid £5,450 but now the council have built lots of brick chalets themselves so we're losing the sale of our huts and we don't pay as much. It takes about a yard and a half of canvas to a deckchair. I can remember when it was 1s 11d a yard, and now it's 75p.

Cromer hasn't changed so much to live in but we get a different class of people and everything is more untidy now that so much food is wrapped. Kiddies pull off paper and throw it on the ground but I suppose that's typical of any seaside place. It's noisier too because of discotheques and bingo. In the days of the big hotels everybody dressed for dinner. You saw the gentlemen parading on the prom or up on the clifftops with their ladies in evening gowns. That's all over. There was a concert party on the pier all summer, two cinemas, a rep. company in the town hall and the old-fashioned lantern slides in the parish hall. Now we've one cinema which is used for bingo some nights of the week, only one summer show on the pier where the seats have been cut by half, and no rep. The place was built with narrow streets so we haven't got places for car parks and we can't get people into the town. The railways are almost done for and very few buses come in. There are lots of retired people who can afford to buy a bungalow somewhere out of town but they don't add to the holiday trade.

Speckled with red-brick buildings and the inevitable holiday camps, Mundesley *is* a bit characterless. But the town was smaller when George Cox senior moved down from Cromer. His son now aged 40 seems poised slightly uncomfortably with a foot in each generation. Moulded by the old way of life, he maintains the pace of the new. Though he is comfortable enough in his modern house where four youngsters scoot around his pretty wife, there are signs of the tensions of adapting. In fact, increasingly with the next two speakers, one becomes aware of the change since fishing sons followed unfalteringly in their fathers' footsteps.

In the old days if you were fishing for a living you didn't just rely on crab pots. You had the gear for everything that was available to be caught at different times of the year. You had crab pots, whelk pots, shrimp trawls, fish trawls, herring nets, salmon nets and your lines all stored away in a shed.

The last commercial fishing here finished in 1937, just before the war, so when we first came there was nothing being done at all. My father left Cromer because it was getting too competitive. The fishermen would always help each other out if they could when a bloke's boat was broken down or anything like that. I remember we borrowed a boat from Cromer on two occasions when we got some trouble but there was always someone who seemed to be either a little bit jealous or frightened that you were going to earn a little more than him. My father had a way of thinking that if you go to sea on a Sunday, you've only got to do seven Sundays and that's another week's work, but a lot of them at Cromer disagreed. They just didn't like working on a Sunday. My father wanted to be independent and on top of that, although Cromer might be central for crab and lobster catching, that's all it is central for. Mundesley is not far from the main crabbing and lobster grounds and it was better for what used to be herring fishing, mackerel fishing, shrimping and trawling. Most of the lining was done here, too. He was the same vintage as 'Shrimp', Jack Davies and 'Tuna' and they virtually all followed a similar course, apart from the fact that they stopped in Cromer while he moved out here. We'd been at Mundesley a year before I started fishing for a living but Father had done crabbing all his life and my grandfather before that. He came over thirty years ago and when he was alive and in good health we had two boats running. If that was fine enough there'd always be one of them in the water. Every day.

Creeping further round the coast, we find the type of fishing is slightly modified.

We used to start off crabbing, then round the second or third week in April we'd turn to mackerel with drift nets and that would go on until the end of June if you were still getting something. We once did twenty-one nights on trot in a crab boat after them but when you got mackerel catching night times, hauling crab pots in the day and then the job of delivering all your stuff, you didn't have much time for anything else. There was Father, myself, my elder brother and, the latter part of the time, my younger brother who is now at Cromer fishing full time. After the mackerel had finished we used to be lining or trawling. It was a recognised thing with Father that if you had to be on the beach at three o'clock in the morning to go off, you'd get there at two instead and go trawling for an hour. That wouldn't cost you any more. If you got something you were all right, if you didn't you hadn't lost anything. But invariably we found a few soles and that all helped to pay a bill of some description. Satisfaction is all my father possibly could have got out of it. He loved the sea. He loved working on the water and that was his life. He wasn't rich, didn't leave a fortune or anything and if he earned £5 he'd spend £4.50. But he enjoyed himself and I think if he was to come back he would try and do the same again.

Once the mackerel had finished we'd still be crabbing and lobster catching, but as soon as we put the nets away the lines would come out for roper or skate. You didn't do it every day because you couldn't always get the bait but probably once or twice a week, provided the weather was fine. Then, towards the end of the summer as crabs and lobsters dwindled, you did more and more lining. When I was share fishing out of Yarmouth on the drifters I had a basic wage of £3.10 and a share of profits after the costs were paid. For six years we went drifting during the herring season—three out of one family. They all used to go. The drifters would go to Aberdeen April–May time and fish down there for about thirteen weeks, come home, change the nets and go to South Shields for another thirteen weeks, gradually working nearer this way.

65

Round about September you'd start your home fishing in the North Sea where your gas platforms now are, then just before Christmas you'd be into the English Channel working your way between Dover and Calais. You'd come home for Christmas but you'd keep your boat going and work what they called the Cape fishing — Cape Grisnez. That voyage would normally end round about the middle of January and after that came the Plymouth fishing. Then virtually you'd stop, come back to Yarmouth or Lowestoft and start your season all over again.

A cran is a herring measure averaging about 1,100. If you have less than 900 or more than 1,500 there's an old law which says they are not to be sold for human consumption. One cran should weigh 28 stone. Later on, longshore fishing, we used to get the bulk of our herring here before anybody else had started because Father was always prepared to have a go at anything and nine times out of ten he'd be rewarded. If you had a lot of pots in the water, and some boats worked 200, you couldn't really haul them all day and turn round herring catching all night with paid hands. But being a little family concern we got round that. Two of us went after the pots and two with the nets to share the work load. Had there been thirty-six hours in the day I'm sure Father would have found something for us to do. He wasn't a taskmaster but he always made as much use of the time as he could.

I stopped fishing full time about six years ago and carried on for a while part-time, just working fifty or sixty pots. I opened a wet-fish shop in the village to see if we could work the two in together and get a living but it didn't work out so I carried on poodling along until I got this job. The shop never paid off — never has done and I don't think it ever will. Two started in Cromer but only one has survived. There are so many people in Mundesley who remember the price of fish twenty or thirty years ago and they think that's all they should pay today. So when I got this offer with one of the gas companies, I went. My only regret is that I didn't go six years ago. I'd be far better off now if I hadn't tried to hang on with the fishing.

Mr Cox brings up an issue that has always been red hot amongst crab fishermen. He is surprisingly vehement since he hopped from one camp to the other himself.

Another reason for the declining industry is my little pet hate — the use of crabs for lobster bait. I know it still goes on

66

and some of the fishermen know it too but for some reason nothing is being done about it. I caused a hell of a stir on the coast about it some years ago because at the time several thousand were being used daily. Some have packed it up but the volume of crabs being used is still the same as it was and you can always find out who is using crab as bait because he'll have that many more lobsters than anyone else. As the law stands, no Cancer pagura crab may be used for bait, if it is you are subject to a £50 maximum fine for each offence. But they use any crab they can't bring home to sell. Some blokes have been caught but when we've had them in court the old judge has fined them a minimal sum — ten pounds, twelve pounds, something like that. When I went fishing with my father, going back twenty years, we used as much crab bait as anybody. Then we changed our minds because there was a decline in the crabs and we realised one reason for it was we were breaking too many shot crabs, the ones that just shot their shells. They're the crabs that would be carrying spawn by the next spring and they're the breeding crabs. We were breaking two or three hundred of them every day and we were getting lobsters, but when we settled down and thought about it we realised what we were doing. My father had actually passed away before we went to this meeting at Lynn and they brought it all up. They knew what I'd been doing, I openly told them. Maybe for a year afterwards there was a decline but gradually the practice is coming back again and I'm afraid unless they do put a stop to it, that's had it. It's good lobster fishing this year mainly because it's been so fine, but another reason could be that there aren't so many crabs. You never do get a lot of crabs and a lot of lobsters at the same time. I still maintain that if they increased the measure for crabs, in the long run there would be bigger ones about but it's not for me to talk now I'm not doing it any more.

What draws the fisherman to the sea? They say fishing is 'in the bones' or 'in the blood'. Is it something perhaps too deep for words?

I am satisfied with my present work to the extent I know what I'm getting each month. I work a week on the rigs and a week at home and if I can get to sea three or four times during that second week I can keep going. I don't know what it is exactly but I have a lot more peace of mind. I shall never pack up fishing altogether. I like the sea that much I couldn't live ten miles inland, or if I did I'd be commuting to the beach all day long. Anyone who's been brought up to the sea knows that even if it's not possible to go out, even if he has no gear out there, he still makes that ritual walk down to the edge. Edna says 'Where are you going?' and I say 'Just off to the cliffs'. There's something makes you go. If one of our children wanted to go on a trawler out of Lowestoft I shouldn't say no, but I wouldn't want him to work night and day from the open beaches because it would be even harder today.

It is a brisk Saturday morning. You could almost slice the air at 5 o'clock when the Sheringham fishermen reel down the stone steps from the heavy-lidded town. 'Morning' one calls to another as they leap into empty boats and play the engines or chop up bait on the slipway in the moonlight. One of them slips a long galvanized metal quant, or pole with a V-shaped head, into the stern of a boat while several heave shoulders against its side and another man slips skeets — iron rollers in a wooden frame — in front of the bows. Smoothed pebbles crunch as, jerking and tumbling, the boat progresses down the beach and into the water.

There is a boy amongst the fishermen. No spectator, Fuz Middleton is working. Asked to describe himself he said 'I'm 15, short and tubby', and laughed. Snub-nosed good looks belie his age and a forceful character. Fifty years ago he would already have been earning a living at sea. Instead of which society is still trying to condition him. He will not be conditioned! Perhaps he was born too late.

I'm still at school, worse luck. Leave in just under a year. Sort of quiet personality, I think. I like to keep meself to meself. Sometimes I go up the clifftops and just sit and think. May sound silly but that's what I like to do. In the summertime especially and take the old dog for a walk. I've never thought about anything else really except fishing. I've got me own pots what I've been getting the last two year. My father's been making 'em and giving 'em to me. I've bought a few, not very many but a few. I've got the strength to rope them, but I just hain't got the technique right yet. But I hope to very soon. I can braid, just about. I've got a shank and a boat that's now being done up. That's going to take all my savings. About £100. D'you know 'Shrimp' Davies at Cromer? That was his old boat called the *KP & K*. It's twenty-year old. We're now had new timbers, washboards and thwarts put on, and we're generally done it up. That's over in Happisburgh where two boys ha' done it. They're done it very well and I should think it will be ready in another three weeks. I haven't actually hauled on me own, only once with Richard Little and he had a hauler on. But that's a lot different from hand hauling. We haven't got a hauler, it'll have to be by hand.

Fuz is definitely being discouraged from going to sea. Fortunately he has great determination.

At the Secondary School the teachers say 'Well, what's the point?' I don't know, I just want to do it. They keep on telling me to go to university and all that but personally I don't think I'm bright enough. I went up to the education officer and told him what I want to do and he said 'Well, you can go trawling'. I have been thinking about this and I might go in to learn and then drop out. Learn all the different ways and that, 'cos you can do that. They take you on six weeks trawling, teaching. Then I'll carry on from there. But I went to Hull this year on holiday and I looked at some of the boats and the stench put me off altogether. The old rotten fish and that was enough to turn anybody up. I know it's different when you're at sea but even the boats didn't look clean, and near enough that broke my heart to see the fish going to waste. All these little dabs about three inches long being killed because they just get caught up and can't get out of the net. There's millions of them killed every day. It's a great waste. I can't stand it if I see a little old crab crawling about in the boat. I have to take it down and throw it in the sea. That seems silly but it's just the way I am, I suppose.

I used to go railing and netting. I'd say I first started about five. Used to go Saturdays, just watching. I'm the youngest. There's only two of us and my sister, she's twenty-three. I went out with my father, it was rough some times. Very rough and I was frightened—scared stiff in fact, but I didn't say anything. I'm very often sick, specially easterly weather but, there again, that don't worry me. I just go over the side and that's it. For about half an hour I slow down, then carry on as normal. Back to work. I like the sea. Just the sea. I don't know why really. I suppose it's part of the family. Many generations they've been going to sea here. Especially in this family. Both sides. So that's just bred into me.

The others at school take an interest. One particularly asks what's fishing so he can get an idea what's to be got on the beach. If I say there's nothing about, well he won't go, but if I say 'There's a lot of cod about', he says 'Well I'll have a go Saturday.' He's the same age as mine but we're in different classes. I'm in the bottom. I don't work. I like geography but I get fed up with history, just can't see the interest in it. I'm interested in the history of fishing, yes, but when I went up to the teacher and asked him could I do a project on fishing? He said 'No, that's too complicated'.

I like to have company when I'm in a boat. I couldn't go there all day without anybody speaking to me. It's cold and miserable sometimes. But I still like to work outdoors, that's the main thing. I mean with any job outdoors you're in the cold, the rain and the wind, aren't you? But I happen to like it. I couldn't work in a factory, noise. Being closed in. I like to look around me. I've been in cities. I've been in London for two or three days and to tell you the truth I was right glad to get out of it though I never told anybody. I was right glad to get home. I was lonely, no friends up there of course, just my father and his friend. I felt I couldn't breathe right. I like the smell of fresh air coming when you take a deep breath. Cool. S'nice. To smell the fresh air and taste good food, it's just my liking. And I just like to do things my way. If I get told to do them another, well. I try that way and see if that's best. And if that isn't I go back to my way.

From the baiter-upper's point of view I know just about everything, without being big-headed. There isn't much to it. All you've got to do is switch the hauler on for the bloke, take the buoy and anchor that for'ard, clean the pots out, stack them, and throw an occasional tow over your head. I mean that's quick. You don't think about any of it while you're doing it. That just come natural. If a pot come up with nothing wrong, straight away I bait it up. I feel round it, I don't look, I feel round it with my fingers, and if there's a hole, I say 'There's a hole here' and pass it to my Dad to mend. This does occasionally happen and it's quicker than looking. Some people just don't care whether there's a hole in it or not, especially paid hands. I know some of them who couldn't care less. I do care about fishing. When I get home at night I say 'How many today Dad?' He'll say, 'Well we got so and so, and so many lobsters.' I'm glad to know that they did well. After we've finished here I'll probably go down and do the bait. Just drift down the gangway and have a look at it. That is my homework more or less.

I'm called Fuz 'cos when I was a baby I had fuzzy hair. I had one big blond curl in the middle of my head and the nurse called me Fuz. That's stopped with me ever since. Even the teachers, some of them call me Fuz up the school. I prefer it to Bennett because my name's Bennett, my father's name's Bennett and it gets all complicated. You're calling everybody Bennett. 'Fuz' sort of stuck to me and I like it. Something different. I like to be something different when I want to be something different and be normal when I want to be normal. Just be me own boss, that's all it boils down to all the time.

3

WHELKS

Aye, aye, its a peedie helicapster:
There's lots are caught in the sea off Scrabster.
— *Ian Findlay Hamilton*

The tide is low, only a trickle of water finds its way through a mile of bleak marshes to the sea. The sun is past its highest point, it is August, midday, and the shops in Wells have closed for lunch. So the bustle has halted temporarily. A number of people sit on wooden benches against the side of the Shipwright's Arms, ale in hand while gulls peck about on the sand between shreds of bladder-wrack, and halyards bat against aluminium masts. Below the gaudy amusement centres a bevy of children splatter in salt puddles. On the West Quay, the first sail unfurls as water begins to flow in.

On the East Quay there is movement among the low black sheds. A fisherman stacks up sacks of bait on a small platform jutting above the water, then he hops down the wall on an iron ladder to retrieve a piece of floating wood. Behind him fires are lit beneath still water in the coppers and four chimneys let out ruffles of grey-black smoke. Someone throws out food for scrapping gulls.

Now there is activity on the second landing stage. More bags of bait are dragged over the grass as the sheds are being brushed down. I look again at the water. It is deceptive, the dribble is becoming a stream. Swirling, eddying round; leaving first a sandbank to this side, then one pricked with worm casts to the other. Just below the wood and breeze-block wall two boys fix an outboard motor to a small blue dinghy. They tug and haul it into the deepest channel they

72

can find but it lodges firmly in the sand. In the bottom shed Alf shovels more coal onto the fire.

Fishermen are standing or squatting on three jetties, looking out where the creek curves at right angles through the lavender. The boys are still pushing their boat down to meet the tide. The sun catches the forward line of each ripple; it bends, crumpling into a network. The water is blurred amber in the shallows turning to green at its deepest. A gull flies high, its shadow dips across the water. The halyards rap more quickly in the wind, almost tinkle. Bigger ripples eat up the creek, diminishing sand islands and the pebbly mud beneath the wall. A group of children have collected round the sheds, buckets in hand, to scrounge the odd piece of bait for catching shore crabs. The wind blows black smoke horizontal from the tops of the chimneys. A tern swoops and skims. Only half an hour later the creek is full. Black heads, currants, dot the water as the mast of the first fishing craft is visible creeping up to the bend in the creek. Laden with whelks, an old lifeboat grunts into full view, runs parallel with the quay on the far side, turns sharply towards it and draws alongside, facing the incoming tide. A second and a third boat turn the corner until soon all six are unloading their catch. Some are simply carried up in hessian sacks, some are swung by rope onto jetties, one net bag at a time, while others are trundled into a shed on trollies.

For anyone wanting to hear about the beginnings of whelk fishing at Wells there is no better way than to look in at the sheds when the tide is low. In rooms hung with nets and coils of rope; piled with pots, balls of yarn, tarred rope ends and knives, there is work in progress. If the pace is quieter, slower than that at sea, it is nevertheless an important part of the enterprise. Net bags are being knitted or braided with wide plastic needles, keeping an even tension by pulling outwards from a hook or nail in an upright. Regulating the size of the loops with two fingers of the left hand, the needle goes through the next loop, round behind, in front and under as

in making a string shopping bag. It is not easy at first, but
with practice one improves. Then there are pots to rope, a
task that requires neat precision and a strong pull. The old
ones have spent the best part of a life at sea, though they
delight in gentle leg-pulling, and mix up the stories a bit,
sometimes adding a bit of their own.

At seventy-five 'Loady' Cox is slight, almost frail and feels
the cold. But his hands, long-fingered and pale, are amazingly
supple and he still goes up to the sheds to work each day. He
does not feel it is right to stick around inside, does not like it
either. Convinced that life has gone to the dogs, he blames
high wages and education, based no doubt from experience
of schooling that fitted him scantly for fifty years at sea. He is
jealous of his family's position, puckish and sharp, but if he
has lived through rougher, tougher times than today's young
men are likely to see, he does not complain. Indeed he
sometimes expresses contempt for them. I do not think he
merely possesses a talent for self-deception. He worked when
not to work was not to eat, when life was unpolished but
vital. He notices young people's leisure and compares.

His shed is a hive of fishing gossip, scarcely a morning
passes without company. In the winter, to the chilly sparkle
of a little fire, he sits on his bench, lights a paraffin lamp to
char the ends of a cord, gets his pipe going and tells his tales.

I left school when I was twelve and come up here with my
dad. Doing odd jobs around the shed. Stoking and helping
out. I first went out to sea at eight or nine. Went out many
times. Didn' do it for a liven till I was fourteen or fifteen. I'd
haul the pots in then, it was part er the work. Hard work didn'
seem to hurt us. We used to wear long leather boots. All hand
made. Stitched in leather. They wouldn't roll down so after
being out all day in the salt water it'd be a job to get them off.
Then the next mornen they'd be so stiff they'd stand up so's
you'd have to practically jump into 'em. They'd hurt yer feet
too—all hard and tough. Every Saturday evening, after we'd
finished for the week, we'd rub them with tallow to soften 'em.

The first one to whelk here was my father. There weren't

74

many men making much of a living from fishing afore the Shannocks arrived. There was a bit of line fishing and the mussels. That's all.

In the 1890s my father moved from Sheringham. He went to Whitstable afore that but he wasn't too good [well] so he went back to Sheringham. There's some of our family working at Whitstable still. Young men used to work all over the country then, here one week, there the next. Didn't think nothen on it. Later he come down here and others followed him. Coopers and Grimes are still here. First he used to sail right over before whelking, then back home at the end of the week. There was too much competition at Sheringham what with crabbing and line fishing. It was hard to make a liven there. When he moved he just loaded up the boat, chairs an' all and come down here. Not that there was all that much to take, it wasn't a bed of roses living in Sheringham then. They had the little boats. Not like these whelk boats, not half so big. No cabin. Nothen.

My father married a local girl. They had eight children, only five was boys and we all went fishing. Jack's now whelking — he's the youngest. But the girls never went near the boats. It was a man's job. My father sailed out to work all weathers in a square-rigged boat. They had gunter sails, lugs you'd call 'em. A single sail cost 4d a square yard an' it would have to last the year. If the wind dropped they rowed. I remember that. The oars would dip in and out. That was so mechanical like it was almost a dream. We didn't have motor boats here until 1915. Weren't no winches either. All hand hauling.

As 'Loady' explains, whelk men use heavier gear and go further out to sea than crab fishermen, so they require bigger craft.

We had the hubblers to whelk with down here first, 'hovellers' you'd call 'em. They were double-ended, like the crab boats only they was bigger. They'd be about 15 or 16 foot on the keel — 18 or 20 foot overall. They used to use them for herren an' mackerel fishing and for cod-lining. They did a lot 'er that wintertime. I have known them to have a lid cover at the head, a cuddy where you could get out of the way of the weather. You could put bunks in there and a stove for a cup er tea when we were netting. We used to be away all night and fry herren an' all sorts. They had more arruck holes than the crab boats, four or five instead of three. The for'ard ones would be bunged up with sacking or a large cork from the

herren nets. There was two sorts of cork, the little ones and the
real old-fashioned herren cork, five to six inches broad and
about seven to eight inches long. They come off the head
ropes. We used the square mainsail and sometimes a mizzen
and a foresail, depending on the wind. If they had a big job on
they used to get a big crew. Two boats would join up together,
six or eight in a hubbler and two in a crab boat. They'd be
relations who'd take a share of the profits after the expenses
were paid—like the Scots fishing boats only they called
themselves a company at Sheringham. If we went drifting we'd
be out about twelve hours and if we got 3,000 mackerel it was
a good catch. You might get ten bob. Of course, that was
worth nearer £10 then.

We use much larger boats now. There are three old lifeboats
down here. I was the first to go out in one, 1954. We had two
and they are over 30 foot. The *Elizabeth* now, all her fittings
and her keel is made of brass. She sailed up the Thames in the
last Coronation. We got the old lifeboats when the new self-
righting ones come in.

'Loady' and his youngest brother Jack have generations of
fishing behind them yet their father received a dubious
reception before becoming established at Wells. With a weary
walk from Sheringham behind him and then a trip to sea, he
was still not allowed to leave the creek without being stoned.
Another whelk fisherman, Alf from Brancaster, has been
round long enough to have found a niche although he
remembers what being a newcomer was like.

When I first started fishing I don't think I had any friends
because I was more or less an outsider. My father fished a bit
years ago but he had a pub on the green. I started outside. I
weren't a relation to them what was in it and they didn't like
that you see.

Two others, Vic and Roger, are still asserting their claims.
The distinction is important to other fishermen and reflects,
of course, their own behaviour and outlook.

After the Second World War people outside the old fishing
families started filtering into the business, generally working as
paid hands. New fishermen bring in fresh blood, new ideas
and a healthy disrespect for unproven tradition. At the same

time they have to be more militant in order to stake their claim, in order to survive what is clearly an extremely parochial climate. There is a certain closeness, a caution amongst the established that marks them. Loady remembers life in the fishing community at Wells very much as an insider. His memories are suffused with the certainty of belonging.

There was eighty fishermen's kids on the East Quay, in the houses round the tiled yards. Some of them houses had great big cellars for the smuggling but they've mostly been filled in. We lived behind Jolly Sailor's yard—that's all holiday people now. And down there next to the pub, where you park the car, that was the drying yard. All this washing'd be flapping about with the sea down there below. I remember the petties. They was outside in the yard and when you went night-times you had to cup your hand round the candle so'd it didn't blow out. We al'us had a candle to go to bed with. But we didn't have television. Not any of the entertainments you got today. We went after our own. Cor, there was fighting in the streets, particularly on a Saturday night. We youngsters used to watch and cheer them on. Then we was always fighting with the children from the west side er town, the sons of shopkeepers and agricultural workers. We al'us won!

Our family wouldn't go out to sea on a Sunday, but most of them would go in the pub. There was about fifty pubs in Wells 1903 and they was open all day long. You could just about walk out from the door of one into the next. The men would have lunch in there. Penny for a roll, penny a pint er beer. Sometimes my father and a friend would go up the gasworks for a barrow load of tar. Rope round his neck tied on the handles. Because the whelk pots all have to be tarred. It comes from Colchester now and the smith makes the iron bottoms lives at Hindringham, but when they were made here they used to have the owner's name on the bottoms. Some from about 1918 are still being used. They was better, the bars were all part of the base, not welded on. They used ter be four smiths lived in Wells. Anyway, 'bout three hours after my father left we'd have to go and fetch the tar. Pick up the barrer from outside er the pub and fetch it. We knew where our fathers was. Wouldn't get farther than the old pub. See they'd pass, meet someone they knew and they'd never get that tar.

If 'Loady' and his brothers were able to swim, it was unusual at the time. Bob Rushmer, a retired fishery officer, said:

It's only very recently, within the last twenty years that young Sheringham boys have learned to swim. Now they learn at school because everybody else does rather than because they want to be fishermen. Few of the old ones could keep afloat. When he went to sea my father wore a three-quarter length yellow oilskin and heavy leather sea boots with steel clates on the heel, a half moon on the toe and studs in between for tramping up and down the shingle. If he'd been thrown overboard the boots would have filled up and he'd have gone straight down. I think they reckoned swimming only prolonged the agony. My father couldn't swim a stroke and if one of the old fishermen had said he was going for a dip they'd have run him off to Norwich (Asylum). They were supposed to carry lifejackets but I don't think they ever did.

Now 'Loady' remembers:

Women never went to work — not out to work. They had big families, seven or eight, so they were busy looking after the kiddies. My mother never went out at all except to an auction or rummaging for clothes. The auction was held about once a month. The women would leave in the afternoon, then they wouldn't be back until about nine-thirty. Al'us cooking and scrubbing. They had a rough time.

When I was ten or twelve a boat called the *Blackburn* was wrecked ten mile north-east out of Wells harbour. She was a steam boat and it was early in the year. She must have hit something because when the worm diggers went down they found all these bodies so they sent off carts to collect them. She went down so quickly no one knew anything about it. No lifeboat or nothen. They buried them all down here in the churchyard; carried the coffins on their shoulders, each one with a Union Jack. And all the big blokes on the council come down. Every coffin was led by a stool-bearer — they weren't allowed to hire school children so they hired you the day after you left. You walked down the middle of the road with the round seat of the stool of your head and the three legs dangling down your back 'n sides, while horses and carts come whizzing by. I was stool-bearer several times. Four or six men carried the coffins because there weren't hearses then. The fishermen

78

got five shillen for carrying and we'd get two for the stool-bearing. When they had to stop and rest, like at the bottom of a hill, we'd put the stool down in the middle of the road and they put the coffins down on top. They made the coffins from plain deal with cast-iron fittings. You'd clear the whole lot for nine pound ten, because sometimes whole families were wiped out and there was nothing to pay with.

Malting was an important industry in Wells until the maltings closed down about 1930. Most of the men would knock off fishing to help with the harvest. Barley come in by boat and by cart. I can remember eight teams of horses, all brass and ribbons, making a lovely sight down on the quay. They'd bring in about two ton er corn to the malthouse.

At Wells and Brancaster, as well as at Sheringham, fishing was more varied in the old days. But now stocks of some species have either disappeared altogether or greatly diminished. One of the reasons is greed. 'Loady' explains how the cockles vanished and Vic confirms that marauding of the oyster beds still goes on. Starting with 'Loady':

They didn't only whelk in my father's time. First there was oysters. They've all gone. After that there was cockles and they've gone. There have always been the mussels but they've just about gone, too. Isn't nothing you can do about it, the harbour is all silted up. The oysters died out when there was no more at sea to plant; I reckon the cockles disappeared because of all the holiday-makers. They used to come down here and take loads er them. The trains going back to Runton and East Dereham was full of cockles on a Saturday night. And later on they used to hire a lorry to collect them and pay for it out of the profits. My father also went off after plaice. He used to go and dig dew worms [earth worms] for bait.

Now Vic Pells from Brancaster:

A few years back I found some small oysters on the old grounds at sea. I went back the following year when they should have been marketable size and never could find one. We have a lot of starfish on this coast, and there are so many other pests. The native oysters that used to be here were big. The Burnham oysters were well known. They came from an area off the coast called Burnham Flats and were called the 'Burnham Grounders'. There were once oysters dredged and landed in all these harbours but disease killed them off in 1923. It's ideal oyster ground with a mixture of salt and inland water and they can only survive in areas that are not polluted. But there's just nothing there, no spat — that's young ones. The Shellfish Division of the Ministry of Agriculture, Fisheries and Food are trying to grow artificially reared oysters at Thornham. Pacific oysters. They are a different type that matures in a couple of years instead of taking four or five. Some fishermen have bought the spat but I never would have any because I knew what would happen and it's happening now. People are pinching them. Over the years there've been people pinching mussels and cockles out of the lays.

Even Loady's memories of marketing carry an undertone of caution, of wariness:

They use different measures for whelks all according to where you are. At Wells we measure in pecks, three pecks to a bushel. A London bushel is four pecks but Lowestoft, Grimsby and Whitstable measure in washes. In the Midlands they deal in hundredweights, so you have to work it out roughly. A peck weighs about a stone so that's what we reckon on.

Years ago we sent them all over the country. Billingsgate is a dump market. We never know what we're going to get for 'em. If they're in short supply they send a telegram saying 'Prospects good' but it never says how much they're worth. I went up to Billingsgate two or three times; the first time about thirty year ago. At six o'clock all the pubs opened and the dealer give you a stiff milk and rum before you started work. You weren't allowed into the market until 6.30 or 7.00 am, when you found out who you were delivering to. They had great big rough fellers for porters. One of them would give you this brass disc with the name of the merchant written on it and you'd give him the whelks in exchange. One disc for each box. They're smart boys up there so you had to be careful or they might whip them onto a lorry and be off. That's a sight early in the morning with the porters carrying all their boxes on their heads. They've got big heavy boots on and they come charging along. It was all wet and slippery, you had to look out you didn't fall. You couldn't sell the whelks within a twenty-mile radius of Billingsgate because the porters wouldn't get a fee. The merchants hire the porters for so much an hour and hundreds of lorries were lined up, so you had to tip the police to let you in. Thirty years ago you had the barrer boys buying

80

from the fish merchants to sell through the London streets and that was even more chaotic then.

A drive south along the coast finds much the same thing happening at Brancaster on the first swell of tide. One boat is hauled up onto a little red tractor from the main quay and the whelks are taken inland to boil, but three other loads are cooked on the edge of the sea. A narrow lane, sprouting a fuzz of cream angelica runs down to the old malthouse-boiling sheds. Here two of the four boats are decked. They fish nearly twenty miles out at sea, which causes some comment from the inshore trawlers which are prohibited during summer months from trawling between three and twelve miles offshore by the North Norfolk Prohibition of Trawling Order.

Several photographs of Vic Pells' fishing craft stand in his home with a tablet reading 'Fishermen never die, they only smell that way'. The boat is half decked, with a small wheelhouse to fend off the worst of the weather, the only one with a loo.

Vic is forty-two, powerfully built and tanned red-brown. He lives with his mother at Brancaster in a green corrugated iron house tucked away from the road. He does not strike one as a bachelor. "Aren't you the marrying sort?" "Well the way I see it, when you can buy your pint of milk a day why saddle yourself with a cow?" His father, Barney, was a colourful local figure who 'liked his pint'. But he did not own a boat, he worked for somebody else. So did Vic to begin with, then he bought his own. He barged in. "Now his heart is in it", even the older ones concede. He is inventive, progressive and more unusual, a political activist casting about for support. People respect him for behind his laugh there is a sense of responsibility, a concern for others. He speaks easily, his words roll off the tape, but he can well be serious. He knows that at Brancaster as elsewhere, the fishermen ought to be banding together to protect their own interests.

Years and years ago, when the whelk sheds were malthouses and brickwork sheds, there was a brick quay that all the cake and grain boats used to come up to. You can still find the remains of it below the old coastguard station. The quay existed because there was a sluice gate and a pound, or reservoir, on the west side of it which used to fill up at high water. Then at low water the sluice was opened to clear out the quay and the creek for the fishermen's hard. Well in recent years the sluice gate fell into disrepair and the sailing club have filled in two-thirds of the pound so the fishermen's creek is slowly but surely silting up and will continue to do so. In my opinion, when the National Trust took over this area, the brick quay ought to have been preserved because it is essential to the fishing industry and it is part of the history of this village. But now the National Trust have leased the area which was the pound to the sailing club.

I blame the parish council and the Fishermen's Society for allowing it to happen. I've been on about it at local meetings but I've not got the backing. In fact, I've been as far as to get a copy of an Act of Parliament which clearly states that no person, whether he holds the leasehold, freehold or copyhold of any property below high-water mark, shall do works to that property without the permission of the Department of Trade and Industry. This is a coastal protection act, according to which, if the fishermen like to get up on their back legs, they alone could make the sailing club reinstate that property to its original condition. We could make two completely separate and independent quays.

Vic also has strong feelings on what he considers the Government's penalisation of the self-employed.

Self-employed people in general in this country are being left behind. The FOS [Fishery Organisation Society] is fighting for the fishermen. There's a move on to entitle us to a type of dole. But I'm convinced that they could win providing they all banded together. The unions today have got too strong but I still wholeheartedly agree with the trade union because I believe that a worker needs protection. It's just gone from one extreme to the other. I don't want to go back to the times when a man worked for a crust, this is where the trade unions started. They've done a good job but it's got out of hand. The Welfare State, too, it's a wonderful thing but for the self-employed it's no work, no pay. It annoys you to watch people in industry earning fantastic sums of money and then going on the dole for a percentage of their income. We get no dole, because we are classified as share fishermen who are self-employed. A share fisherman has a basic salary with a bonus on whatever he catches. The only thing we've got is social security but basically the self-employed won't go on social security because this is why he's self-employed. He's too damned independent.

Vic's father, Barney, could never have been a proper, pucker fisherman. His character would not allow him to work methodically. In fact it is surprising he produced so single-minded a son.

Barney was born at Stiffkey. He went to sea in the old sailing ships, starting off as an apprentice. And that's where he spent most of his life until they began bringing in all the discipline, then he backed out. Of course he was called up in the first war. Of all things, he was a dispatch rider before he went into the Royal Inland Water Transport Service. Afterwards he went back to sea until he packed it up and did all sorts of jobs on the land. Like yacht skippering — he was with one family for 15–20 years. Then he went fishing for a bit but you could never say that he earned his living wholly and solely from fishing. He was still doing the odd yacht delivery jobs off and on right up until the last war when he joined the Local Defence Volunteers. He was issued with a rifle and ammunition and used to go out patrolling the villages. Then someone thought there should be a bit of organisation in the ranks, so they formed the Home Guard. That was the end of it. They couldn't make him join because he was too old, so he worked at the aerodrome this side of Docking until the end of the war, when he went back to fishing. After he got his pension he didn't have to worry too much. Just collected a few cockles and mussels to subsidise it. He always was a beachcomber; sold quite a bit of timber off the beach during the war as he was twenty-four hours on and twenty-four hours off at the aerodrome, which gave him a bit of time. He also spent a lot of time in the local, because he had travelled around a bit he could spin a good yarn.

Wild-fowling was frequently a fisherman's sideline.

Until about 1947 Barney went punt-gunning. I often went with him I know because he used to swear at me when I wouldn't keep still in the boat. There was no limit on the number of Brent geese you could take then. He might kill twenty or thirty at a time and they were worth 6s 6d each. There was nothing else in flocks big enough to use a punt gun on. But with a hand gun you could shoot mallard duck, pigeon, curlew, and even oyster catchers and seagulls. Even blackbirds and starlings were worth as much as 3d each. You could earn a living shooting any damn thing. The bad winter of 1947 was ideal for wildfowling because everything ashore was frozen up. All the ponds and lakes like Holkham Park always freeze before the sea does, then all the duck come down onto the sites for food and you can shoot them on the salt marshes. But Brent geese were protected soon after that and then there was nothing left. Wild-fowling certainly deteriorated, because by 1951 or '52 there were loads of farmers inland interested in sport. They were making duck ponds with decoys and holding organised shoots over gravel pits so that killed it for us. If duck were getting well fed on barley a couple of miles inland they were not going to stay on the salt marshes. The old type of punt gun was a muzzle-loader. It had a percussion cap and a firing pin on the side and drove from this pin down into the chamber of the gun. You put the powder in the end of the barrel, let it run right down to the bottom and then most of them used to put wads of newspaper on the top before ramming the lot down. Pour your shot in, more newspaper on top of that and they would kill geese at about a hundred yards. Muzzle-loading guns were used long after the 1914 war. There were still a lot about up until the '30s because a breech-loading gun that fired cartridges was expensive. Barney used his until 1947, right up to the end.

He would get to windward of a flock and lie flat in the bottom of the boat. The gun wouldn't swivel round, it was fixed so the whole boat had to point in the right direction. The gun had a lanyard on the trigger and when it was pulled that would fire it. One firm, Pettits of Reedham, would buy anything in feathers, and rabbits and hares as well. Feathers were used a lot. They took the oil out and died them or bleached them for making artificial flowers and all sorts of decorations. Pettits had a stand at the Royal Norfolk Show and I've seen the flowers there. They plucked the fowl, though what they did with the flesh God only knows — I expect it was made into potted meat or potted fish. It's tough and so fishy you could never eat it straight, but Brent goose would make good fish paste. They must have done something to have paid us so much for it.

In order to make his way, Vic has needed more thrust than an established fisherman. Many are dedicated, newcomers need self-reliance and confidence in extra measure.

I went to sea when I was about seven and could hardly see over the side of the boat. I went with an old boy, Harry Loose, whose wife sometimes went with him. He had a special small pair of thigh boots made for her and I shall always remember when he gave me a pair—it was the first I ever owned and I was thrilled to bits. To have a pair of thigh boots just like any other fisherman! I wore them with an oilskin and a sou'wester and that *was* something. When I was at school I used to go weekends, then when I left I took up engineering like my brother. I did about three years and got fed up with it. We were both apprenticed at the same place and he's still in it. I broke my apprenticeship and went to sea. I've no regrets. I wouldn't do anything else.

I went with Harry Loose to begin with, the same as Alf and Laddy, worked with him for several years and then I went with Alf after the war up until 1962. Then I started on my own. I bought a boat—a decked 32-footer with a wheelhouse from Dover. I used her until 1969 or so when I bought my present one. She's really a Norwegian fishing boat but she was fitted out as a motor cruiser before I had her. I took part of the cabin off and converted her to what she is now, adding one or two little bits and pieces later. Automatic pilot, radar and radio telephone. I've got two radios in the boat. I put the medium frequency ship-to-shore one in for safety soon after I bought the boat. It has a 400-mile range and I've often talked to the Dutch coast or to ships down in Grimsby and Humber. If I or any other boats are in trouble I always inform a lifeboat. I've had one standing by once or twice. That's only sensible. This year I have enrolled as an auxiliary coastguard, so I've got the coastguard's own frequency on my VHF, a different radio, shorter ranged. I towed a boat in last year in pretty nasty weather so I called Humber radio to have the Wells lifeboat standing by. We didn't need it but I never knew if the weather was going to get worse. It did but not too bad to do the job. Somebody asked me just recently if I thought it was worth their buying a radio. Well, I said, if they did they could shout a lot further.

My father volunteered for the lifeboat for a short time but it had a shocking name because they could never get the crew out of the pub. Boats from Lincoln used to pray before they left port that nothing would happen until they got down Sheringham way. A ship once went ashore on the Gore Middle sands in the depths of winter. The tide went down and the lifeboat crew actually watched men running about on the sand, trying to keep themselves warm. They were all drowned. But ships were all right when they got down towards Sheringham and Cromer. Our lifeboat disbanded in 1935.

The newcomer joins fishing with certain freedoms unknown to the traditionalist. Roger, for instance, freely admits he does not always know the right answer, that he makes mistakes, while Vic's dedication is not to any particular aspect of fishing, just to life on the sea.

If I won the pools tomorrow I'd still spend all my life at sea. The only reason I'm whelking is because it's about the only way of earning a living on this part of the coast, and if you are fishing you spend most of your time at sea. I'd love to be able to cruise the world. I could do that if I won the pools but I'll never get rich whelking. A good lot was made after the war but nowadays expenses are so great. So it's not nearly the job it used to be. But I'm independent. I don't know what I particularly like about being at sea. I don't think anybody can tell you, but when you get out there you leave everything else behind. You're free at sea, aren't you? There's always a certain satisfaction, even if you just go out to haul whelk pots. If you are out on a bad day, especially when none of the other boats are going, you're on your own. You haul your gear and come back. It's not that you've beaten the others but you've beaten the weather. The same applies if I go across to Holland with yachts. Say I'm bound for Rotterdam, I get this satisfaction in making the landfall the next day. I've done it. I suppose Chay Blyth felt the same sailing round the world. He'd done it. He wasn't interested in being a hero, he just wanted to prove to himself that he could do it. I can understand that. When I'm on the boat and it's calm, I'm scheming all sort of things—new types of whelk pots and what I'm going to do with the boat. Alterations here and there. But when it's rough you think about nothing but the weather.

'Loady' makes pots for the Coxes, Alf and his son Terry help one another, but newcomers like Vic and Roger have to find their own. The old methods of making gear are extremely time-consuming, so, instead of rope-bound iron pots, Vic uses plastic ones.

Plastic pots were never used before I had them. That was just something I dreamed up in a mad moment. You see you can't get the rope for a conventional pot and it takes so long to make. Having once made it you've got to tar it and even then it's not fit to go to sea for about six months. Strictly speaking, it should be left until it's bone dry, then re-tarred and dried again, otherwise you just wash the tar out and lose your preservative. I think plastic ones are successful although no one else has taken to them. I once made all mine but recently I've got a blacksmith to help with some. I try to do everything but you can't.

Roger, too, is open-minded about new ideas but most of the older fishermen are very suspicious of change. Vic gives an example of this:

The first motor winch at Brancaster they took from an old Austin 7. After that they all used Austin 7 engines for years. Went miles to find them. Didn't ever seem to think they could use anything else until one day someone used an Austin 8 engine. They were surprised it was just as good. I first fixed a hauler that drove off the main engine instead of having two, but they all have that now. Then later I put in a diesel engine. It caused quite a stir when I started using polythene rope. They didn't think it would work. It has disadvantages but they're outweighed by the advantages. In a gale the old manilla rope lay on the ground, swung back and forth and chafed like sandpaper. We've had it worn out in a couple of days. But polythene rope floats clear of the ground and it's easier to hook with a grapnel or a creeper—that's an iron bar with a series of hooks on it. We pull it across a shank of gear to hook the rope. Now the rope floats it's much easier.

I lost some pots yesterday to two ruddy Belgian trawlers. In real bad weather a whelk buoy takes some spotting. In fine weather you can see them quite easily on the radar but they trawl at night and in a blow where it's a bit sloppy you get so much clutter on the radar, so much interference from wave action, you just can't see them. We assume they went straight through because I lost thirty pots, but not all off one shank. They came off four, which is much worse. They pull all the other whelks out.

Alf Large is seventy-four and still goes to sea, sitting to bait the pots while his son hauls. People wag their heads and say he should not be out there, but he says it is his life. A large man with a rosy face and a grin that only just surfaces above layer upon layer of blue, white and buff sweater in the cold months, he looks every inch a fisherman. But he is secretive and very shy. Until recently he would not talk to anyone, still he does not say much. True, perhaps to the archetypal Norfolk inhabitant, he is 'Sharp, hard, acquisitive and distrustful of strangers, but a good friend when he knows you'. Occasionally he gleefully fuels the village's old reputation for feuding and rapacity.

> That used to be bad years ago I've heard my father say. He said they dussn't go down the beach unless they'd got one of these hand rakes. Somebody might attack 'em. You see it goes back. Their fathers tell them what their fathers done or what they didn't do and that's how that keep coming back. It's more or less the same now nearly. It's just like a little village. It don't show on the surface but if you catch more than wot they do. . . . Other fishermen are friends, they talk like, but you can't trust some of them. They keep watching how much you got. Yes, I watch them too.

That afternoon, while waiting for me in his shed, he was dragging sacks of whelks into the back of a van. 'I can finish 'em', says Terry. 'Nearly done now', Alf carries on. When they reach the end, Terry hops into the seat and drives the van out of the shed. We sit down beside the steam baths and I ask about Brancaster whelking in the old days.

> Just after the first war there was masses of whelks. Four years give them time to breed and about fourteen boats went after 'em, same as they had at Wells. But if storms stopped the Grimsby smacks from coming in to collect their bait, we would wait a couple of days, hopen' they'd make it, then boil them up an' try the cooked trade. Ours was always sold last in London and 'cos they wasn't fresh, see, we got a bad name. Whelking was no good in the 1920s and 1930s. It wasn't the catches. There was no trade. You didn't get anything for 'em. I cleared ten shillings my first season. Then all the boats knocked off

and we went after trout for a few years, sea trout, that is. We used a seine net, about 150 yards long. One man stood on the shore with a rope, say 30, 40 yards. The boat went off and we'd shoot the nets right round in the shallow shores. Then fold them up and drag 'em in. That was hard work and it weren't a good living either. We sold trout in the village at two bob a pound. Sometimes there were three go together but like us, we were only two. We never had so much to square up then! About twenty years ago we was catching trout again. Off the beach all the way to Heacham. We'd whelk all day and trout all night.

Before the second war we decided to try whelking again, doing it quietly so they shouldn't all know. It wasn't much different from what it is today only we used to hand haul then.

My boat now, she'd be worth £18,000–20,000. She's 36-foot, only four years old — built for me at South Shields. She's a seineing design with a modern fish finder to discover the soft sea bed. See, the others have dials, but mine charts a line. Where it's soft there's whelks.

Bait is of vital importance to the fishermen. 'Loady' and Alf discuss types used in the past and Vic brings what is becoming an increasing problem up to date. 'Loady' says:

Shark is about the best bait for whelks if you can get it but most kinds of fish will do. They feed off dead fish or crab, not rotten, just dead. We used to spend a whole day, every Friday, catching bait. Fresh mackerel was sliced down the middle with a little salt to keep them stiff, then we used them to bait up lines for catching billies (tope). It was called 'sweet william' at Grimsby, I don't know why. Al'us 'sweet william'. Dogfish used to be popular until about 1930. Then the Londoners began eating it, called it rock salmon, so the Grimsby trawlers come and took the lot. Today they use what they can get.

And Alf:

Bait must be in good condition. We used to have herring from Yarmouth. You can take the jacks (hermit crabs) out of the whelk shells to catch the green crabs to catch the whelks with. We've used razors for bait on the big tides when you can get 'em. The tide come further in and it go out further, too. Well you get fair-sized tides every month, but you have exceptional ones spring and autumn. And right down by the sea, as far out as you can go, the razor fish'd be sticking out three or four inches easy. We never used a shovel. What you really want is a bread knife to cut into the sand and hold 'em quick from going off down. Otherwise they'll be two or three foot deep. You can get dozens and dozens like that if you're on your own. Your friends make plenty of row you see and when the razor fish feel the vibrations they're off. They're good to eat if you slit the shell with a knife. Take them out to fry in deep fat. Not for long. Next year we are going to set up lines for dogfish and pick them up when we come in.

Vic feels:

The crisis in the trawling industry is pushing up the price of fish offal astronomically. We use cod's heads and small whiting and herring. Years ago we used nothing but herring. Now you're lucky if you can find a few. It's partly the result of the pet food industry. All your Kit-e-Kat, Whiskers, Paws and Topcat—there's no end of them. Imagine half a cod's head in a tin—because they grind the lot up, bones and all are just wonderful for puss. If you realise the price of a tiny tin is nine or ten pence, the price they can afford to pay is high because nobody complains about pet food. They put it up another 2p in the shops and you still go in and buy it. But, in fact, you're buying our bait.

In the old days, Alf continues, whelks themselves were chiefly used as bait.

When they used the long lines for catching cod and other deep-water fish, they'd need masses of whelks. Those old cod smacks had lines stretched several miles and every hook would be baited with a whelk. They had to smash the shell first then put it straight on if the weather was fine to go off fishing. A whelk would stay there a long while—that's the idea of having them, because they keep on the hooks. But you mustn't let a whelk die because the scent go out of it. If you could kill it, that was all right. They kept the whelks in wells of sea water; that's like a watertight compartment in the bottom of the boat, or they'd hang them over the side in nets—using the sea like a 'fridge. The smacks at Scarborough we sent the whelks to used to work about fifty miles off the Yorkshire coast. Supplying them was quite a good business that time er day.

He is old enough to have heard about and seen types of whelk pots unknown to younger fishermen.

They used basket pots made of wickerwork in the big oyster smacks before I was born. They was weighed down with old bits of iron. More or less like the ones we got now but not quite so tall and they used to haul them oftener. The smacks used to lay out there and on the slack tide they'd go and haul them. Chuck them out again for the next slack water. Then they used the hoop nets. We tried them about two years ago. Caught a few off them, never had many. We thought we'd try after what we'd heard. That was just an experiment and I think we failed because the net was synthetic and it kept on moving all the time in the water. They don't like it. I know they used them years ago for whelks and crabs, too, because we used to pinch them out of these storehouses for hoops. A small row boat would take about fifty, stowed on top of each other in the stern. They were shot about five fathom apart. You only left them down ten, twenty minutes, so when the last one was shot you'd be ready to pick up the first.

The Grimsby pots are wide at the bottom and small at the top, and heavier than ours. You should hold one of them! We shape ours out more in the middle to catch more whelks. The boats they use in Grimsby are about 50 foot and the pots are heavy because once a gale of wind blows they go over on their side. Ours were designed for the crab boats and up this end of the coast we just increased the size. Took the shape but increased the size. First thing to make a pot is get a nice bit of rope, make it fast on to one of the rods and keep on going round and round. Work all the way down right from the top to the bottom. You got to pull on it, and you put in like a curtain of net to stop the whelks escaping because they can't climb upside down. But if there's a little hole in the pot all the whelks will find it. They're all gone out. And after two days that would be empty. I can do a pot in under an hour. I done fourteen in one day and finished 'em off. Started four o'clock in the morning.

Whereas crab fishermen are always within sight of the shore, the whelk fisherman is out on his own, with his mate and mile upon mile of golden green water in every direction. Unless it is rough, Roger thinks about improving techniques, Vic plans labour-saving devices, while Alf is caressed by soothing memories.

You are lonely at times when you're steering on your own. When it's coming daylight, in the mornings, it seems to be lonely then. You're out there, well your father and mother've been dead years but they're still alive out there. You know what I mean? You don't think they're dead. You're still near to them. I don't think about things as much as I used to years ago. Now we've got a wheel house but years ago we used to go in the open. Well that seem to be different. I think you were closer to the work before.

Fishing has a fascination for spectators who envy such isolation, envy such strength. It is easy to admire the whelk man's pact with the elements although to Vic or Alf there is simply work to be done. Of course a fisherman is unable to regulate his working hours. Even when he gets to sea he can not compel fish to be lured, indeed there may not even be any fish where he hopefully dips his net. Yet the chief differences between his work and a land job are probably governed by the unpredictable sea itself. I have been out in decked and open boats but naturally I can pick the right weather. Usually the sun has shone, the sea sparkled and the wind merely pulled the water to the gentlest of swells.

There is plenty of activity in the apparent emptiness of the North Sea. Tankers and large Norwegian vessels creep by on the horizon while small Dutch coasters steer brightly across the bows. There are buoys at intervals to alert the skipper who navigates by watch and compass, and countless birds reeling and dipping after fish. Already there is work to be done; sack mats to be shot overboards and relaid or perhaps bait to be sliced into sizeable portions. The land opens up, a panorama, then begins to fade. Pinewoods blur darkly and church spires retreat to a haze. As the boat approaches the right spot, the crew search for a tattered flag buoy that marks the first shank or line of pots. It draws near until one of them makes a grab for it with a hooked stick. Jack Cox, skipper, explains the routine.

You pick the buoy and then start to haul. You haul with the tide and you must remember to keep the boat uptide of the pots. It's a matter of experience and knowing the tides which go round clockwise. It is tricky when that's rough. I think the best haulers are probably those who started off doing it by hand. There was more heaving to do but also you had to be right over the pots so they'd rise vertical, otherwise you'd drag them over. Taking the rope over the moving bollard or hauling winch, the pots are brought in in a big coil aft. The shaker-outer shakes them out and the baiter-upper takes the pots from him to put his bait in. Maybe two haddocks and a couple of herring. He traps them in the bar, that's two strings, and pulls the button up tight so they can't wash out with the tide. Then he stows the pots in the fore end of the boat, clear of all the ropes, ready to shoot away when you come to the last one and pulled your last anchor up. That's the best way, the old traditional way with three in a boat. There's thirty-six pots on our shanks, I believe they work about thirty at Cromer and more, about fifty, at Grimsby. There's ninety feet or fifteen fathoms of rope between each pot. In shallow water you can work fourteen fathoms but we keep it to fifteen so when we drop into deep water there's that extra to play with. There's a buoy shank with the flags on and an anchor on each end. You recognise yours from the odd bits of colours and you put your name on your buoys in case they get lost.

You've got to know exactly where the beds are. On the Norfolk coast I suppose there's twenty miles square of whelks thick and thin. There's Race Sand with a buoy on each end, then there's Dudgeon Shoal further out. We keep clear of the sand banks, working just inside them or just outside. If you're on a good place, you just turn round the buoy and shoot up again within a yard or two. If anyone trawls through the pots he pulls them all to pieces. He can pull them for miles until they break, or cut them away. With a storm in the wintertime they roll up in big bunches and you've got a job to lift them.

When we finish with the hauling business we turn round and have a piece of food and maybe there's about forty bushels to dig up and measure into the nets before we come home. While we've been shooting the pots the shaker-outer's been digging up but he won't have them all done. If there was a lot of hermit crabs you'll be all the way home picking them out. I leave the tiller and help them out. She'll steer herself home nearly. Besides hermit crabs, there's what we call bullets [slender spindle], butterfish and dog whelks. Almond whelks,

the yellow ones with a smoother shell; we don't get many of
them so we throw them in with the others. They taste fairly
good, sweeter, that's all. Then you get what we call the 'five
fingers', the star fish. We don't fling them back, we chuck
them on the back end of the boat and let them dry up in the
sun or throw them back when we come inside the harbour so
they die up on the sand. You get a bed of five fingers on
whelks, they kill the bed off.

If we've an hour to spare waiting for the tide to clear the
harbour as a rule we spin for mackerel. You pick up a hundred
some days, might pick up ten the next. That do vary quite a
bit. There's two ways, spinning or what we call jigging. The
first way you have your weight, about 3lb, and on the end of
that you'd have an ordinary spinner which is some shiny metal
revolving with hooks on it. You travel at a good speed with it,
two to three knots, and the boat drags that through the water.
The other way is to stop the engine, drop down with the tide
and drift with it. You have a trail of about eight different
coloured feathers on the hooks with a little lead just to go down
to the bottom. You keep pulling it up and down with your
hand to flash them through the water as if they're small fish
going up and the mackerel notice them. You've got to keep on
moving it, jigging. If the mackerel are thick, feathers are the
best but if they're in patches and you've got to keep chasing
them it's best to keep on the speedy side with the spinner.

You've got a hard tide underneath the boat coming up the
creek, so you turn in sharp here on the corner and then start to
unload. Wash the whelks by pulling the nets through the
water, onto the cart and then into the whelk house for boiling.
The first thing a boiler's got to do is fill these coppers up with
water and lay his fires. Years ago we used to fill them up from
the pump and carry all the water to the coppers, but now
they've just got the tap there with a hosepipe to fill up. We've
got two oil fires now but, of course, they were once all
hand-fed. About an hour before the tide come he lights up and
brings the coppers nearly to a boil, just keeps them simmering
until the first lot of whelks go in. He drops them in with a
double pulley over the top and a single at the bottom, a
three-fold block, to take the weight off his arms. When the
cold water on the whelks hits the copper that simmer down
again and up it comes in four or five minutes. If there's a bit of
scum come to the top they clean it off and fill it up with fresh

water. They're shot out of there into the baskets to cool off and two more go in. Boiling ain't a very good job because there's steam around you all the time. In hot weather it's not very nice. I've done lots of it. The whelks want to be absolutely cool before they go into sacks otherwise they sweat and they wouldn't last so long. But if they stand in the baskets three or four hours they last two or three days. Then they're sacked, tied up and sent down to the cold freeze factory where the women pick them out of the shells and freeze them in small packs. The rest go to Billingsgate. We used to have private customers but since they took the railways away transport has gone. You can't push three bags here and three bags there, so we finished that sort of trade altogether.

It is left to Roger to speculate what the present position might be if fishermen had worked in together.

Once upon a time there was nowhere else to send whelks except to London and you used to chance what you got. There was a lorry load out of here every night. But now we all supply different people. We should get together and hire a lorry. This should have been done years ago when the freeze people moved in and took the cream. We went to London and saw three whelks for three bob and two dozen shrimps for the same. Somebody reckoned they came from Wells and it makes you think. If the whelkers had got together years ago and bought a cold store or a factory they'd be sitting pretty now.

Something more than Jack's personal aloofness comes out of the next bit, something of the deep faith that the Sheringham people once lived by.

You are alone a lot out there. If you're steaming to gear, say 2½-2¾ hours when you're working out twenty miles. And you've got to steam all the way back again. Five hours standing on that damn tiller. But I don't mind it. I often wander alone on these marshes anyway. It don't worry me one bit. I got up this morning and took a small boat out for a couple of hours on my own. I respect the sea. You get gollywogs in your stomach sometimes, you feel a little funny feeling but I wouldn't say you were actually frightened because if you was really frightened you wouldn't be there. You wouldn't stop at the job. You'd get out of it. Yes, to be afraid of the sea's the wrong thing altogether but you've certainly got to respect it.

You're only a puny thing, only a small thing there you know. It's much bigger'n you are. There's an old saying the fishermen used to have at Sheringham. 'You watch and pray'. I think a lot of people go through life and they don't have anything to bring them down to size, do they? It's the job that counts. If you're a coal miner, I think that bring you down to size in the same way. Quite a lot I should imagine. In a storm you get more or less excited. You're like a dog running about in rough weather. The sea is glorious. But it's like a woman isn't it? Full of moods.

Being an artist does not make Jack any less of a fisherman, but it does help him to record what the life means to him.

I started painting in Scapa Flow during the war. I'd only done sketches before that, not anything in colour. I always could draw though I don't look at things now when I paint them. Maybe tomorrow morning I could wander along this bank just looking at the tide and the boats, and in the evening I could come home and paint that scene. I look at it two or three seconds, then it hold in my mind. I've always done boat pictures, harvest scenes and wild birds flying. Duck, geese and things like that. I might stop going to sea and paint all the while. I'm sixty-two next birthday. That's getting on a bit. When you've got hard work on the water you're not like a young man of thirty. I'm not painting much at the moment—I don't get the chance but what few I do I sell pretty good. People keep coming around wanting them.

If I was going to paint this scene I'd put my easel up here and say, right, there's a grey sky. Grey-blue sky and the grey-blue water. And the water is a tone deeper than what the sky is. That's your two big colours. Then you've got the hard going down to the boats which is a more umber colour to me, with a little bit of yellow ochre picking the stones up. There's this big black boat and the bank with all this brown stuff on. And in the distance you've got the trees going back dull grey-blue which is good for distance. That's faded out quite a lot. You've got your middle distance and it's faded down past this old black boat. It loses its intensity of colour. And as you go back further it's bluer and bluer. You'd slap in with a two-inch brush all that colour in the sky, then you come down a tone on your water, throw in your bank, the hard and your boats with a smaller brush. I quite often do birds. I think I know them. Gulls are the hardest to tell of the lot because they change so much according to season. There's a Glaucous gull, the great black-backed and the lesser black-backed and the ordinary herring, the black-headed, the Sabine gull, the little gull and the Mediterranean gull, but I couldn't tell them all straight off, I'd have to watch them through binoculers.

I'm trying to combine two lives, yes, fisherman's and painter's. I think one blends in with the other. People say why should they? Well, a fisherman looks at skies most of the time, or he should do anyhow because to him that's weatherwise. And I think a painter, especially in Norfolk, he looks at the skies. You see quite a lot of things when you're a fisherman because you're up early in the mornings, late at nights. Other people are probably sleeping then. One could probably do a lot easier job, a clean job and get more money but when you're brought up as a boy to it, it's in you. You either like it or you don't. If you like it you carry on. But that's not money what counts. I should think the most important thing in life is to have good health and strength, you can always earn a living then. And to have an appreciation of good things around you. That is important because if you don't appreciate nothing you're not living are you? You're just existing. If you've been out on the water all day, say it's come on cold on a winter's night and the wife's got a lovely big fire roaring. Isn't that nice to sit down and appreciate it?

'Loady' spoke of pub life during the early part of the century. Jack affirms that fishing and drinking still go together.

When that's rough you go down the pub. I mostly go to the Shipwright's, it's nearer home, that's all. All I've got to do is put on a pair of slippers, walk from my house and I'm there. And most of the fishermen get there, too. I think it's the company more than anything. I mean you may want to go along and talk with somebody about some fishing or whelks or weather. We don't get drunk like they used to. But I hain't got many what I call close friends. I've got acquaintances but I don't make strong friendships with people, not with men anyhow. I wouldn't be too keen on having a friend and going everywhere with him, all that business.

There is only a public bar at the Shipwright's Arms, a narrow room with a counter running the length of one side.

A yellowing paper on the walls is hung with framed pictures of coastal birds. Three tables sit snugly, one behind the other; indeed there is no room for them any other way. A door at either end only just relieves congestion of a Saturday night. 'Weren't no bloody room for us in our own pub' is an August grumble. 'Bunged up! — You could hardly move'. Yet you can scarcely move in there any weekend in November or December. Or even in February when the spring winds howl fit to flatten the building perched at the edge of the quay. Loping navy forms emerge from a silver mist, overcoats huddled round shoulders hunched up against the cold, and stamp at the brave sight of a fire. Known as 'the fishermen's pub', it is only a stone's throw from the place where they live and work. You can sit outside in the summer and dangle your legs over the bare creek where gulls tumble in the air.

Early in the evening groups around the table start playing cards or dominoes. 'Three's and five's' is a game of adding dominoes so that the sum of the two ends make multiples of three and five. It has been played here for over sixty years. Whiskies interlace mild brown, the tone is intimate and gently riling. Lilting voices rise and fall, swearing is automatic. 'Say, were you in the herring fishing picture in the EDP last week?' shouts a scrawny man with several pints behind him. 'This lady says there ain't no bloody herring fishing no more'. They are highly critical of attempts to portray their life-style on the media. 'See us on TV a week or two ago? Like a lot er bloody parrots, all saying the same thing one after t'other'.

In the Shipwright's Arms there are not only local fishermen but ones from up and down the coast, 'Shrimp' Davies from Cromer and 'Skipper' Woodhouse from Caister, sometimes amongst them. They prefer one another's company to that of non-fishing people from the same villages who, in turn, regard them with admiration, pride and some despair. Faces blush pink above bleached slops, and strong arms like rope, protrude below sleeves. The atmosphere is animated by an occasional roar from the tables. When they knock off work, the men who guard their fishing secrets spontaneously enjoy one another's company.

At thirty-five, Roger Bishop has the advantages of a younger man, with sufficient faith in his own abilities to thrust his way through. Besides a wife, young child and a house on the council estate, Roger has shares in a boat, whelk sheds and a business. He is tall, strong and dark, vigorous, bearded, open-faced and volatile. In fact he has several selves. One curses life roundly while another is sociable. One is adventurous, perhaps even foolhardy, while another is hard-working and shrewd. He probably needs them all, for his background is from the slightly lower status of worm-digging. He built up his future from there.

I think the Bishops on our side of the family originated from London. My grandfather came down after oysters, first to Lynn and then down this way. My father and an uncle dug for worms and I started in 1958. My sister married a fisherman and my one brother dug for a while before he packed it in to join the army. Afterwards he took a course for teaching at a technical college. He got out before I did. He had more sense. Anyway I had ten or eleven years of it then I went whelking for two years and after that I went out spratting.

The spratters all come from Whitstable. There were about six here to start with, had their boats on a White Fish Authority grant, only they weren't making enough money at Whitstable to pay back the White Fish so when they found some sprats here, round they came. They made a fortune to begin with. They were going out on the first of the tide, loading up, coming back and emptying at low tide. That was in the early 1950s. In the summer we were roper fishing when weather permitted, from May until August, then I used to pack up and go worm-digging until the sprats come, end of November time. That was good because it's the best worm-digging time in the winter. I'd sprat until March, then have a couple more months digging, then back to roper.

As with crabs, marketing sprats is aggravated by the fact that these towns and villages are cut off from big market outlets.

The sprats are here again this year but the trouble with fishing from Wells is that whatever you catch you've got to send either to Grimsby or Lowestoft. That works all right if you're catching plenty but it used to work out we had to catch nine ton of sprats before we paid for the lorry. Whatever you got above that was profit but if you got under nine ton you might just as well dump them back over the side because all you were doing was paying for the transport to Grimsby. Mostly they were only going as fishmeal anyway. We did get one cannon order, I think they were going to Rob Roy's to sell to Woolies in tins. It was all right if you got big sprats and nobody else was catching big sprats but if they were catching big ones further north, well the factory was closer, they didn't want to pay for ours to travel from Wells to North Shields.

One time we went up to Grimsby cod fishing, only there was no cod so we come back and went right round to Yarmouth, but we still couldn't make a living and we came back here. I said 'We've either got to catch some fish or I'm getting out of it'. So we decided to look at Lynn and see what we could find there. They said 'You're just the blokes we're looking for, we've got a cannon order and can't meet it. So we went down to Lowestoft, bought a net for £40 and shot it over in the Wash. Well when it came up I've never seen nothing like it, like a bloody sprat bag, so we were doing the all right then. But that's better than it ever was now because they're shrimping all the year round.

Somebody was going to set me up in business so we went to have a look for a boat all over the place. Then when we got one, he backed out of it so that left me out of a job completely. Then I went on the oil rigs for a year, only I came back when the boy was born. Clive and I had always talked about going fishing and I said 'If you're going to fish from Wells it's no good going trawling because you're only fishing half the year.' I think the most I ever did earn there was £430 in a fortnight, we were doing it nineteen hours a day. The £400 was all right but if you did nothing for the next two or three weeks, you had nothing. You never hear a whelker shout about what he's doing—it's not like spratting and shrimping. One day Clive met me in the pub and said 'Do you still want to go whelking?' So I said 'Yes, but don't talk about it over a drink. If you still feel the same way in the morning, come and talk to me.'

When he come round he had got somebody to lend us the

100

money for a boat, so we planned it would take us a year to get everything together and a whelk house organised, and we kept an eye open for a boat. A week later there was one advertised in the *Eastern Daily* at Brancaster, so I went over and had a look at it. It was just what we wanted, so Clive come and had a look, too. Right, we got a boat. We thought we had a whelk house, too, then someone decided he was going to grow oysters in it. There we were with a boat and gear but nowhere to go. I had the idea of seeing Gricks to ask whether we could borrow their boiler. 'Yes, lovely, as long as you sell the whelks to us'. So we were away.

When we knew we were going to start I went to work at Fakenham and got a job nights so I could come home in the daytime and do the gear up. I used to take my twine and needle to Rosses and sit there knitting. I learned that when I was spratting but making a net is easy compared with mending one. It was the 3rd of November when we decided to start whelking and by May we'd got the gear together, packed in our jobs and gone. Well we weren't catching many the first year. I'd never hauled before, I'd only been at sea with somebody else. Clive was an engineer, he'd never been to sea to work, only pleasure trips. So when we started I couldn't haul and Clive couldn't shoot away. I shot while he was steering the first time. At least we got the gear down, two shanks at sea and away we went hauling them the next day. You can guess what happened, it was pulling and tugging until at last we got them up. It's very very hard to keep the boat over the pot while you haul, this is something you've got to learn by practice. It's a great help if you've got somebody there to say, do this, do that, but before we could learn anything we had to make mistakes and get out of them. Well, any rate, the first day we hauled we got four whelks. We've still got one of them up here. It says the 9th of the 4th, '74. All we had out of two shanks. Oh they laughed. I mean I would have done.

The next day we went, we still got them on the hard just outside the harbour, and I took another shank out to south-east Docking before I hauled the two on the hard. We got a bushel and a half that day, so we were going up. But every time we come in with only a few it made me more determined to carry on. I knew a little bit about the game because I'd been whelking for two years. I knew what I'd done wrong but you can be whelking a lifetime, baiting and shaking

101

out a lifetime, and if nobody says 'Are you going to have a haul?' or tells you something about it, you don't know. They won't let you try. This is the thing, once you can haul you can whelk. Why should they teach other people if they're paid hands. If you can haul they're out. Anyone who can haul holds the trick card.

We were working on the gear and slowly getting things organised. We had a garage to do the gear up in and I think about twenty-five bags was our best last year. We had to have somewhere to keep the bait, so we borrowed a whelk house at Brancaster. We were taking our bait there, salting it down, then running over to fetch it all last summer. We were at it all winter and the longer I was hauling, the better I got. I made mistakes but I gradually worked and worked at it. Sometimes I could er bloody sat down and cried because I couldn't get the boat to do it. Our boat, the *Concord*, is easier than the lifeboats to haul in; she was built for whelking and you do it over the side. But we haven't done too badly and I reckon in another year I'll be as good a hauler as any of them. Clive had a go and nearly smashed his hand on the bollard. He isn't going to have another, but with the engine he knows it all. I don't know what the other boats' garage charges are but we never pay anything, he does it. I'm quick tempered and he's just the opposite so we get on great together.

We had a lot of help from my brother-in-law and several other fishermen but when we first started some of them wouldn't say a word for three or four months until we got this whelk house down on the quay. We still unload near the Shipwrights but we've got the whelk house going now. We pulled the worm hut down and we've got two coppers and a bit of canvas. Jack, he hung on for us inside the harbour when it was rough one day and we'd had the whelk house five minutes when they rushed in, so now I'm accepted as one of them. We worked five shanks all through the winter and now we've got six, the same as the others, and one at home. This winter there have been gales. We haven't been going out much but that was a blessing in disguise really since when we weren't going out we were doing up the gear. I think out of the whole year we had one day off and that was when we went to London to watch Norwich play. We still haven't had a holiday now for three years. We'll have one if that's rough but if not it'll be a long weekend. You have to rope the pots up; that I knew but Clive didn't. To do a whole pot completely takes about two hours. There's going to be a time when we want another man and the only fair way to do it is to put him on a share, even if it's a small share, then you get no grumbles. If you catch nothing, you don't get nothing; if you get a good catch, then you get a good wage. This is why I like the partnership idea. You're working for the same things and you're satisfied, not running round looking for a crew all the time. I mean even those who've got crews lose them every so often. If there's two or three ships come up into the quay, they go and help unload because they earn more money doing that than they could going to sea. So the boats are often one short, or they don't go at all. Whelking is really a three-handed job, there's only one two-handed boat here besides us for the simple reason we can't afford a third. With two it's just one mad rush and when the gear gets fouled you need three. We've only had a small foul. We cleared three shanks and brought one home, and cleared the other one the next day. But I've seen three shanks rolled up in one. We got all the pots off and the heap of rope took three of us two days to unwind.

So we're looking for an old boy to help make the nets up. At the moment we still use sacks but we can't wash the whelks as they come through the water, our boiler washes them all in a tub and boils them in baskets as they do at Brancaster, but when we get alongside the quay we can't hook the bags on to lift them up so we've got to go in for nets. They're a lot easier to handle, too — there isn't anything to beat them. That's like a whelk pot. Whoever invented one knew what he was doing. But this is where expense comes in because the pot was designed so you could use all your old things up, like sisal tows that weren't strong enough to pull the pots with, could be wrapped round them. But now we're using synthetics and they're no good for roping pots, so we're buying brand new stuff.

We didn't intend to start whelking until this year so really we're a year ahead; things went that fast for us. I'd never do it again. I weighed fifteen stone when I started and in three months I weighed under twelve. But I think in five years we'll really be established. I can still get into muddles, like when people start shooting over me, and things happen like this. It's all right when all is going well and the pots are full but you can soon get disheartened if they don't come up.

103

Why am I going to sea? I'm doing something I like and making a living and I'm home to bed every night. Those are the main reasons. All right, there's big money travelling but you're doing six weeks out then a week at home. What's life? Only one fisherman's son here has gone fishing. I don't know why people go fishing because that isn't an easy life—it's bloody hard work, especially the way we are two-handed and trying to rig up gear and whelk house and everything else. It helps to be in the right place at the right time, know what you're doing when you're there and have a hell of a lot of luck. But I think the challenge is it. The more people laughed when I was coming ashore with ten or fifteen, the more I thought, they're laughing now but one day they'll sit up a bit.

4

WORM-DIGGING

My sole employment is, and scrupulous care,
To place my gains beyond the reach of tides.
— *Thoreau*

'It don't give you muscle, it shrivel you up it do', said a slight,
sinewy digger, emphasising his last word with the Norfolk
'du'. 'I can tell you it's pretty hard work'. He had been at the
job since 5.00 am. It was 7.30 on a pale, clammy morning.
Pools of water left by the retreating sea were grey. The light
was dull opal, the sand grey and the bleak line of marshes a
deeper grey. The air hung heavy with rain. Only seventy
worms. The sand was too soft, it was a poor dig. But he had
gone to some trouble to dam a stream of water across the
ebbing flow. A wide arc of sand was pricked up around the
area he was working, in holes seeping up with water and
sloppy mud. So he plugged on rather unsuccessfully.

Between Cley and Thornham, centred in Blakeney and
Wells, there are more than a hundred men digging through
the winter, although less than thirty do it all year round. The
worms are sold to long-liners during the winter and prices are
good. In the summer there are only amateurs to supply.
Unless a digger happens to live near Cley, on the spot for line
fishing from the beach, it is scarcely a lucrative trade. Before
the war the price was less than ten shillings a thousand. Just
after, it rose to a pound and today it stands around ten.
Occasionally they got a really good dig — 3,600 in about four
hours. But that was a long time ago. Some work for a king
digger at Wells. You can watch him pack the worms up from
a little tin hut on the East Quay before he takes them to
Norwich.

105

There are tatty letters pinned to the wall:

Dear Sir, I regret to inform you the last consignment was twenty-five worms short . . .

Dear Sir, Your last consignment was short on . . .

Dear Sir, Can't your men bloody count?

'Is it ever possible to miscount worms?' said an old hand widely known as 'The Professor'.

> No, no, how can you miscount them? Those worms are like quid notes. As you dig 'em up so there goes another ha'penny. Your mind don't go on the worms, it's what they're worth. That's what keeps you at it. When you're digging 'em you think about how much they're worth, then you can turn round an' think about other things when you've finished. You got to think what you can do with the money. What you can achieve with it. That's on everybody's mind. It's just the same with all people who are working. When they bring up so many pots of whelks they think about what they're worth.

On the whole worm-diggers are an independent lot — the scourge of the men who work the cockle beds and mussel lays. There is an acknowledged difference between them and fishermen. The digger's workshop is the open coast, his requirements a gritty determination and a supple back, his only tool a fork which needs replacing every half year. But the relationship is more subtle and to some extent they are part of the fishing community. After all they drink side by side at the Shipwright's Arms. However whelking would not have suited The Professor.

> I did go out four or five times in a boat along er the warden but I didn't care much for it. You're in one place, you can't get up and say I'll wander a couple er miles or have a walk round. Because many a time I've spent an hour walking. I'm a great wanderer.

'Laddy' Lane, jack of all trades and owner of mussel lays has scant respect for what he believes is an easy life.

106

Sometimes he even goes to the trouble of prosecuting worm-diggers.

You won't get a lot out of worm-diggers because you might open the ball up. They don't work because they're mostly on security. Some of them haven't for years. They are earning a pound a hundred, so if they can dig 500 a day that's £5 on top of security. That's a lot of money. There's some days I run my motor boat all day and don't get that. When you can get a bucket and spade and earn £5 with no expense there's nobody going to work. The two I prosecuted a couple of months ago got away with it — said they didn't go and read the notice board until after they'd been digging. They had to pay their lawyer but they got off. There are easily 150 doing it now, all on the dole. You can't wonder why the country's in such a stew.

A Brancaster whelker's opinions are probably more typical. 'Most fishermen think of worm-diggers like pirates. They put nothing back. They've got to earn a living but we cultivate. They don't. Just a fork and plastic bucket. We got on all right, but we don't class them as fishermen.'

Barry is a tall, well-built young man, a year-rounder who appears to take the work in his stride. Philosophically he says 'I reckon it's not a good living but it's not a hard life either. I can get home by midday on an early tide. Job over. My father and my grandfather done it. I work to an order. Had to get 1,400 this morning. It's good digging to get a thousand on a tide.' Barry's father, The Professor, is an aristocrat amongst worm diggers. He dug to make a living, but he enjoyed the thrill of wind in his bones, the polish of the sun in his eyes. It kept him at it for sixty years.

My father was a policeman [he told me] and we went from one village to another. I was the first and all my young life I was travelling about so I went to school in about a dozen places. But my father left the police force when he done about seventeen years and come down to Wells. Then he took up worm-digging as a livin'.

I didn't do much schooling after thirteen, I was generally out at work. There were eight more of us, all younger, so I had to start early. I can remember in them days when it was a rough morning all the worm-diggers used to stroll up and down on the quay and if a young feller like me walked behind them to see what they were talking about, he got a smack on the ear. You weren't supposed to listen. My mother were a little woman and my father was six foot two and weighed eighteen stone. He was fair coloured and curly. He did most of his digging down here in Wells and at Stiffkey, in a place we call Black Nock.

My father wouldn't sell them locally. He sold to a chap named Sallinger in Yarmouth. They went away by train in his time. There would be about three or four of them working in together—it was always a matey sort er business. I know the fishermen are not all matey now. The more money there is in it, the less friendliness. And I've found out, the harder you're put to it, the more friendly you are. Oh, I cried many a time with the cold. We only had hilos, sort er small leather boots that come up somewhere on your calf and we got wet feet. I've been out and broke the ice on the water, had bits er sacking wrapped round me legs and walked right across the Low, five miles, and when I got there my father'd say, 'Come on, get on, put something into it!' Four of my brothers come up to do it as well. My brother Hector, who now lives in March, had a very short spell digging because Father got wrong with him about something or other when he was about fifteen. Hector didn't like Father talking to him so he picked hold of the big wet sack what all the worms went on and nipped Father across the face with it. Father was chasing him round the whole place and the next day he didn't come home no more. He went on the *Old Emmanuel* along with Captain Gray. They give him the job as cook for half-a-crown a week but he was sacked after the first week because he broke a plate.

'The Professor' has an enquiring mind and ideas of his own about worms.

Worms are best in different places different times of the year. Beginning in the spring, I worked on Moorstone Freshes and Garsborough—those are names for sandbanks at Blakeney. Then I went to Black Nock at Stiffkey and on The Low and East Bite at Wells. Some time in May I moved over to Overy, working my way round the coast to Brancaster. One season when things looked really bad and there wasn't a worm to be found anywhere I got a 'message'. I tried the beach off Tarrington St Clement, deep in the Wash, and there was plenty there. Later on I worked at Butterwick, the far side er Boston, before starting off all over again the next year. I've bicycled everywhere on this coast. I've done more'n thirty mile before I ever started digging, thirty mile back; then you pack 'em in vermiculite or peat, even newspaper. Anything that's dry. Christ! I got home and I worked two hours getting off little parcels all round England.

'The Professor' was a familiar sight, plugging away at his old bicycle, a huge square basket on the front and bucket strapped behind, or digging on the shore while his mind was busy hatching schemes. He was endlessly curious. Not content merely to dig, he 'conducted research'. You could watch him counting out worms, pondering, laying them side by side on the sand. He is seventy-six. Almost certainly he has never heard the word 'hermaphrodite', so he would not know that the lug worm is bisexual. Instead he has done what men of fertile imagination have done for centuries — found a hypothesis to satisfy the inexplicable. And if worms do not voluntarily leave their burrows, even for reproduction, some of his conclusions are not far from the truth.

I weren't satisfied in digging worms. I wanted to know all about 'em. There's worms that come within only a hundred yards of one another are quite different according to the texture of the sand. If you've got black mud under the bright top, now that worm won't keep well in the summertime, but if you go over to the coarse and brittle, what we call chaffy sand, they'll keep. There's muddy sand, chaffy sand or stoney sand — that's coarse and the worm need a thicker coat to get through. Then in Brancaster you come on to the ironstone and the worms are twice as strong and twice as thick. Even in the heat er summer they're still alive and kicking after three or four days. No other worms seem to live like 'em.

Every worm has a ten-year cycle from the day it's born. Of course we've got a lot to learn about sex and all different things. So much to learn about. Now there's a hundred females to one male. The male worm is rather blacker, with heavy wrinkles where it moves its body. They 'aint got no spawn inside 'em. Deep under the ground the female gets the urge to procreate before big tides at a full December moon. The

109

spawn is in a bag that gets bigger and bigger and bigger until it burst her skin and kills her. It gets spit to the ground and lays there in a blob. Then the male come and scatter sperm on the top and the two mix. So the actual fertilisation happen outside, it happen mechanically and that's how the new worm come into being. The blob turns into tiny white ones which, as soon as they are free, burrow down. Like in the Bible, those what hit good ground survive and those what hit bad ground perish. Some time every year there is a whole lot er young worms swim over the bar along with the sea and up on the Freshes to put themselves in everywhere. Jack said to me one day on the quay, 'There's two million worms now come over the bar, there'll be plenty next week.' He was just pulling my leg but that's exactly what do happen.

When you're digging in the creeks where the food is good, you get good long black worms but you have to find the water level. You have to know the best place to block that creek up to drain away the water. You put a dam across and bale the water out of the middle. You've got to be like a land surveyor to know exactly how the water fall. In some parts, as soon as you block it up, the water come down so quick and fill up, it rises over the top er the dam.

Worm-digging suited me because I had plenty of time for reading and I never was one for mixing with other people. I didn't make friends. Had dozens of acquaintances but I didn't used to make friends. And I like the life. I can tell you exactly what it felt like. You've got an 80-mile an hour blowing — and frozen rain and you're walking ahead of it with half a hundredweight on your back and your fork cutting into your shoulder. Then you try to keep moving it over from one to the other all the time. And the very fact that you're battling with the elements does something to you. Makes you a man. A challenge, that's all it mean. That's all my life have been — a challenge with danger, and I liked it. See, if I hadn't been challenged from nature I'd have got myself into trouble doing something I shouldn't. I'd have had to've got some excitement somewhere, but that was enough for me.

Like many of the fishermen, The Professor was deeply effected by his physical surroundings. Jack Cox is able to express these feelings in paint, Jimmy Paris or George Cox give them inexplicable almost magic properties while Philip

Green in the next chapter is so close to the edge of the sea, he is almost woven with it into one vehement ebb and flow. The Professor verbalises, sensing the reality again as he speaks.

And the other thing I used to like. I'll try and explain to you now. We've got a grass of hills on the east side where the Crawfords used to farm. They'd bring all the corn down on flat-bottomed boats harvest time. And the mill at the top of the Jolly Sailor's yard was where the wheat was ground. There'd be hundreds and hundreds of meadow pipits — they make a noise sort of like a lark. Just like a lark, only they don't go up so high. They fly up right quick and down to the ground quick. And when I went early in the morning — because you had to go whenever the tide suit you — you'd leave perhaps at four, and by a quarter to five you'd be a quarter across the meals and the sun would then be shining. There'd be a lovely morning in June and the sun would come up blood red, plenty er rays in the sky before it happen and then, all of a sudden up go a meadow pipit. Then as you went along another one gets up until the whole marsh is filled with a chorus of birds. On the ground you'd see little white tails nipping along of the rabbits, 'cos it's full er rabbits. And as you come along they'd be dashing into their holes out er the way. Well there was wild lavender, the sea lavender, and that all made your life. I can remember the pink feet, too. Gaggle, gaggle, gaggle up in the sky, the geese. We don't get them now. There used to be dozens of them all flying over and wild swans. Then if you looked on the stones you'd see at least fifty Danish crows. You never was tired of seeing these things; you always looked to see 'em. It was a pleasure to you. It's just the same as if you'd gone to see a bit of a play.

The first time I walked on the quay in Overy harbour the sun were playing a game all along, chasing shadows across the marsh. And as the shadows went across there's a light green and then a dark green and the colours all finished in the far-away hills. So I said that's my front room. That's what Overy looked to me.

5

MUSSELS

And light. Always light. And of course the sea. It
got under your skin, you became part of it, until
you came to feel that you could live nowhere else.
It was like love.

— *Sybille Bedford*

For pure physical slog there is no fisherman's work more
arduous than mussel fishing. The hours spent on the job are
long, most of the methods have not changed for hundreds of
years and in the end, as the men themselves point out, they
are dealing with a relatively low-valued commodity. Just how
to bring it in line with the 1970s is a problem to which there
is no obvious answer. Philip Green describes one concession to
the times:

> About twelve year ago we went to an engineer who lives
> inland saying he wanted something to riddle those mussels — if
> possible driven with a motor. If you do it by hand it means one
> person turning, one feeding it and another picking the debris
> out, sorting and measuring off, so that's three. It is cheaper to
> buy a tiny two- or three-horse motor, plonk him on and then
> work two. One throws them in from a five- or six-ton heap and
> the mussels go round and round inside a barrel. Little ones
> drop out and the big ones fall down onto a revolving tray at
> the end of the belt. The other person stands there picking out
> a shell or a stone and as soon as the basket gets level he whips it
> out and shoves another under. It's exactly like a carrot riddle
> except for the grading of the wire.

Yet Laddy Lane is wary. 'They've got these riddling
machines at Wells and Brancaster, I don't like it. Too much
messing. I like to be on the hard when I'm riddling, to keep
them clean. I think by hand, the way we do them is the best
even if they do double the quantity.' Like the old agricultural

labourers, fishermen have esoteric faith in the power of direct manual labour. So Mr Lane, prodding with a fork, shifts them up and down the lays in endless rotation.

There's more hard work to mussels than there is to whelking, because you've got to keep on turning them over in the lays to give them fresh ground. That whole bed has got up out of the water and the mussels are too thick but I'll work at them, cart some out and put them further down. You've always got to keep at work on 'em. A lot of people ask me what I feed them on but they're eating what comes in with the sea. They keep chewing and chewing and spit out the mud, which all turns to sludge. You don't see it but that's how they feed.

Some harbours are better than others. Overy always was good. But I think this sewer has killed the job a bit. They aren't so good this year, though we had a lot of rain and that may be it. Mind you, I think the creek is cleaner now because there were a lot of cesspools running into it, polluting it. I didn't sell all one winter, they wouldn't pass. Today you've got to have good mussels otherwise you get stopped, even when you send them to market they're inspected to see if they're clean. If they catch mud in 'em you've had it, especially in London. They're most fussy in London but you get a better price for them, I believe.

Though a comparatively young man, John Henry Loose has only just decided to procure a mechanical riddle, a dozen years after the first one was introduced.

The difficulty is that I have to increase sales to cover costs if I use more machinery. Things have got to be economical before you go out there all day killing yourself and finishing out of pocket. Although we use more machinery now, there's depreciation on it. There are two mechanical riddles down there at the moment and I'm getting one but there'll be no increased output as a result, it just makes life slightly easier. You can use tractors on the beach but you can't get to the mussels. That's the difficulty, you can't use conventional machinery because it won't go through the mud. It would be possible to devise something like your combine or sugar beet harvester but the cost would be terrific. Then as soon as metal touches the salt water it's going to corrode.

113

John Henry, like Philip Green and his father before him, uses a special type of rake for loosening mussels and bringing them to the surface. Called a 'dydle-rake' at Brancaster, a 'wim' at Stiffkey and a 'lab-rake' at Wells, it has about seven teeth fixed to a handle with a curved iron frame attached to a net. The handle, ash or larch, something that bends, varies in length up to about 18ft according to the depth of water in which it is used. For scooping mussels out of the shallow washing pits he has a similar tool, one used for clearing out rivers for centuries, called a 'pit dydle' or simply a 'dydle'. Instead of prongs, there is a metal blade along the bottom, a little more 'flow' or bagginess in the net to hold mussels, and the handles are made from hedge elm, cut locally and bent with a piece of string. He knits his own dydle netting as well as the nets [bags] for carrying mussels.

Despite the Eastern Sea Fisheries' belief that mussels offer the biggest trade expansion potential, this is not a tale of a thriving industry but one that is just ticking over. At Blakeney, musseling has finished altogether, at Overy and Stiffkey it is petering out, so Brancaster is one of the last strongholds. Two fishermen who spend or spent most of their working life musseling, one at Brancaster and one at Stiffkey, tell of its present and past.

An October mist hangs over Brancaster Staithe, tinging the faded sea lavender to a yellow smudge. Below ramshackle whelk sheds, the base of the fishermen's quay and boats scattered on the mud are enveloped in a white haze echoing with the throb of an electric riddling machine. Upon closer inspection several brief wooden frames are visible; some hung with bundles of drying mussel nets while others are roughly draped with tarpaulins to form the rude shelters fishermen crouch behind in windy weather. One is squatting there now, refuelling a large round hand riddle from a net sitting on a barrow, shaking the small ones through and packing the rest into a sack. 'Yes it takes longer. I hain't kept a-pace with the rat-race, but they keep better this way,' he reasoned. 'That's like the difference between an apple picked from a tree and a windfall. They're kind er bruised from the machine.'

Beyond the hand-riddler are ten or a dozen cleaning pits; wooden-sided and concrete-bottomed, some sprinkled with mussels. Beside them a man is working the electric machine, throwing mussels in at one end using a deep-seated fork with flat-tipped prongs. Water splashes on to them from a pipe leading up out of the creek as they clash round and slip out down a chute at the other end. He crosses over to the receiving side to remove pieces of seaweed as they drop into a plastic basket.

Another blue-slopped fisherman rows up in a boat and jumps into one of the pits to clean the mud off his boots before joining a third group where a wispy yellow-haired youth is emptying out mussels in a heap on the ground. Behind him stands a long row of tied sacks. A brown-slopped fisherman followed by a pink-cheeked child walks with sliding steps towards his car. They get in and drive off. It is John Henry Loose, only fishing survivor of a big fishing family. He tells us something about them:

> The Loose family probably came from Holland—they've been traced back to a wreck in these parts. Mother lived at Briston. Her father was a farmer who went out of business in the 1910 floods—when all the corn stood in the fields, cut, and went grey again—it was a complete loss. So he went bricklaying at Sheffield, then at Scunthorpe. He came back here when he was fourteen or fifteen. Father lived here. His father was a fisherman but he's an intellectual. Always studying. He took a Doctor of Philosophy in the sciences, and they went as missionaries to India at the time of the second war. Stayed there about seven years and came back a few weeks before the 1947 freeze-up, when even the sea was iced over. I was just over three when they returned and I don't remember anything about it. They came home with the intention of returning again but they never did. My father went teaching at Fakenham School. In the end he was there for twenty-seven years.

On several counts John Henry stands apart from other

fishermen. For a start, he received a good education, then he slipped back a generation.

I went out fishing with my grandfather and I always was very keen. As early as I remember I used to go messing about in boats and I probably went to sea round eight or nine. I left school at seventeen, just a few months after he died, so everything came to a head. Either I started straight off or lost the opportunity for good. My father never seemed to try and influence me. I've got four brothers so perhaps he used his influence elsewhere. The eldest one went in for electronics and started his own business. Then there's me. The next one went to university before teaching and the youngest is at Cambridge now. I'm not the type who changes, I'm thirty-one and I've adapted completely. I couldn't do anything else. There are advantages in the work. It's great being your own boss. You come and go as you like. You have to do a certain amount but you do it at your own convenience. Last winter I had a terrific slog. I went out day and night but today we've had a regatta and we've just been out in the boats amusing ourselves.

He is probably the sole fisherman in Sheringham today who has only once been to the local pub.

You get quite a bit of community spirit in the White Horse don't you. We never go so we miss out on that one. I've only been in there once in my life, when I was a little lad at school, so I must have gone in with somebody else.

If there's money about, fishermen will go for it. I've been working here for fourteen years and found the standard has altered now the older ones have moved on. At the moment a six-peck bag has only got five pecks in it. When they were young they had to work hard all the year round to survive, but now, when the season is in boom and you get four or five months' good weather, a fisherman can make hundreds of pounds. They adjust their standard of living to the boom period, which means when the winter gales come on they've nothing left. But this is not peculiar to the fishing industry, it seems pretty general throughout the country—it all comes over through the box.

Fishermen are so independent that you don't really know what other people are getting. I mean you send your mussels away almost side by side but you aren't supposed to know what

116

they're getting for theirs. It's all the biggest secret imaginable. That gets round eventually but nobody goes to someone else and says we're going to get such and such a price, let's agree to it all round. One or two are coming round that way but there are various reasons why it never works. I think everybody should be free to fix their own prices. I don't agree with the union principle, we all get together and you pay a certain price or you don't have them. That's one of the ruins of this country.

Working in together would take a terrific amount of organisation and because of that it will never happen, or not for a very long while. It won't work because as soon as you start getting together somebody is going to put in poor quality stuff. It's been tried before and there are very few people who will play fair all round. You get a good price for a bag, well next time you'll put a few less in or you'll not bother so much to get them up to standard. You see they feel under no moral obligation. I think that's more important than what you get out of it in the long run. I'm not condemning anybody, they get away with what they like — it's up to them. But if everyone was prepared to give a bit more for what they got it would be a lot happier place.

The Fishermen's Society is organised under the friendly societies. There's an official body and certain acts and rules relating to how they are run. It started mainly so we could obtain various garments and equipment that fishermen need. Dick Everett did it for years and years in a voluntary capacity. Not only fishermen belong, but a newcomer has to be accepted by the committee of the society. Nobody yet I think has been refused. The members pay a pound in, we deal with various firms and get gear together, then they come along and have it but it is on the decline because now they all get out and about buying their own stuff. They won't support their own society. I honestly think most of them imagine I do it for my own benefit. They get the impression the profits are all mine, whereas in actual fact I'm out of pocket every year. I'm sure of that. There's a fixed rate, an honorarium they call it, of 5 per cent on the stuff that's sold but it doesn't cover my costs for running here, there and everywhere and paying up for people who don't pay. Right now I can't even get the stuff.

I should think about fifteen fishermen belong, then there are a few of the older ones who have almost retired, perhaps twenty, and about ten or fifteen other people in the district

117

who are interested. At the last annual general meeting I think there were eight there. Nobody bothers. They don't realise that if they came and bought more it would be better for them and better for all the fishermen in the village. We're affiliated to the Fisherman's Organization Society, a body in London that oversees all the local inshore groups. They have a general secretary who comes down every year to supervise the AGM and he says the problem is the same everywhere. Until there's big money at stake or their livelihood, nothing will wake fishermen.

Which brings us back more or less to where we began, with a comment from Philip Green:

The trouble with musseling is the money. You've got to collect the mussels, grow them and then hand them over to the fellow who's selling them. If you've got good stuff, whether it's eggs or anything, you can mostly get rid of it, but the fellow who's selling them is the dominating factor. He can say so much a bag — say twenty-five bob — and how the hell can you get a better offer? That's improving now but then the price of everything is going up. There's no real value in the things.

These remarks are echoed by John Henry:

The man who takes our bags drives the lorry down. He can ship them off to market and make more money in one day than we can in a week getting them ready. There's a terrific amount of work preparing them — getting the ground ready and putting the mussels there before you get a penny for them. You've got to provide your own boats and various equipment, boots and coats — they've all just about trebled in price in the last three or four years. Whereas all he has to do is buy himself a lorry, or get one on HP, drive down here, pick the things up and call the tune at the other end. If we could get together and buy a lorry we could sell to the market itself. Prices have gone up recently but mussels are sold to the customers for over ten times what we get. It's exactly the same situation in farming, only farming is a much bigger industry and now they're getting together and selling direct.

Mussels are cultivated on lays, but the lay must be replenished from banks or 'scalps' at sea where they grow naturally. Since bringing them in is half the battle, John

Henry has a definite advantage in renting both scalps and lays.

A lay is just an area of land where mussels grow readily. Those in Brancaster are numbered up to a hundred — they were standardized about 1920 into roughly 50-foot-length strips. But very few are being used now, perhaps ten or twelve. Much of the harbour is deteriorating. Many more could be used if work was put into clearing them up but there are only five or six men still musseling full time. The lays have been passed down in the families and we pay a nominal rent to the National Trust. We pay the same rent even if we don't use all of them.

Grandfather passed on six or eight lays and I work about three. Of course it is entirely governed by tide and weather. You could say we work according to the moon. The season ends roughly at the end of March when most of the mussels are gone. I've been taking them off 3–4 inches long but the job now is to tidy up and dig away the mud. As soon as the weather improves I shall start bringing mussels into the lays from Hunstanton where I hire the whole beach from Mr Strange. Billy, my grandfather, took over the scalps in 1935 when no one else wanted them. Before that, they had never been let out of Hunstanton. 'Scalp' is pronounced 'scorpe' though it is spelt 'scalp' or 'scaup' and that comes from a Dutch word meaning shell. If anyone wants mussels they pay me now but I'm not obliged to let them on, anyway they're not in great demand. It all requires too much work. It never ends. All summer I bring the mussels down.

Philip Green is in his mid-sixties. When John Henry's grandfather had the run of the scalps, Philip's father used to collect mussels from them in his old sailing hubbler, and as a lad Philip went along too. There is little of his apprenticeship he does not remember.

'The Greenway' reads a hand-painted sign just inside Stiffkey, at the edge of a turning off the main Wells road. One or two cottages lead to a row of modern bungalows the last of which, set back in the corner of a piece of farmland and fighting a battle against an invasion of nettles, belongs to Mr and Mrs Green. The road leads on right up to the edge of the meals where it peters out into a stony thoroughfare. At this point the impact of light is tremendous. Stretching forwards and sideways over miles of salt marsh is a wide clear sky. Only a ribbon is land, the rest is sky.

It is November and patches of squat samphire have turned crimson between stretches of spent thrift heads, sea aster and lavender, here and there dotted with scraggy bushes of seablite. The terrain is blotted with large, muddy, bird-tweaked circles and intersected with gulleys of sea water. Clumps of grass bend in the breeze; a flock of curlews flies strongly overhead in an uneven chevron, letting out liquid bubbling trills. Ahead is a one-sided bridge over a wide creek, its black slopes netted with grey-leaved purslane. And beyond that, far away over the marsh a little white houseboat tilts uncertainly to one side. Despite a wind, warmth pierces the earth in thin streaks of white light.

Further away still, seawards, there is a tussocky ridge of marram and behind that a lower, reedy, shell-speckled area that gets washed by the tide each day. A bunting lifts up from the ground. Holkham woods nudge the horizon on one side and Blakeney Point on the other. Still there are miles of sand before the sea. But a figure is bobbing along in the distance—someone dragging a length of wood. When he reaches the edge of the line of marsh he hunks it up onto his shoulder and plods on. Old corduroys, a blue slop and beret pulled down over his ears, short and wiry. It is Philip Green, never so happy as when he is on the meals.

Like John Henry, he is a family man, essentially practical, who goes his own way. Whatever the job, Philip has his own method of doing it, nor does he want or seek other people's advice. Life for him is like the sea, by turns, grey and hostile or vigorous and untamed. He is constantly refuelled by it. Perhaps if there were one word to describe him it would be vital. He has all the attributes of a born narrator. While he speak, he gesticulates continually. The fireplace is his canoe, the mantle the mule, and the hair carpet, simulating a sail,

120

gets slapped over one knee and tucked down behind the other. His wife unobtrusively straightens it out as he carries on:

I never did go oystering. It got so slack that it wasn't worth the time. Whether it was constant dredging or whether it was pollution, I couldn't truly say. There used to be three going out of Stiffkey after them; my father went when he was younger. They'd leave on a Monday morning for the deeps off the Dudgeon or Back-of-the-Falls, work all one day, one night and the next morning then come back in the afternoon. You could sell them locally if anyone was ill and had a doctor's orders for oysters, but you couldn't sell them commercially and you knew damn well if you lay them here for four or five weeks they would open up. They wouldn't stick the warm temperature and the sun coming through the water.

My great-grandfather was a whaler, he went out from Lynn on some of the last old whaling boats. The Yankee whalers used to sail down to the south and they'd be gone for a couple of years but he'd leave in the spring, have the summer up in Davis Straits and all round there and then come away home when the fall set in. There were five Greens fishing in my grandfather's time.

My father ran away to sea when he was eleven or twelve because he thought he'd get more grub there than he did at home. He lived down the street and he'd start talking. Everybody would be quiet and listen to him and he'd just be going on like a tape-recorder about what he done. 'I walked to Blakeney', he said, 'Saw this skipper and got a ship', because there were little ships from Blakeney going down to Newcastle taking grain and bringing back coal and cattle food. He took some clothes, not that he had many. Probably pinched his brother's hat and someone else's stockings to make himself a bit of a rig, and he buggered off about one o'clock in the morning, so he was down about nine. But they missed Giles, my grandfather called him Giles, where'd he got to? And my grandfather who was fair at thinking and slow at talking, give the table a thump that knocked over the breakfast things and said, 'He's got his leather boots on, so he's gone to Blakeney, gone to sea!' Well they walked to Blakeney and found my father. 'What you doing here?' My father was trembling and shaking. 'I've got a ship and I'm going to earn some money'. So

121

my grandfather went to see the skipper, because they all knew
one another. Told him, 'Keep an eye on him, make him do as
he is told'. He was only a boy but he soon turned out fairly
handy. He was several years in various old ships, some old billy
boys, 70, 80 and 100 tons. Later he went to Yarmouth and he
was walking on the quay where they used to fit the luggers out
when someone said, 'Boy, do you want a boat?' So he went with
a fellow who owned a fleet of herring drifters. His wife would
take the boys home to look after them and what money they
earned. She'd write to their people and say their boys were
being looked after and where they were. They'd keep a decent
crew like that. At any rate he was with them for quite a long
time until he went off on a tramp steamer. There were twelve
on her, a little old lugger, about 48 foot. They'd fill her up
with herring, salt them down and then when she was loaded,
sail home. Of course he said it used to be a race home for some
of them. That's a fair old stretch from the Dogger Bank to
Yarmouth.

When my father was a boy it was his job to get buckets of
horse muck from the lanes and down the road because in the
springtime when they were refitting, putting patches on the
boat or anything like that, they'd always have a couple of bags
handy. Then he'd get chalk out of the pit or alongside the road
and grind it up right fine with a wooden mallet. Put it in a tin
and mix it up with tar until that come like pudding. They'd
daub it on the crack or the patch, always liberally, nice and
even all over then the horse muck and tar and chalk again. I
should think that was a binder like they used to put horse hairs
in mortar years ago. Just recently they were taking the wall
down from an old pub in this street and a chap noticed the
horse hairs. If you'd got a damn big patch going on to a smack's
bottom it would need to be tough, so presumably it had the
same effect.

The 1953 floods smothered up my lays. There's about three-
quarter mile of sand with a big high outer bank and the flood
came in from the west; it must have filled it up three or four
feet deep right across, completely burying everything. Then
the channel had to bore its way through again. This is a good
creek, it comes through from Wells, through the marshes and
past what we call our meals to the hand bed lays which my
grandfather started building up with faggots. A faggot is a
bundle of sticks; they chopped gorse or bull thorn [hawthorne],

put it together into long bundles one top one way, one the other; one root one way, one the other, then took a piece of wire and pulled it round right tight. They're sometimes six foot, as long as you can make 'em. The idea is as old as the hills, the Romans used to build up marshy ground with them and lay a road on top, so it has come straight down from their time. You drive in two stakes for them to lie against criss-crossed, hammer them down and twist the faggot wire round the tops. Then you go down to what they called the hard ground further down, load up the canoes with stones, chuck 'em on top of the faggots and they'll bind up the mud to make an artificial bank. You could use a load of pit props of all sizes that had come ashore. You'd sharpen them up, drive them in and then put boards along, perhaps two rows and fill the middle up with stones. The faggots were OK if the bottom was suitable but if you had a big gap that was a more substantial way.

On the mussel lays there used to be a lot of this old snapweed that visitors pick up to tell the weather with. We also call it kelp. Well, we had an invasion of the blasted stuff on the mussels. It would stand up in the flood and, of course, the sand would collect and the poor old mussels you wanted to keep clean were buried underneath it. We had to go round scraping the weed off so the tide could get amongst the bunches of mussels and we'd use it for collecting up the sand. The other modern way we used on a hard bottom was to make a ridge of stones and throw some loose mussels on — in no time they would build mud and there'd be a bank all made by the mussels themselves. You can build up sand with old spartina. Simply take a fork, dig bits up and shove them in zig-zag or diamond-shaped. That flops over and the sand builds up like billyho. In no time you've got a ridge. The north bank is all hand-made. God, they'd be down there before that was daylight and working away until after dark when my father was a young boy. It must have been before the beginning of the century they started on it. Both my father and my grandfather museled, then the one flood just went woosh — after all that work. They put more into that than eleven Leymans put into a day's effort.

We built a flat-bottomed canoe, we built everything. We'd got a pair of hands and a little brain, so anything you wanted you'd just got to turn round and make. Well, actually, what

123

you did do is lay the boards down, say for a sixteen-footer. You'd need a good inch and a half thickness of wood on the bottom, then you put on your clamps, just squeeze them together, not too hard, just gently and make a middle line down. Say we'll give her three-foot six or four feet according to what beam you wanted. Then you chalk round near enough as long as the damn thing's going to be and plane round. You plane the edges just a little bit out, so the sides stand slanting then you lay your floor down. There'd be about four boards across, clinked [clenched] all the way through and you're away. Put the lower plank round, only before you do this you want to stick a wedge of wood under her head to bring the bottom up a little, about an inch and a half. Because if you leave it perfectly flat, when you get them on the mud you can't move 'em. The buggers sit there like an old sucker fish. But if you make her bevelled she'll be all right. I never got stuck because when you're so high it's knocked into you by the other generations. The average one will carry about 20–25 bags.

To be honest, the sails were any damn thing you could scrap hold of. There were several ships come ashore and if they were a total loss, we'd buy the whole lot—masts, spars and bring them ashore to sell the wood. The bits of sails would come in useful for the oyster smacks and mussel smacks. You see everything had to be done on the cheap. And, of course, they used to make them themselves, which is a hell of a laborious job. My father'd have his needles and several different kinds of palm. A palm has a steel disc full of indentations let in two layers of leather—shoemakers use them to force the needle through leather. The roping palm, for sewing the rope round the sail, has a small raised disc and the ordinary palm has a big flat steel one. You stick a thumb through the leather and the metal bit catches your needle when you push him. If he was roping he'd use a fairly big needle with double twine. He'd lay the sail out flat to cut it, then he'd get the strips tucked over his knee and go push-pull, push-pull, working all the way along so the stitches were almost touching one another. Imagine going slowly up thirty feet and coming back on the opposite side of the seam another thirty feet because the canvas is only so wide and you probably got to do twenty seams altogether.

There's a place called Black Nock that was all salt mud and eelweed, the little thin grass that swans and ducks live on; and winkles, young cockles and young mussels used to accumulate there. Lovely little mussels, they'd vary from half to quarter of an inch. You'd think a mussel is a mussel all the world over, but they aren't, they're as different as people. Some are long and narrow, some are broad, some are short and stumpy and some are blue old buggers that won't grow at all. The only thing I can think of to compare them with is people. And these mussels used to grow like the very devil. You'd shift them off and put them in the lays, when you'd cleaned them right down to the shingle. That would be all mud and slush and you had to rake it about so the big tides came and cleaned them up.

You'd lay them in about six feet of water, fairly thick, mostly on the south side because the north was a bit sandy, and they'd lie there five or six months. Meanwhile you had the big mussels you were working on right through the middle. You'd start cleaning them up in September, finish about March, then you'd shift the little fellers into the middle where the mussels were actually growing, then clean them off. It's a game of repeat, round and round; laying them at half to three-quarter inch, growing them on the sides until after about four months they'd be an inch or an inch and a half and then, by the time they'd been seven or eight months in the middle, in the deeper water, they'd be just big enough for sale.

We used to have an old Yorkshire mule, a big sharp-ended Scarborough herring boat, which my father took up to the Wash. The Wash is a big area, Lynn control one part of the fishery and Boston control the other. It's all split up into different scalps lying on the outer edge of the sand at low water, some of them as big as a field. And as the fishery control the scalps, you have to write to them to get a licence, then they'll send you a hell of a great form about ones you can work and you have to pay about ten or twelve bob for a month, which, mind you, was March. Of all the rotten months of the year to go from here — load and try and get back in such short days. And March is mostly easterly winds when it's buggering hopeless to get home, especially sailing. Some tomfool fellow on the fisheries' committee — they're all shopkeepers and retired colonels — toss up the forms, take one out and that decides which scalp you can go on. Sometimes they were up there all March and half way into April, they'd loaded and tried to reach home. Got as far as Hunstanton where they would lay near the pier in the lee, stay there two or three days and the mussels used to stink because they'd only keep about a week. You'd run up to Heacham, chuck the damn things out on the sand somewhere and go ashore for some food. The journey wasn't wasted because you were still stuck up there. You'd wait until you thought it was turning fine and go back on to the scalp, load up and repeat it over again. You'd just get as far as Hunst'on with a nice little freight in, all washed and battened down, the wind'd turn easterly so there you had to stop. Then the buggers would start to stink and off you'd go again. That was when my father went but I've chucked three loads over in a motor boat. It's OK for the Brancaster men because they've only got to come round Holland Point through Brancaster Bay and into the harbour, that's enough. Wells is a little more than enough, but if you have to come to Blakeney, well sometimes that's like trying to jump on to the ruddy moon because you just couldn't make it.

John Henry has much the same attitude towards officialdom on the Fisheries Committee as Philip.

Each fishing place has a representative on the Eastern Sea Fisheries, some have two, but half the committee are just businessmen. The inspectors come round about once a month or once a fortnight and try to get you to tell them how much stuff you've sent away so they can put it down in their books; that's all they want to know. One comes here and guesses how many I've done. I don't tell him what's not true. I don't tell him anything at all. If he puts a figure on it and I've done that many bags I say 'yes' . . . the fact that I've done perhaps another fifty as well is beside the point. He doesn't ask, so I don't tell him. They're just a nuisance.

But back to Philip Green on the vagaries of mussels:

The scalps vary a lot, it all depends on how they're worked and how they're controlled. I've seen them spread over several acres, tons and tons of ruddy mussels. When 'Little Billy' Loose hired them off Lee Strange, my father used to go there in his old hubbler, she was only about 23 foot and she'd carry about eighty bushels. Those days we used to get a shilling a peck, which is four shillings a bushel when we retailed them, so we weren't handling a fortune. The trouble was, even if you once got them and laid them here and they really got growing, you could still go and lose the lot in one big tide. Every blasted mussel would be swept clean away. You'd go down there to a

126

beautiful clean sheet of mud, and that's your winter's work. It happened when the tides were big and it blew hard, which it mostly did when the winds came from the west or nor' west. The disturbance in the water soon started them moving. Boy, it was just like leaves blowing in a drive. You don't see the buggers any more so you start off again.

When we took the mule, there'd be Old Uncle Nat and probably my grandfather. They'd go round and get three lads out of the village who used to go oystering and faggoting with them. They were thick in the head but strong in the arms, good old labourers. So there'd be five of them because she was well on 40 foot, built-up and decked-in, and she'd carry three or four hundred bushels of mussels. You got onto the scalps, take a 10 foot stick and look for a piece of hard ground with a pit of water and a nice bed of mussels. Somewhere not too hard to work in because if you was plonking about in mud all day it was damn hard work. Anyway, you'd jam the old stick in and tie the smack up right on the edge of the pit so when the mussels came dry all you had to do was to wim them off and ferry them in your little boat — that was the flat-bottomed canoe. You wanted a wim that would really bend because you put some weight on it. You'd stand in the canoe, wimming mussels over in perhaps seven or eight feet of water, chuck it out and let it sink. Some people had heavy wims to let them sink quick, but that's hard work. The thing is to get a good handle so the whole thing is well balanced. You feel it hit the bottom then you rake towards you, prodding away, twist it over to collect the mussels in the net. If you're a good hand it would come up heaped on a scalp where they lie nice and light, but if you're wimming on a lay they'll be dug in. The thing to remember is not to dig too deep because you'll get mud and dead ones. You only want about one layer thick. You drag the line four or five feet before you pull them through the water to wash and there'd be a little old twenty bushels in twenty minutes.

The small tides are ideal for collecting mussels because the tops of the scalps will come out of the water, they raise the mud seven or eight feet, so it's all hills and holes. You can get over the side and fork them into the canoe. They don't fall through the prongs because they're all matted together so you just slide your fork under and as they come through the water they'll wash. You do it quicker that way. Don't put your boat

127

too hard on the ground because you've got to take her from there to the smack, chuck the things out on the smack and then off again as hard as you can. You've got to do as much work as you can when that's possible. The big tides will probably allow you two freights. Then, when you get a nice pile, you bring the canoe alongside the big boat and one will stand with a shovel to chuck them in. Because once the big boat leans, the sides are too darn high for you to hunk your nets and rakes over. Probably you'll take two tides over 'em. I have done it in a tide but mostly it's two to get a really good freight. If the tide comes in in the evening you'd get aboard, trail your canoe astern and wait. You wouldn't move the smack — you'd be too damn tired for one thing. You'd simply give her a bit more chain so she had about twelve or fifteen fathom in fine weather, wash your hands in the bucket because you'd be splattered with mud and sweating like a pig. By the time you'd had a bit of food and a lie down it was time to turn out again. It's dreadfully hard work hopping about in that mud.

When you'd done, you'd think we'll drop away with the last of the ebb, so you chuck the canoe aboard, put her onto the hatches and come away home to Stiffkey. In the sailing days they preferred to work in with the tides if they could because it's much easier. It might take a day, a day and a half, or you might do it in a matter of hours if you had a good breeze because some of those old things really could go. I never went sailing up there for mussels, thank God, we always had a motor and sail so we were fifty-fifty. But my father used to do it the hard way; well none of them would have understood how motors went. My grandfather wouldn't have one in for a start, they were no mechanics. They used to carry three or four long oars on the smacks, then if the wind turned light they'd get the bloody great things out and drop the old rowlocks into her rails. The stem of them might be about two and a half feet long. It would be two people standing up facing one another, one pulling and one pushing like the gondoliers. Old Nat would say they'd do more in a quarter of an hour with the tide than they would in an hour and a half when it come against them. You could get the old girl up to possibly two knots with the tide, so after three hours you'd get a long way. They sometimes used to row the things almost the whole way. But if the tide set up fairly smart against them, they'd have to bring her up and beach her. I still took the canoe in the old-fashioned way because, providing you used hand labour, you couldn't improve on most of the old methods. In the end I went down in the old clinker-built Blakeney lifeboat. My father lent me a hand to deck her in and we never chucked one load out with her. She was a lucky old boat. Several times she only just scraped home.

By the time they got home, if the mussels had been in three or four days and the weather had been hot, they'd be wanting a drink. If they were really bad you'd have to wait until low water, otherwise when you chucked them out they'd all go floating away like millions of little black boys because they'd open and let a few drops of water out and they'd be light. There wouldn't be enough inside to sink them. They'd float with their nibs out — that's the round part of the mussel where he drinks. The beard and the other end attaches them to other mussels. Anyway, in a bushel load, half if not three parts floated away. But if you waited until the water was fairly still, they could get a drink. You'd see bubble, bubble, bubble as they were going down. I have known a time when there was a good current but they had to get them out fast, so they put a but net round the bottom. They all hit the net and after they'd been in the water a few minutes they'd sink. Of course, you couldn't afford to lose the darn things.

Sometimes we used to bring a load for ourselves as well as a couple of loads to sell, because if you could make the odd bob that'd keep you ticking on. You'd fill up the bushel skep nice and level — that's a wicker herring basket with a handle each side — and either empty it into his canoe which he could take off to his lay, or else somebody would say chuck fifty bushels over here, drop her down a bit and chuck another fifty. Then they'd put them down in their own time. Every five skeps you'd shoot one mussel in a bucket and everyone would sing out 'three', 'four', 'five', so when you counted the mussels up each one would represent five bushels. That was one way of squaring up so there wasn't any argument because nobody wanted to lose out.

Then you'd turn round and put a couple of tons of sand into the old boat to balance her. You could turn it out when you reached the scalp and balance yourself with mussels so she would take an extra sixty bushels. You reckoned out roughly thirty bushels to the ton of seed mussels, which was another three pound. We got a shilling a bushel for carting them backwards and forwards — years ago mind.

For many years Stiffkey was the centre of the north Norfolk cockling. In fact, the name of the village, in local dialect, has been immortalised by its cockles — the 'Stewky Blues'. Philip Green's recollection of the industry are touchingly lyrical.

All the poor people used to live by the sea for mussels, cockles, winkles and whatever they could get, so the cockling must have gone way back. I remember it about fifty-five years ago when there was little industry here — you've heard of 'Stewkey Blues'. There must have been about thirty if you put the full-timers with the half-timers, women and men, more than three parts women. It began to phase out in 1938, dawdling on a bit at Stiffkey but the gun camp killed it elsewhere. They stopped altogether about thirty years ago. Carts would come in from Melton Constable, Langham, Binham and Briston, little villages inland, selling the odd farm produce but chiefly red herring they'd bought from Yarmouth. Everything was done by carrier cart then and in the big families herring was a good cheap food. They'd sell it from two or three hundred little wicker hampers and they'd know the people who would really buy. If a neighbour was there she'd say 'Get us a dozen herring', so one woman might buy for the row. Then they'd fill up the cart with mussels and cockles. Mussels started in September and went on 'til the end of March. It's chiefly cockles through the latter spring and early summer, then the samphire would come on early to mid-July if it was a good season and go right through until early September when it started to seed. They'd come about four days a week but Saturday was the big selling day. The horse and cart could carry about 24–28 pecks of cockles in the wintertime and about four pecks of winkles.

Old Becky, I remember, as a dear little doll of a woman; when she was dressed up she looked just like a little old Danish crow. She was a wonderful old lady who used to go down cockling well into her nineties. There was no real reason. By that time her family was quite well off and she had relations to look after her, but it did her good and she felt she couldn't exist without it. She actually used to gather them for herself and then hawk some round the villages. Warham and Whiting was her round. What stopped her in the end was poor old Tommy, her pony. He got so old he couldn't drag the cart. So she said when Tommy packs up, I'll pack up.

They went down in their second best gear from the village to the bottom of the greens where they'd dress up with all these things packed into their baskets. My God, they used to carry some gear with them because out of these big old two-peck wicker baskets would come a massive dress to go on top of their second-best skirt. They'd bring it up and tie it round the knee so it was like a Dutchman's trousers. They had fairly wide leg pieces that wrapped round and round about two inches over the knee boots, then up to the knee so that the muck and water wouldn't go down their boots — a bit like the puttees they wore in the 1914–18 war. In the summertime they'd wear a big loose blouse on the top and in the winter it was a variety of short coats and tops. Then they'd have wrist bands round to keep the arms a bit dry, and what they called hand pieces made from old stockings cut off so that was a long tube of wool to go just over the wrists. Chiefly if they kept their necks and wrists warm they were warm all over. All the palm would get sodden and soppy but the hand was so active that it didn't matter. You couldn't have much between your fingers anyway because it would get wet and the sand would get in and chafe. On their heads they'd have a straw hat in the summer, but mostly a big old felt one with a long brim. Then they'd put a head scarf over the top, pulling the sides down over their ears and tie it under the chin. Hence there'd be a sort of peak coming out in front. It looked strange when they peered from under the peak with their red faces and tiny bright eyes, but that was really sensible because if they were working in bad weather they could look down the tunnel and they wouldn't be affected by the wind, rain, blowing sand or anything.

We used the ordinary little cockle rake down here. Really we made one from wire nails which were as good as any. You'd get a piece of hard wood, push a half-inch hole through and cut a stick out of the hedge for a handle. Knock him in, then get about a quarter-inch drill and make the holes about three-quarters of an inch apart. Put it in the vice, then just a touch of grease on the nail and knock it through. You could make one in about twenty minutes. The women very rarely used a rake. They'd work in a half-inch of water, preferring it reasonably dry, otherwise water would fly up their arms. But in the deeper water where the drains were there'd be some darn good cockles because they'd be drinking all the time.

You'd stick the net on the ground and pull the cockles into

it, give them a wash and they'd be just that much bigger than they were on the dry. Sometimes when the sand was dry and fluffy you'd pull the rake through, keep shaking the net and it was a quick way. If you were pulling an eight- or ten-inch rake you were covering a good bit of ground; you might get six pecks an hour while the old women knifing would take two or two and a half hours, perhaps three.

The knife they used for cockling was four to five inches with a bent blade that narrows into a wooden handle. The local smith would bore the handle and knock the blade well home. They'd hold it in one hand as they bent over, resting the other on the basket turned on its side. Then they'd scratch at the cockles which were about half an inch under the sand. After a four-inch scrape they'd see the nibs of the cockles and if they were really thick they'd know at a glance. Then they'd have to scratch two or three out to make a start and, collecting them in the fingers, throw them back into the palm of the hand. As soon as they'd got a handful they'd throw them in the basket. If they were a mixed lot, they'd only pick out the big 'uns. They'd go as quick as lightning, so you couldn't see their fingers moving. I've done it myself and got forty-two pecks one morning working from 3.0 until 7.0. They'd know exactly what they wanted before they went down, though of course the real limit would be the number they could carry. About eight pecks was a good load for a woman. I have known one carry nine. You could say 6½ to 7 pecks is a hundredweight.

When they had the gear ready to go, the cockles were in hessian bags and they had what they called aprons to carry them with. This was a square of really strong hessian with two ties at either end. The woman bent over with the apron hanging behind, tied round her waist, while the other two would pick up the sack between them and lie it on the apron. She'd put the second ties over the top of the sack and round her shoulders to hold them, settle them in the middle of her back with a wriggle and hold on. That's rather like a rucksack. When she was loaded she'd tuck the ends through her waist to leave her free to help plonk another sack of cockles on someone else until they'd gone round all three—because they used to work in little gangs of two or three. Then they'd all get the baskets under their arm and set off wibberdy-wonk, wibberdy-wonk, with these funny little hoods and the bell-bottomed trousers.

They'd go out all weathers. Sometimes it rained incessantly from the time they left until they finished, and sometimes they'd be down there in the winter and the sand would be frozen that hard they couldn't get their knives in. They'd hunch up round and shift bits of ice, go into the drains to try and scrape up a few. But boy! the conditions would have to be impossible before they'd pack in. They'd walk until they got to a creek, when they'd go down ever so carefully in well-trodden footholds, jamming the basket in the mud to hold and supporting themselves on it so they didn't slip. When they reached the top of the marshes they'd leave the stuff on what they called stages — that was four posts knocked into the ground and a rough platform built across. The cockles would sit upright until the cart came down when the driver turned it round, dropped his tail-board over, backed up to the staging, untied the bags and shot them loose in the bottom of the cart. Then he'd hand the bags on the railing for the women to pick up again. Of course, they shifted about from different beds as the years went on and the seasons changed.

The women picked all the nice branchy bits of samphire clear of the weeds, then took a basketful to the water to wash it until the stalks come up beautifully white. If there was clean grass there, they'd lie it down or if there wasn't they'd put a couple of bags down and spread it all out so that it would dry off. If it was packed wet and slumpy you'd get a peck and a half in a peck measure, but when it was dry it stood up crisp. You could also deliver it in better condition. There was so much competition that no one could afford to lose even one customer. The cockles went in the cart first, then the samphire loosely packed in hessian bags went on top to be treated with the greatest care. As the old boy sold it he'd have a little square box and keep shooting a peck or two pecks into this box and then quarter-pecking it out from there. That was hard work because they never had no machines and everything was hand done but in my father's time they was contented, that's my humble opinion. It didn't change as much in my father's time as it had in mine. Look at my mother, she was buggered off down to the Isle of Wight with a ticket tied onto her coat when she was eleven. Sent down there as a kitchen maid. The train coming into Wells was about the most exciting thing she'd ever seen before that. The donkey and cart took her from here to Wells station because they just couldn't keep them at home.

133

Blast, she said she couldn't even tell the time. Well you see that was hard but it didn't seem to hurt them much did it? She's as bright and as cheerful as anybody and she's what? ninety-one.

Yet neither John Henry Loose nor Philip Green would swop jobs with a city dweller at any price. They are tied to their pieces of coast more closely perhaps than they realise. Very close indeed.

John Henry assents there are advantages to his work:

The advantage of living in an open place, I mean there's nothing much but the sea and sky. But when people ask me why I go musseling, I usually say you've got to be daft to do it. You can get as much money on the dole. It's all right for me because I own the scalps, whereas other people have to get them and grow them. I've only got to fetch them. That's about half the work. But even then it's not necessarily economical. It's all right when you're young but I think it's as far as I shall ever get. I don't suppose I shall ever do anything else.

And Philip knows there is only one place where he belongs:

I wouldn't want to be cooped up inside. It's bad enough when you're indoors a couple of days when you aren't well. You've got to tolerate it but you'd bust out sooner or later. You want to be adrift.

If you're out on the marshes, well you've got a living to make. That might mean keeping your eyes watching out. There might be a good lump of wood; well, perhaps that's a fiver and if you weren't bright enough or knowledgeable enough, you wouldn't know in a certain part of the marsh this stuff was dry. You got to keep your eyes open for that and you've got to work another job in, perhaps gunning or one of a thousand bloody things. If anyone come down and say 'You mustn't do this', you'd just say 'Go to hell!' straight away. I mean you wouldn't be rude, but you aren't going to have every Tom, Dick and Harry telling you what to do and what not to do. Why the hell should you? You come on this life and you can surely do what you like. You're not going to raid anybody's house or anything but like they sold the marsh to Matthews, if he just put a gateway across the road, well that'd be conveniently burned down and that'd be that. And if he come down to stop us we should have to say 'Well. . . .' No you want to be adrift. Think for yourself. Do what you want.

You want to be working twenty hours a day and do something; really do something your way and think how to get on with the bugger. The whole of life come up one day or up a week, or maybe a fortnight and right down rock bottom the next bloody week. Holding your own the next one, and — well that's a fight against nature all the time. Weather, wind and tide. Sometimes you get sick and tired of it but you still keep going at it.

If you go inland to any little village or any little town, how much room have you got to manoeuvre? Unless you're travelling on the public road, it might be a little park, a little bit of green, a couple of square yards and you're onto somebody else's property. Here, what you've got is right the way from Wells East Hills through to Blakeney, h'aint you? All that ground which you could call your own. I mean I can call it my own. I can use it just as my own. I can shoot on it, wander about on it, sit down on it, take who I like on it. There's no restrictions. And there's so many things to see and explore, to do and find that each day is different. You see, being next to the sea, the whole damn thing is changing. By the way, I seen the old Brent geese come in yesterday, about 150 of them. I think yesterday they probably landed. That's October 9th. One time there would be tons of fish, flats and mussels to go and get. You might have an idea and perhaps build a little boat, go down and try it. There's little passing yachts, there's always something different. I've seen a good many places — Norway is a lovely place, Iceland is a barren old hole and I think you'd get fed up with the bugger. Here, that's flat, but there's so much to see providing you educate yourself to get interested in what's there. There's flowers, plants, insects, birds, changing all the time. You do sit up and take notice. Like in the summertime they're laying and coming in, you see the young and you get to know the different ones. I aren't too good on the names, half-way good. I aren't like these birdwatchers but a lot of these birds get so familiar with you, the same old ones meet you each day. There was a one-legged oyster catcher and some little ring plover and stint; they know you, they'll wait for you and if you're worm-digging they'll come and pick off your heap, if you're musseling they'll come onto your boat. I've seen them actually sitting on the side of the creek when we've been rowing up. They fly over, sit on the stern of the boat, then when you chuck the stuff out they'll get on the heap and pick about. And when you're riddling they'll be there just the same. I mean we know each one lives for the other.

6

A LITTLE OF EVERYTHING

Fishes that tipple in the Deepe,
Know no such Liberty.
— *Lovelace*

In 1909 W.A. Dutt described Overy as 'a bleak little place on
the landward border of the marshes with two little inns, a big
old buttressed malthouse, a quay with a wooden bench for old
salts, some painted boats belonging to the mussel-rakers, and,
when it's not overpowered by the indescribable odour of
shellfish, a fragrance of sea southernwood.' Perhaps when the
wind flattens the marshes and bustles up East Harbour Way,
when the tide retreats, leaving the creek mullet-nibbled,
when the rain drizzles and boat masts hum, then Overy is
bleak. It is a village of many parts. The malthouse has been
converted into a boathouse, there is one pub and only one
mussel-raker, seventy-eight-year old 'Laddy' Lane. Broad-
shouldered, slopped or jumpered, always capped and spec-
tacled, with a confident, challenging independence and a
rugged friendly face. He has spent nearly all his life in Overy,
exchanging more recently a pebble cottage for an impeccably
neat red-brick bungalow. He is part of the place:

> Grandfather used to live at Burnham Norton. I don't know
> what he did. My father was foreman of the maltings here and I
> don't suppose he ever went on the water. Fifty years ago you'd
> be down there all day and not see four people near it. You'd
> never worry about them treading on the mussels them days.
> Mother lived just down the road. There were fishermen here
> then, but only one or two. My father got fifteen shillings a
> week when he was foreman, farm labourers got eleven
> shillings. There were two granaries and a coal house on the
> quay and all the road outside was boarded over. Five or six

136

men were bringing in coal all the time. It was my father's last job at night to bring the steps down and close the gate. After they shut up these malthouses he went along Everett's mill; there wasn't any work in Overy.

I was born in 1897 in Flagstaff Row. That make me seventy-eight next month. Five of us were born up there. But we were six boys, six bonny boys, no doubt about it. You'd have had no job to get a husband then. Only one is alive, my youngest brother, and he lives in York. He was a builder, foreman builder, his son have took his job and he's retired. My oldest brother worked on the railways Cleethorpes, all his life and my second brother died of brain fever when he was eighteen. It took my mother bad so's she was more or less an invalid. Sam was chauffeur and gardener, then Ted, he worked at Scunthorpe, engine driver in the Stanton works. Then there's meself and then there's Connie, we used to work building with Welcome. Flagstaff was only a small cottage, that's why we had to come out. Two up and two down. No carpets on the floors, they used to scrub the bricks. You could eat off of 'em. There wasn't one woman in this place had a carpet on the floor. Had a hearth rug and that might er been a sack cut open. My mother used to tell I wouldn't ever be no good, yet if she was to have had a place like this! After we grew we used to bath ourselves in the kitchen. She used to boil a big saucepan, 'cos you know they used to have fireplaces then, the big old dixie. Like as if they was making a stew, used to be hooks up the chimney to hang the boiler on. My mother used to bake her own bread. And cakes. She was a good cook, so was her mother. We used to love to go up there and have some of her cakes. Used to think the world er that. We ate half an egg or half a herring. Never had a whole one when we was kids. Porridge was our breakfast. That was our main food, because I used to get separated milk every day for nothun'. 'Cos I worked over the farm and that was in my wages you see. That'd be a half a gallon, so my mother never had to buy no milk. You wouldn't see families about the streets in the evenings because their fathers wouldn't let them. Most of the fathers was strict like that. We had one of the deepest wells in our garden, there wasn't any other water. But we were happy.

It was a good little school here but we didn't learn nothen. Write your name, that was just about the lot. Do you know the biggest education I had? Playing darts. Counting on the board.

137

But we got past all right. I never do read, only the paper. I *can* read. But what do you think the boys used to do at school? Knitting. I used to knit for all the grandchildren. Some of the families never had boots to go to school in. Wore nothing. Bare feet. Go up that here yard and up them stones, didn't take no notice on it. Their feet was as hard as what their heads was. I always had boots. I suppose really we were a little better off because my father was getting three shillings extra to the farm labourer. You'd get a pair of boots for a shilling or eighteen pence. But being boys, we was big boys too, we wore a lot of clothes up. My mother'd always be a-patching. She had to. Couldn't afford to keep on getting new ones. But we always had clothes and we was always fed.

And Christmas time we'd get a ha'pworth of sweets and a pocket handkerchief. We used to watch the coal boats coming up and we boys put hours away sliding and skating beside the sea wall down in front of the chapel. We used to have pram wheels on an old trolley and we'd shoot down the stone pit in that. We had the best regatta on the coast, all the working people would go in for it. Must have started after the first war. Later on we'd walk to Brancaster and to Wells regatta. I used to take the *Annie* to sail and row with Welcome every year. We had chapel three time a day on Sunday. You had to go just as much as to school. These villages lived their own lives.

According to a local paper dated 15 September 1910, a Burnham Market farmer was hauled before Hunstanton magistrates by 'Frederick John Lane, a lad in his employ'. The farmer pleaded guilty to assaulting young Lane 'under great provocation'. He had been having a great deal of trouble with some of the boys, he said, and 'Laddy' had been the ringleader. 'Laddy' remembers the incident well. He had a harvest job and the farmer ordered him to rake behind some wagons with a broken rake. When the farmer refused to supply a new one, 'Laddy' went home. He returned later to ask for his wages and was horsewhipped for his pains. The magistrate fined the farmer 12s 6d, including costs. It must have been one of the first major battles 'Laddy' won.

I used to work weekends when I was eleven. You see an old farmer used to come and borrow me. I left school when I was twelve or thirteen and worked for 4s 6d a week, that was seven days, milking cows at Sachels. I give it to my mother and she would give me 2d back. Old Sachel came round with a stick sometimes. I remember once we were loading oats, handing down huge bags, and I was too little to take them. The oats fell out and he was after me so I just left. I worked for Richie, the coal merchant, then for his son Billy, hawking coal from door to door. We often ended up in Brancaster 11 o'clock at nights. After that I was in a stone pit. As long as you did your ten yards it didn't matter how long you were over it. You got 17s 6d for ten yards, picking it, then hand grading. It took me a couple of days from 2.30 in the morning until eight, and during the rest of the week I was out with my gun. I was always out poaching, I was the only one did it. My mother used to say I was the roughest of the lot! Then I used to go out threshing on the marshes . . . anything. They used to stack the corn and we'd do a day's work threshing, perhaps three or four days a week in the wintertime. We used to do all sorts of jobs, we always kept at it. Welcome, his brother Jack and I. We went in the same category — all hungry!

Serving in the forces, particularly in the First World War, was the first time many fishermen left their immediate surroundings. Many died, of course, some were broken by what they went through, a few returned bringing with them new stories, new experiences. 'Laddy' survived.

I was in the Royal Norfolks four years, 1916-20, one of the smartest regiments in the British Army. We were about the only one that had to clean our buttons when we came from the front line. When we were called up we went to Felixstowe for seven weeks training and we were out in the front. In Mespot we had to keep close to the water because we drunk a gallon a day, you couldn't go long without it. When we were on the push, when they took Sannaiyat, that was the only time I ever volunteered in the army. They came round the regiment wanting to know was there anybody who could row a boat. Aye-aye, sir! They said the 13th Division was cut off, they wanted someone to row rations over to them. It went on for weeks and I thought the 13th Division couldn't be starving because we were still there. You see Sannaiyat was a place we couldn't take. We couldn't cross the river, see. We attacked it all ways but we never could get the Turks out of it. They were so entrenched in there. We bombed 'em, shelled 'em but we couldn't move 'em. So we was going to get across and take 'em by surprise. That worked, too. We got over. Anyway one afternoon about three o'clock the Italian orders came, all them that volunteered to row a boat fall in on the right.

We marched twenty-five miles that night up the east side of the river, the Tigris. We went up that quiet that night because you didn't have roads like you do here, you're on a sandy soil that used to be white most of the time with salt. Every gun was lashed hob to hob and when we got to the river, there were the pontoon boats waiting for us. We never had very big guns because they hadn't nothing to move them with. The biggest vehicle out there was a ton Ford, old T Fords with chains on their wheels — you could hear them going up nights, clacker, clacker, clacker. . . . We went over at five o'clock in the morning. I never even had a rifle because I was on the boat. I was the first over, it may have been my luck because the shells come after we got over and a lot of them died. My pal got killed when he was towing the boat back into position, because it was so strong on the tide we moved down a hundred yards. I mean you say the tides turn here. That's nothing!

We took so many in each boat, they were all equipped with two hand grenades because we always was during the war, every soldier in the front line carried them in his haversack. The Tigris wouldn't be more than 100 yards across. I made my pal bowsman and he had the rope. I said 'The minute we get near that shore, you jump and run up and catch her'. As soon as he ran up and catched her he got a bullet. That's how he finished. How I knew was we'd swopped puttees. When you got a corpse and buried him you always took one puttee off and wrapped it round the two feet to keep them straight. You'd be rolled up in a blanket maybe, but a lot wasn't. Hundreds were just thrown in a hole. We had to go back that night because we'd left so many dead there, I think five in the boat was killed. Well, we took them back that night, buried them and then came back again at half-past two in the morning. I was a stretcher-bearer really but I volunteered for this job because of the rowing. When I got back I never volunteered no more. If I got picked for a job I got picked and that was that, but I never volunteered.

I had a touch of malaria after I came out of the heat, it was 130 degrees in the shade. But I was one of the lucky ones, I just

140

took everything as it come along. You knew you'd got a job to do and that was that. I had four years out there and I never really suffered anything. Big people went under, they couldn't stick it. I had a month's holiday in India, lovely place. I'd have settled down and stopped there if I'd known what I was coming back to. But we made slaves of them. While we were there they'd shave you, do you up, clean your boots, you'd be spotless. Only it wasn't right. Although they were black they were human beings.

Back on home ground, 'Laddy' returned to the life he had left — shooting, fishing, mechanical haulage, he would try anything that was going, in fact there was not much he did not dabble in. Harry Loose, with whom he went as an apprentice whelker, came from a different branch of John Henry's family. 'Laddy's' wife was also a Loose.

There used to be a postman from Burnham came round with a pony and cart with the letters. He had more pheasants in that old cart than he had letters. Nobody ever knew. We'd be down there rabbiting on the hills and I shot rabbits when I hadn't even seen them, just the twig of the marram. We lived there, that was our hobby. We shouldn't ha' got a drink if we hadn't a gun or a dog. When I went off whelking at Brancaster I still went poaching. Used to take my gun along the road half-past one in the morning, then if anything was up the tree it had to come down. Never went to sleep. There were fourteen of us whelking and the longest boat wasn't more than 22 foot. You didn't get a Brancaster whelker ever tell you he earn money, they're always starving but they still keep going. I'll tell you something though, they don't go so regular now. I worked eight years with Harry Loose and if you followed his ways you wouldn't be a long way out. He wasn't religious like the rest of the family but he believed in witchcraft. He was superstitious, too. Wore a gold chain round his neck to stop himself being bewitched. You don't see so much of it now but in them days we're talking about there was a lot of witchcraft. Whenever Harry was a-whelking he'd have his watch out and he'd time himself from leaving the harbour until he reached his gear. He'd also have his compass out and when the time was up, if that was foggy he used to say, 'Ease her up', or 'Give me my lead'. I used to give it to him and he would put a lump of

141

grease on the bottom and drop it over. When he saw what was on the grease he'd soon know exactly where he was.

I had to bike from here as I hadn't got enough money to buy a car. That was when we were having the family and you had to turn out early even in the wintertime because we were getting raw bait. We worked out in the Well. Of course, now they've got big boats they're going out miles further, they can do it. But all fourteen of us were working in the Well. Sometimes you would hardly find a place to shoot there was so much gear lying about. There was a lightship at Lynn Well until they replaced it with a lighted buoy. I should think the buoy's just as good because when it's foggy you never see her until you get right up to her. Sometimes Harry would go early and take the lightship some bread — they never had any, only biscuits. So he would sling two or three loaves aboard when that was fine weather and we had plenty of time, and they used to give us some red herring. They were all right. Perhaps we'd put half a herring in a whelk pot, sometimes a whole one if the whelks were a bit shy and wouldn't bite. It's tough and it's got a strong smell, you can't get many whelks without a red herring. Swinners or crabs are all right but you mustn't put them in the bar because the Fishery bloke used to come out and pull your gear up. You had your initials on the buoys, and if they found any crabs in the bar, they'd lock you up. But if that was in the bottom of the pot they couldn't do anything because you'd say they got in. So we always gave them a crack and chucked them in the bottom and where that crab was you'd get a full pot. A whelk would suck all the meat out of the crab, even from it's claws. A whelk can open a cockle and feed off that. Latter times we used to salt the swinners, put them in a barrel and then throw some salt over to kill them before you used them. We caught swinners with pots in the creek, half-a-crown a bag. That was another job I used to do in my spare time. I had about a dozen pots here when I wasn't at sea. When they took the whelks to Burnham Station then they'd come round here after and pick up the swinners. If I could get four or five bags on a tide that was a lot of money. If you earned a pound a day a-whelking it was a good lot, too.

Being opportunists and versatile, both fishermen who feature in this chapter, 'Laddy' Lane and Denis Frary, were quick to jump onto the bandwagon by offering their services to summer visitors. While some simply complained about their presence, the wily ones bought up cheap land and old cottages before they began to reach inflated prices. 'Laddy' says:

When I left off whelking I stopped at Overy with the mussel lays and ran pleasure boats during the summer. There were nearly a hundred huts down on the Island for visitors. You got ten shillings a hut taking down food and water during the week and if they come up it was 6d a time. Billy Hains' boat was called *The Rosemary*, Welcome had the *Welcome Home* and we had the *Golden* and the *Duck*. Then when Fred got fourteen I sent to Hunst'on and bought him a little boat to run some but Fred don't stick it, he never took hold properly. He knows his job, he's been along with me long enough for that, but he's a rambler. Like the musseling. Sometimes he'd promise he'll work them so's I really believe it, then he come down and just go off butting with a fork. I had the *Golden* twenty-seven years and she's still at Brancaster. I sold her the year before last because we had no work here for two boats. I used to run them at high tides and the *Duck* at low water, but you could put what you liked in a boat then, there were no restrictions. Now you can only take twelve it isn't worth doing — you've got to charge so much to make it pay. When you could put a nice lot in and let them go cheap everyone was happy. And the Board of Trade have got to come and pass her before I'm allowed to run though *you* can take out a dozen people any day you like and drown them all. When they prosecuted me for carrying too many I knew there was going to be trouble. It cost me a hundred pound but I didn't care. I just showed them I knew more than they did and I fought it right through. When the judge called me up in court I went in at twenty-to-ten and came out quarter-past-four. The old judge said 'We find you not guilty'. He said 'I suppose you've done that a good many times?' I said 'I suppose I have', and he said 'You'll do it again won't you?' And I said 'I suppose I will'. I said the Board of Trade blokes don't know what they're talking about because if I took them down the harbour and turned them round two or three times when that was foggy, they wouldn't know the way home.

John Henry deplores the steady crumbling of the fishing

community in his village. It is the same at Overy, 'Laddy' agrees.

Overy is finished. Young people can't get houses to live in so they've got to get out. When you close the school up you're closing the village. Then the post office just mornings, and I don't suppose this shop will keep going much longer. I had a haulage business so I was about on the land as well as the water. I sold that about twelve year ago when I retired. I would have given in to Fred to carry it on but he wouldn't take it. I started the haulage thirty or forty year ago, began carting my own shingle off the beach when they re-built Bircham aerodrome. I took off twenty ton a day. You seen that old army boat in the dock here? That was our shingle boat. We took her down to load her and brought her up. You used to have to get a permit from the Crown, that's how I always knew the channel belonged to the Crown. Then I carted it by lorry to Bircham. I used to do sugar-beet, too. I did three lorries once and my brother worked for me for three or four years. I used to cart for no end of people around here, when I sold the business there was a tractor loader and everything. Fred used to do the truck driving, then I would do the tractor, meet him and load him before he went off again. He did four rounds a day at Lynn. I went as far out as Stiffkey, Wells, all round the Burnhams. Used to cart corn to Yarmouth. I've been twice there in a day. Now I'm retired I just plain muck about. I don't do much, few bags er mussels a week. Do just what suits me. I don't know what's going to happen after this year because my boat's not big enough to go up to the Wash and I can't get anyone to bring me a load in.

Today, when 'Laddy' Lane is not working his lays or running a pleasure boat, he is sitting on Dutt's wooden bench, his beady eyes fixed on a pair of binoculars, guarding the mussels. The 13½ acres marked mysteriously by means of buoys and little posts holding copies of his Several Order are something of a legal curiosity, and mixed up in their history are some of the principles of feudalism, capitalism and distributism. They are 'Laddy's' life line.

Took me six years to get the Several Order. We had so many people to fight. Starting with Lord Leicester, he kept me

twelve months. My lawyer kept writing back and forth, then we
went to the Crown. You write them a letter and you don't hear
back for three months. The only way we cleared it was to get
the MP from Lynn. Of course, he didn't know much about the
job, I had to go over there for hours and hours telling him,
advising. But when I got him right, we pressed and the Crown
had to come forward at the finish. My lawyer wrote hundreds
of letters, he had them all on the bench. The village didn't
want me to have them either. That's jealousy. You always get
that in a village.

I had a lot of trouble with diggers before I got my Several
Order and now there's so many worms in my lays they would
pay me to let them go in. But I've said no, they never did play
the game. I wouldn't let them dig one. I put 300 bushels of
cockles in there once and I never had half a peck off it. It will
be the richest place for worms if I hold them off, as I do
because I'm always here. So if ever they break in I've got them
and I don't let them off either. I had to pay rates on all that
ground and they made me pay £500 to get the Several Order.
If I want anything I'll take it and they can come after me if
they want and do what they like, but I'm their daddy as long as
I live in that creek and nobody's going to stop me. My only
hope is that Fred carries it on because that'll keep in the village
then.

His attitudes to marriage is governed by the same principles
that govern his life:

We've worked together in married life. We're had our
hardships but we've battled them. We kept towing along and
nothing stopped us. I mean whatever I start to do I finish. And
I still do. That's what you've got ter do. I mean if you don't
work together in marriage, what's the good of getting married?
We've been married fifty-six years. That's our golden wedding
present, that teapot, over five years ago now. We had to take
the knocks together and we took the other way together. And I
can't see no other way of working it.

Of course I can't go on with mussel trade much longer
though that keep me going really. I love the place you see, I
love the job, I was born to work. That's what's important to
me. I was born for work and I enjoyed it. I've worked seven
days a week all my life. And my father was just the same.
Although he believed in having a master, I didn't. Wanted to
be me own boss. Mind you, if you work for yourself you get to

be a conscientious chap. I started with nothing—just plunged into it and got control. When I can't work I don't know. . . . But there's got to come a day, ha'n't there?

Denis Frary is another example of a fisherman cum salesman who plays the tune of changing times. Prepared to help out here, throw in his lot there, maybe he is a forerunner of the odd-jobbing, part-time fisherman of the future.

On Wells West Quay a crane is swivelling loads of corn from a small German cargo boat into a yellow truck. What for? 'Cattle feed', informs a smiling face from the haulage contracting lorry. 'Where are they going to?' 'Not very far. Stoke Ferry'. 'Don't we produce enough oats?' Evidently not. But when he's delivered this lot he's stopping off at King's Lynn to take a load of English oats back to Germany. Maybe it's the Common Market. I just can't fathom it out.'

Next to the yellow truck three people read newspapers from deck chairs in the last rays of September sun. Beyond them a blue caravan with red and white striped awning declares 'FRARY'S SEA FOODS'. Behind the counter Denis Frary, a short, round, reddish-complexioned man, keeps up a patter of greetings with his customers. He is fifty-one. During the intervals between serving, he tells me something of his earlier life.

> When I first left school I worked with my father, a shell fishermen. He used to work on the beach. Gathered his own cockles and took them round the villages on a tricycle. A three-wheeler with a box at the front and he pulled a box behind. All over the countryside. Burnham Market, Burnham Thorpe and Creek on Friday and the weekends, then during the week he'd go round Melton Constable, Briston and Edgby. He'd take 'em out in his barrow, too. Penny a pint. One and four pence then for a peck of cockles. He couldn't ha' got rich on it but that was a healthy life. I went in the forces during the war, then I started on me own—1946. And I've been shell-fishing ever since. We used to gather them and send them through to Norwich by rail when we had the old railway station.

You've got to know what you're doing with shellfish. That's the reason people come hundreds of miles to eat them nice and fresh. I get people coming from Cambridge, get them from Hertfordshire, Kent, all over the place. That's the secret, eating them fresh. Because everybody can't do it themselves. There's only five shellfishes we sell—cockles, mussels, whelks, winkles and clams. I once collected them all but now it's got so that's a bit too big for me. I go and buy them and do all me own preparation. I don't gather any myself, only the mussels. But I do me own pickling. Buy in the honey jars and the vinegar. I'd work meself into the ground. But that's only just a short summer, you see. I go lugworm digging in the wintertime because they start angling now the last week in September and they go right through till the spring of the year. Most of our bait goes away up north—Newcastle, Sunderland, Middlesborough. I shall work for somebody else this year because after the doctor's advice I mustn't take too much stress on. That was kind of a warning he said.

When the mussels are in season they put them in preservative, in citric acid, and then wash them and use them in the summer. Well to me that's sacrilege because you're spoiling your shellfish. That's not fresh.

Here he brings Philip Green's story of cockling up to date.

What we used to do years ago is go spotting cockles. Find two little holes in the sand about quarter of an inch apart. That's the holes they breathe through and when the tide flows, that's where they take up plankton from the water to feed on through two little tubes. We used to use a finger, or like a carving knife bent round in a hook shape. Soon as ever you touched the top of the sand, the cockle nibs all used to be there. Then things got a little bit more commercialised so you had to find some other method to get them quicker. We used the rake and the net—raking when the tide was first leaving so the sand was sloppy and washed out. From the net we'd put them in a half-inch riddle and riddle all the small ones through. They bury themselves back in the sand with their nibs, which is the yellow bit. The shell open, they'll wiggle about and pull themselves down again. Then they gradually turn theirselves upright and grow. So we'd leave the small ones for the next season. But then the big firms in King's Lynn and round the Thames estuary started ploughing them out. I call it ploughing but the fishermen call it blowing. The boat goes down on top of the sand when there's about two fathom of water and they put an anchor out for'ard. They keep going astern in a circle which turns the prop the opposite way and churns the sand up. So the cockles are blown on top of the sand. When the tide leaves they all lay on the surface and they just net them up. To my idea it's poaching but this day and age you'd never do nothing with the hand raking. I'm worried about this blowing because if you've got a small cockle among the big ones, that crush the shell. But they say that after a piece of ground's been blown they all set thick again because the sand is that bit softer so the small seed will grow.

I've been going down to Overy harbour for over thirty years and even before that. There used to be cockle lays and mussel lays down there, but all the way along the north Norfolk coast the beach has gradually grown up. Marram grass is like a twitch in the garden. If you leave one piece you've got two. It grows in the beach, you get a rough tide, that knocks a piece out and that'll blow somewhere else and set. Once that's set that'll start to grow and you get the wind come along and blow the sand up ag'en it and gradually build up to make a bank. Overy harbour used to be lovely flat cockle ground, but now that marram bank's at least twenty feet high. That's why the cockles have disappeared. We used to cockle on what we called West Lake on Wells beach, but now there's no West Lake left. The marram grass is gradually taking over and that's forcing the foreshore further and further into the sea.

There's a lovely recipe for mussels. Get some nice and fresh from Wells or Brancaster, or anywhere on the north Norfolk coast. The shellfish there are the best in England. They keep talking about Southend cockles and Whitby cockles or Mumble cockles, but ours is the best. Boil them, clean them well and take off the beard—a little piece like a nylon weed which it clings to the bottom of the sea with. Otherwise the tide would wash them away because they doesn't bury under the sand. Get your frying pan nice and hot, and your egg and breadcrumbs. Dip your fresh mussel in them and fry 'em in deep fat like you fry scampi in the fish shop, only scampi can't touch them. They're magnificent. I love them. I love everything—cockles, mussels, whelks, a shrimp or a winkle. Of course, a young person today wouldn't know what a clam is. But I'm no man for an oyster because you swallow an oyster. How can you enjoy an oyster when you swallow it?

You meet some nice people on this job and I like meeting people. We have a lot of Midland people: Leicester, Coventry, Derby, Nottingham, Sheffield. I have a woman from the other side of Grimsby, she's been coming now for this last eight or ten year and she always take two pecks of samphire back for pickling. If you go in the creeks where that's pushed tight together, that will come up as one straight stem, but where it grows out on the open plain that'll bush out. That's the best stuff. That's just like trees. We used to call it 'sheep's samphire' years ago. That took it's name from the sheep that feed on the marshes. Like the cattle do now. There were sheep rights for all the farmers to use the marshes.

At weekends the wife helps me to serve and she also helps me to cook the mussels, pick the whelks out and take the sand bag away. Eight out er ten people don't even know there's a sand bag in them. That is also called the 'worm'. Actually it's the trunk what they feed through. Like the gullet in a chicken, like a trunk. Now we take that out because it's very rubbery. It takes hours to prepare. That's me evening job. When you've done eight or ten hour down here, you've then got four hours preparing again for the next day.

I think my son is coming with me when he leaves school. But I feel fine now, which I should do. Just had five weeks holiday in the middle of the summer. Start about six getting stuff ready. Come down the quay about half-past nine. This'll be the last whole week, then we carry on till about the third week in October, just weekends. I started the stall about sixteen year ago. First I sold 'em from a van but when I found I got on so well with different people I bought this. I should think I'm the most known face on the East Coast.

7

THE FISHERMAN'S WIFE

Now night comes on, waves fold behind villages
— *Larkin*

Joe Pegg recalled with endearment, his mother's dab hand at serving pigs' trotters, her industry with a sewing machine, while Loady Cox remembered his mother's well-stocked larder, the rows of pickles and jam, and Percy Feek, who laid his nets for herring, believed the woman who brought him up to be 'one of the best old ladies ever lived'.

The fishermen's wives cared for large families through the vicissitudes of good and bad fortune, taking a fair share of the 'griefs and cares'. Their own life was largely one of drudgery; of making ends meet and day after day providing meals for a growing family on an unreliable and slender budget. They were giving, selfless women, shy to the world but founts of strength inside their homes.

At least they were well-trained for a rigorous life. Most of the classified advertisements in old files of the local press were for domestic servants. The rate in 1900 for a 'strong, clean girl' was about £10 a year and, as Philip Green related, families could ill afford to keep them at home so off they were bundled like parcels, fresh from the sea breezes to a world of scrub and scour. 'When I was thirteen', said a fisherman's wife from Eccles, 'I was sent to Derbyshire to learn cooking'. Beattie Everett had a similar experience.

A little more than eighty years ago the first whelking was begun at Brancaster by a few local fishermen, among them, Old Everett, whose father used to fish in smacks off Iceland. Old Everett's son and his wife are eighty-four, still living at

Brancaster Staithe. She said:

> I passed my school examination when I was thirteen, came
> home and went to work as a general in a house looking over
> the coalyard at Sheringham. I spent my fourteenth birthday
> working for Miss Smith and Miss Knowles, who had a school
> for all these people who could afford it and I used to do for
> them all. I did everything. Big old grate ovens. I was there for
> nearly three year before I came here, where I was cook. It was
> usual then for girls to go into service.

Since their livelihood depended upon it, wives were involved
in their husbands' work. It was unusual, even exceptional, for
them to go out in a boat but there were fishing jobs
considered their domain — mending nets and hanging them
up to dry in the fields, breaking out whelks for bait with
beach pebbles and carrying a reviving brew down to the
returning crew. People living in Sheringham remember the
sight of 'all the old girls up there on the cliff top with shawls
over their heads and steaming hot jugs of tea'. Whilst any
spare time was spent teaching their husbands to read and
write.

There is a dream-like quality to Mrs Everett's reminiscing
that suggests her involvement was total. The shore was an
anodyne amply compensating for a great deal of tough and
tiring physical slog.

> I didn't know nothen' about the sea before I was married,
> my father was a shepherd really. Then we was married. Every
> day when the post office closed on a Thursday, because my
> husband worked up the post office latter years, we'd make
> cheese sandwiches to take down and I'd eat raw onions while
> Dad had a tomato. We'd sit on that beach until the water was
> running round behind us and the same time it was coming out
> of the heavens. Sit and watch them bombard a ship they had
> for target practice during the war. I love the sea. I can
> understand anyone drowning in it. It used to make me feel so
> quiet and peaceful. Tranquil. Sometimes there was hail out
> there, but we'd go, never mind it. I'd give anything to be able
> to go on the beach now — you've got everything down there.
> Here a pile of whelk eggs and further on something else.

151

Ladybirds! I've seen so many the shore was blood red with them. We used to collect coal and square bits of wood so's they didn't have to be chopped.

I caught swinners for bait in the whelk pots and sold them to the whelk fishermen but they wouldn't pay much for them. Seemed to think because you were neighbours, they ought to have them free. So we'd sell them to the next village because we had to make a living. I would go and pull the boat for my husband when it was vertical, up like that, in the rough weather and I went winkling and cockling for a living just after this last war when times were bad. He lost everything he had through the gales and that's the funny thing, he was the only one that did.

We used to sell cockles and winkles, a quarter-peck a time or half-peck a time and a pint of winkles. They was generally on order. People would come and collect them from the house, but the shrimps we used to sell out. I used to go to Brancaster with them when my husband's father, Grandad, went out with the whelk boat to get them. They would be down the harbour here, out all night shrimping. But he couldn't clean them properly at night. Of course you had to wash them. They had to be washed and washed and better washed because their little feet hold the grit. Oh, ours used to be clean! You wouldn't find a bit of grit in them, I used to crank up buckets and buckets of water out of the well for the two big baths. First he would wash 'em down below, then he'd bring them home and wash them in the big bath, then in another. We had nets to hold them in because we would get large quantities when we went to sea. Then we'd go right through to Overy with a horse and cart and through to Tichwell this way. We hired the horse and cart for about half-a-crown. No more. We only got 4d a pint for shrimps and it was 4d a quarter-peck for cockles.

Philip Green brought attention to the hardships of winkle picking. 'They were buggers', he said. 'But they were paying things. Picking them up in the wintertime, one by one, all of a certain size in about four or six inches of icy cold running water. Boy oh boy, your hands! There's sixteen pints to a peck and you'd need to get four pecks to make a day's work.'

Beattie Everett corroborated:

We picked up winkles against the hills on Scolt's Head, one

at a time. I had to be careful I didn't put in any little ones where my husband was, I might tell you. He was strict over things like that. I've been at it so long he had to pull me up. It makes your back ache. I used to crawl on my hands and knees a lot. Then I wore a skirt, trousers weren't in fashion for women but I'd pin my skirt up with a big safety pin. I *have* been cold. I only had the short boots, there weren't women's water boots in those days. I got wet through and through. But if I hadn't been wet with work, I was wet through my husband pushing me in. Many a time I've been walking along arm in arm with him, talking on the beach. We used to be on the beach by ourselves, walking miles along to Overy. And all at once he'd put his elbow into me and pushed me into the sand warms — that's an old-fashioned word for the holes — and I'd come out dripping wet!

We often used to go down with the boat when the tide was out. From the post office we'd cross two creeks — my husband made pathways over them with shingle and stuff — and then get into the boat we called *Judy*. Oh, he's taken me out in dreadful weathers and I just loved it! Old Ernie Loose used to say to Dad, 'Why have you taken her out? She ought to be at home on a day like this'. In the boat he'd shout sometimes. He'd say 'Don't you know your right from your left?' Well it wasn't any good saying 'port' or 'starboard'. I didn't go right out to sea, mind you, only once or twice. But I've been out salmon fishing all night. I walked along the beach and helped with the net. One night Dad took out Aunt May, Miss White and me, and we were all big.

We used to get samphire, too. My goodness it's a filthy thing to get. You've got to pull it up first. If you wash it down there it would take most of the dirt and seaweed away. We used to shake it about in the net, throw it right out into the tide and squeeze it about. That would get a lot of the mud off, then you'd have to wash it two or three times when you'd got home. Pick all the rest of the seaweed out and snip off the tails with a pair of scissors. Though we didn't cut the roots off what we sold. We'd sell it in wooden measures, half a peck a time. It's better to get samphire off the mud. It feeds better there.

The boat came in from Grimsby to take the whelks about twice a week before they went by train. One time a gale come up off Thornham and the boat didn't know if it was out of the port or not. The whelkers amalgamated together then so it used to take so many whelks off each boat. All the orders used to come to mine. I'd sit on the bank, then if an extra order came in I'd stand on the bank and shout to them in Trump's Hole.

Dad used to panick the sails and some of them used to do their jumpers, slops we called them. He generally had the blue ones so they didn't go in, but if you'd got a bit of carpet, or anything you wanted done, you popped it in. You'd buy the bark—cutch they called it—it's just like rotten sticks. But they didn't use to buy it in his father's younger time. Anybody felled an oak tree, they used to get the bark because that was the best there was. They would seep it and seep it before they boiled it up, for weeks, perhaps months, and they couldn't beat that for colouring or for lasting on sails. Later on they bought wooden boxes of about half a hundredweight. You could see it came from trees of some sort because it had bits of leaves in it. We boiled it up in a great big copper. There were coppers specially for the job because once you had done barking in them they weren't much good for anything else unless you spent a lot of time scrubbing them out with caustic soda. You would boil up the oak, then leave the fire off and put your sail or nets in. You'd keep turning them over and over, then put them on a piece of corrugated iron and let them drain back into the copper again before they went out to dry.

I've been down picking mussels with Grandad during the war when my husband was away. We'd do it at night with a lantern because we wanted the mussels for the next day when Mr King took them to the station at Burnham Market by horse and cart. Perhaps he'd take a dozen bags off Grandad, six off somebody else and three off somebody else to make up his load. Grandad used to put a board across two sharves—that's the handles of a barrow—fill it up full and I would put my feet over and sit on the board to pick them into a basket. My father-in-law would sit down next to me and you had to throw the smallest away.

A retired fisherman-cum-lifeboat mechanic at Sheringham remembered that nearly all the fishing families took in summer visitors for board and lodgings. 'I don't know of a house in Victoria Street that didn't up until the time I was a young man.' It was the same at Brancaster when the summer trade began to flow. Beattie Everett said: 'Every year I used to take in summer visitors in the house behind the post office and cook all their meals for them. Lots of the fishermen's wives did it in Brancaster Staith.'

Both Beattie Everett and Mabel Harrison married into fishing, and both threw in their lot willy-nilly with their husbands. But, apart from the twenty-five years that separate them, different backgrounds influenced their aspirations. Mrs Harrison's commitment to her family is total. She is well-spoken, well organised, helpful and friendly, matter-of-fact and conservative. Her son has not gone fishing.

The Harrisons and the Davies are the last of the thorough-breds at Cromer, shall we put it that way? There are four boys out of one old family and not one of them is going to sea so there'll be no more Harrisons anyway. I think the fishing probably is on its way out. I feel it very much because I've got one son and we had one big ambition — to give him a good education — which he had and he did very well. He's a captain in the Merchant Navy. We never thought of him going fishing. Never.

Today it's much more of a rat race. But things have certainly changed. I've been married nearly forty years and when I first married the boys went to sea automatically — my husband, his two brothers, and their father who was the kingpin. They went and caught their stuff, brought it ashore to put on the train and it would go on the open market. But now that's all gone, the wives have to work so hard. Perhaps there were a few more boats coming in, a few more youngsters starting because they thought they could make a fortune quickly, and although you had your own merchants you'd supplied for years, somebody would step in with perhaps a dozen crabs they couldn't sell and let them go 6d cheaper. On top of that they'd say, 'We'll cook them for you'. Well this started the rot because we'd always been used to selling our crabs alive. So we just had to adapt ourselves and cope with it. First the shop people wanted them cooked and then they wanted them dressed. I think the life is getting harder and harder but it's probably partly because we're getting older and older.

My husband is sixty-two and he's been going to sea all his

life. Father-in-law died very young. He had ordered a new boat but when he didn't need it the three boys went together for the remainder of that season, '47. But it just didn't work out so we went completely on our own. That was really hard because my husband had been in the Navy for the whole of the war and we'd got absolutely nothing. Somehow we just sailed along on our own.

The hours are very unsociable. My father lived in Cromer but I didn't come from a fishing family, I came from a horsey family. Yet I've fitted in and we've had nearly forty years of absolutely perfect life together, I must say. My husband, 'Tuna', is a very placid type of man, you can't get wrong with him. He's an all-round sportsman. He's played football for Norfolk and he's still very good at golf. I think if you're a good sportsman, you can give and take so you make a good husband. He's not called 'Tuna' because of the fish. The only explanation I ever had was from his mother and this is very true of him. Never mind what time he has to get up in the morning — half-past one, two o'clock, half-past two — I'll bet you he always comes down the stairs whistling or singing. He still does it. Actually we have our grand-daughters here to sleep very often now so I usually say 'Don't forget the girls'. I don't like to have them wakened during the night.

When we first went on our own my main job was delivering all the crabs. I had a shooting brake. My husband would catch them and I used to do a square round, Yarmouth, Norwich, Windham, Dereham and then home. I did it each day for years, and I used to be absolutely whacked when I got home. Anyway, this went on until I had an operation about eight years ago, after which I wasn't allowed to lift very much. My husband took over the delivery but it proved too much for him to go to sea then all the way round, so we cut out Dereham and Windham. By that time we were having to cook the crabs, so he'd lift the stuff in for me and I got on with the cooking, scrubbing and dressing where necessary.

We'd boil them in ten-gallon electric coppers. I'd have four on the go sometimes. They have to be soaked first. You put them into tepid water because if you put them into hot they shoot all their claws. Leave them for about twenty minutes until they're almost dead, then scrub the whole thing with a brush and boil them in salt water for about another twenty minutes. After that you wash them again when they come out.

156

My coppers hold about sixty. They have to be scrubbed too and put out to dry. To dress the crabs you first open them up and take the lungs out, the feathery pieces, then you take away the mouth bag. You do this with your fingers, then break the two ends of the shell so you've got a bigger opening and you pick out all the white meat from the crown, or 'shekkle', some people say. I usually call it the crown. I do the picking with a round-bladed pen-knife but you can't get them now. I've got three and they get ever so loose. Lots of the girls use a big knife. They swing it over in their hands and hit the big claws with the handle, but I have a little hammer out of my son's carpentry set when he was tiny because I can't swing the knife back and forth. I always keep a $4\frac{1}{2}$-inch crab measure on my table when I'm dressing in case there's one got in anywhere along the line that's under length. When it's dressed the white meat is piled up on top of the brown. I have done 200 in a day but you've got to really go at it. Dressing entails a lot of work. It takes me about three minutes to do one but someone else might take twenty minutes or half an hour. It's like everything else, just practice. We still sell some of them alive because I'll only cook and dress for people who will take them as well. I won't be caught in a web cooking and dressing all of them. It starts in March or April and finishes the end of August and that's how it goes on every day, every day. You might get one really good year but I have found if you can keep the supply more level you're better off. It's a question of supply and demand. If you get an overflow and you've got to put them onto the open market, you might just as well stay in bed all day because they cut you down and down until it's not worth going to sea.

I also do the books. I think you'll find that most of the females do. With VAT on top of it one gets a bit fed up with it all. I was good mathematically but I'm over sixty now and my brain's not the same as it was at forty, not as sharp. Of course, in my spare time I drove the ambulance for twenty years in Cromer. I used to do all night work and weekend voluntary work before the county council took it over. We had a phone beside the bed and it was either 'Tuna' for the lifeboat or me for the ambulance, so actually we've had a very full life.

Things are quite different at the end of the season. We swing round to herring if there are any but we've only wet our nets once the last two or three years. If they go off every night for three weeks and don't get any, they get fed up and so does everybody else because the petrol and oil has all got to be paid for. During the 1950s and '60s when herring were more plentiful the men used to put to sea about 4pm and return about 2am with their catches and work on the beach measuring them out and boxing, then loading the trucks ready for Yarmouth market. Latter years it was Lowestoft. About 5am the men would get home to bed and the women would then take over and get the goods to market. Rose, Jack Davies' wife, Kathleen, 'Shrimp's' wife and I used to try and get on the road about the same time just in case we had any trouble on the way, then we used to help each other unload, wait for the herring to be sold, have a cup of coffee in the canteen, then back home again.

My husband's one of these fishermen who try to work all the winter so he goes whelking up at Bacton. After we first went on our own we made a whole lot of whelk pots, had the frames made and roped them with back ropes off old herring nets. You get a double line of rope where the corks are and the bottom straight line without the cork is the back rope. Whelking is worth while if the weather is kind, though we've known winters before the war and just after when we didn't earn a ha'penny all the time. You just scraped along with what you earned from crabs because there was nothing else to do. If the fishermen can get jobs on the land they do—building or sprout-picking. They'll perhaps gang up with another fisherman who has got some whelk pots and off they go. 'Tuna' prefers to go to sea, it's what he knows.

In her *Recollections* (1890), Emma Piggot records the plight of Hanna West, a fisherman's wife with a great many troubles in her day. 'Nineteen children born, fourteen teeth pult, but the loss of my husband was the worst of all'. But if life was hard for fishermen's wives, it was plainly worse for those widowed early, and there were plenty although they often married again. A Sheringham resident said of her grandmother, 'she was wife, mother and widow before she was twenty-one, left with a baby of fifteen months. Then my grandfather married her.' As recently as 1962 a Report of the Eastern Sea Fisheries referred to the hazards of small boats working on the Norfolk crab fisheries, pointing out that one of the tough, seaworthy vessels operating from Overstrand did sink in heavy seas. Fortunately without loss of life.

Mrs Harrison explained how she feels when her husband is out in rough weather:

> I know my boy goes to sea and he's got a dangerous job working off the Shetlands, but when he goes I expect him to come back. My husband had some very narrow escapes during the war and he's been overboard about three times but I don't expect him to go and drown either. I think that's the only way you can look at it unless you're going to worry yourself sick all the time. I've been very worried once—though that wasn't until after it occurred. It was ten or twelve years ago when he was out herring catching with his younger brother off Caister, October or November, and the net must have fouled the cork that bungs the bottom of the boat. They had seven cran of herring on board and their boat sank under it. Fortunately the corks on the herring nets just kept her buoyant so she was level with the top of the water. They burned their shirts, burnt everything they could but nobody saw her, not even the coastguards, until at last a fisherman did notice and took them into Caister. I can always remember—he must have gone up to the Caister lifeboat house and rung me at about two o'clock in the morning. He said, 'Well thank God I can hear your voice, thank God I can still talk to you'. I thought what on earth has happened, does he want me there? But he said 'Somebody is going to bring us home, will you be prepared to get up early in the morning to go to Caister and help us salvage anything we can?'. It's strange because we had every faith in this boat, she's still being used down at Sheringham. After that I was sort of sick for about a fortnight. But he had two boats. He couldn't use that one because the engine had got water in it, so that was a big set-back, but he'd had the other one built. He came home, got the mechanic to make sure the engine was all right, pushed it down and went off the next night. Just like that, because he had to go again.

Myrtle West sat so much in the web of the fishing life at Sheringham she can claim a large proportion of the community as some sort of relation. Supporting husband and family was always her sole occupation, so her life might have been closeted, her link with the world tenuous had she been a different person. The first time I met her she asked, 'What do you think of this Common Market?' Then, with a rumble of laughter, 'I like to know what people think'. She is eighty-two.

Teddy 'Fiddy' West's shop is not to be confused with Wests', the Sheringham fish shop, or Wests' the toy shop. It is necessary to turn off the winding High Street with its tiny crab windows, souvenirs and coloured rock, down Co-operative Street into Beeston Road. Here a green-painted corner building reads 'T. West, Local Manager'. Its window is three-quarters empty. There are a couple of slops, rubber gloves, two bells and some pom-pom hats. Teddy Fiddy, a slight, gentle, blue-eyed old man of eighty-one picks up a lump of stone from his collection on the window ledge and cups it. Jet, amber, blue john, lead. But recently he and his wife, Myrtle, have not been getting into the shop so much. Myrtle explains why.

On February 28 we finished in the ship's chandlers. It's been over eighty years in the family. We've had it thirty-eight years, Teddy's father about fourteen and his grandfather before that. His grandfather was fishing at Grimsby in the great boats when he was scrubbing and broke his ankle. It was then he got friendly with the managing director and that's how he got in with the Grimsby Coal, Salt & Tanning Company. We were the oldest branch; there was only the head office in Grimsby when this one was built and now they've got them all over the country—Edinburgh, Hull, Lowestoft and Brixham. But this is the second little one they've shut down lately. Teddy hadn't been in it so much the last two years, so he doesn't miss it as much as I do. I used to come in and tell him what I'd sold and he'd do the writing. The first shop was down the road in a house where Teddy was born. All the woodwork was spars from old sailing ships. It was built for 100 golden sovereigns but it's now been sold for two or three thousand pounds. It's gone down a lot but it will make a nice place. We haven't heard that anyone from Sheringham's bought it, it's probably gone to visitors. I can just remember the old shop with oilskins. Like us, they sold everything a fisherman wears: shirts, slops, long blue boot stockings, the boots, everything. We used to have to order nets from Grimsby but he had mitts—they called them 'dannocks'—and abb, that was navy blue wool for knitting stockings. You can't get it any more. Locally they would come in for a ball of hobb—that's what they called it—but when we were ordering we put the proper name. So many balls of Devon abb, two-ply or three-ply. Now they buy nylon socks. They're not so good in the wintertime. They go cold.

If you ask what Sheringham women did in their spare time, the reply is simple, 'Knitten, they was always knitten'. Although a hand-knitted sweater might last for ten years, it took a long time to make. But Sheringham girls enjoyed it and Sheringham was a knitting centre. When I asked 'Loady' Cox if his mother knitted, he simply said 'She was a Wells girl', implying I should have known better. For fishermen at Cromer wore ganseys, but they had to be imported from Sheringham, Caister and Winterton.

There is a fundamental difference between a jersey and a guernsey, known in local vernacular as 'gansey'. The latter is thin, finely knitted and always navy, whereas the former is thick and hairy, usually blue or white. Believed to have been named from the Channel Island where they were first made around 1600, ganseys must have changed less over the centuries than almost any other garment. It was an indispensable part of the fisherman's outfit worn with slop and tough tanned trousers for weekdays and for Sunday best.

It has been suggested that patterns varied in accordance with function, thus in areas like Sheringham, where boats worked off wide, open beaches, ganseys were ornamented across the shoulders so that the paddling could help ease the strain of carrying gear up and down. Sometimes they were knitted very tight and some knitters required the fishermen to return for fittings at various stages. One noted knitter always gave three or four and her ganseys were such a perfect fit they made the men's earlobes bleed as they were pulled over their heads. Alas, today, two machine-made garments can be bought for the price of the wool, Myrtle says even the wool is difficult to obtain:

161

You can't get wool for ganseys but the knitting was a proper long job. They knit them all down the coast at Filey, Flamborough, Scarborough and in the Scottish islands to different patterns, but I don't think anyone in Sheringham does it now. We used to have ganseys with patterns down the front and sleeves. After the war the patterns only came half way down and the rest was just plain stocking stitch. Teddy's mother knitted them. She'd measure the men with a tape to get their sizes so she knew how many stitches to put on. Then they'd go along for fittings. She never used a pattern. No one did. They had it in their head. There were about twenty needles, she'd keep the spare ones in a little wooden sheath tucked in the top of her skirt, and she'd go right round knitting in a ring. When she got under the arms she put a gusset in front and back and took the sleeves up to knit separately so there weren't any joins. The neck stitches were picked up at the end — they were all knitted right through, collar and everything. Very likely the women used to look around when they were in chapel to see what patterns there was. Then they'd make up their own from what they'd seen. I did a lot of knitting when I was younger; I knitted jumpers but never did knit a gansey. The girls used to start when they were right young, like the Scottish girls who'd come down Yarmouth quay knitting. There was a ball under one arm and their fingers were all bandaged up before they got the herring. Most of the Sheringham wives knitted. If they didn't, there was someone else in the family who'd make them.

They were thrifty years ago. They'd make and mend, knit and sew, patch and patch and patch. There never was anything thrown away. I've been in houses where there'd be a little sand sprinkled on the floor instead of carpets. When my mother was a girl there must have been nine or ten in the family and she had a sister in service in London, my Aunt Lizzie. Mother said when she came home with some paper to put on the walls and a lamp for light, her father nearly went mad because she'd spent money on that sort of thing. And my mother said her brothers used to take the long brass candlesticks with candles in them into the shed to see by when they baited their lines.

When we were kids the fishermen'd have the gansey with blue or tanned slops for weekdays — tough tanned trousers with a centre front flap that folds forward. Teddy still wear that kind now. In bad weather it would be a yellow sou'wester with long oilskins when they went to sea, and they always had sea boots that came up just above the knee. Now of course they have the gum boots. On Sunday they went to chapel in blue beaver trousers and a jacket with velvet cuffs and velvet collar. They had braid all the way round the edge and little flat pockets with black braid. The last one I saw, my brother had it. He bought it at Grimsby and we thought it was an enormous price I remember because that was ten pound. He had it on when we got married, that's fifty-six years come Christmas. They had the thick white boot stockings and a round fur sealskin hat or a soft black chummie. That was more like a trilby with a brim. They wear bow ties and collars now when they're going out — they wouldn't ha' done, not if they was going to see the Queen!

All the women wore aprons on top of a black dress, blue or brown perhaps, but they never went for bright colours, generally it was black. They wore head scarves down on the front but I've never seen grandmother out without a hat, and a smart hat, too. She used to say when she went to chapel, 'I'm going to put my best dinglers on my bonnet. I be like the rest, I go to see and be seen'. If the sermon was too long there was one old fisherman who would start yawning. Then everybody else would start until that wasn't any use going on. The parson would have to pack up and they could go home.

They were all chapel people here. We went to Sunday school twice a day and Teddy was pumper for the organ. You had to go. You only got away from it as you grew older. Backsliders, we are! Willie Long, the local preacher, was a great friend of my father's and his brother married my Aunt Elizabeth. I've been to chapel to hear him and Teddy remembers he sometimes went preaching out on the beach. He was a fisherman and he come from a fishing family, lost his father and a brother at sea, but he was very gifted. He learned his Bible that well that when his sight went he still knew which passage to take his text from by heart. In wintertime he used to travel the country as a missionary with Charlie Craske, John 'Teapot' West and another fellow they called 'Little Mullet'. He had a lovely-sounding voice and anything he talked about was interesting. Even if he didn't have much education you couldn't help listening because he was such a good talker. There's a little chapel built at Runton in memory of him.

163

There was a lot of religion here years ago, mind, some of them
was too narrow. Somebody's son who went into the Merchant
Navy used to come across to my mother's if he wanted to clean
his shoes on a Sunday because he wasn't allowed to at home.
That isn't Christianity is it?

When Teddy was a schoolboy he'd wait for the boats at a
bakehouse just round the corner. It was rough one morning
and they wouldn't take him out so he stoned them from the
beach. He'd be sea-sick nearly every time, he'd say 'Never
again', then he'd go the next Saturday. Teddy's father did
crabs and whelks. That was a very bad time for fishing here,
bad for earning. Then when he died they asked Teddy on. He
went fishing sixty-one years. I've always been a West but
although we were both Wests there wasn't any connection.

A Sheringham tradition which accompanied the fishermen
wherever they went was giving each other nicknames, some of
them so wierd and imaginative, 'Coweed' Farrow, 'Black Bob'
Bishop, 'Squinter' West or 'Lettuce' Cox, that their use might
seem to have been mere caprice. In fact they were given for
the sound practical reason that there were few surnames in
the community and even the taste in Christian names was
conservative, so it was difficult to identify the right person.
Myrtle explained:

There were nine different West families lived around
Beeston Road so they were all known by nicknames. There
were thirteen Mr Wests in the town at one time and five of
them were called Henry. There was 'Downtide' who had the
drum in the Salvation Army band, 'Joyful'—my father—
'Doker', 'Teapot', 'Fiddy', 'Raleigh', 'Jacko', 'Paris', 'Oden',
'Nuts', 'Custard' and 'Tweet'. The nicknames pass down like in
'Downtide's' family there was his son, 'Young Downtide' who's
in the fish shop and his son, 'The Boy Downtide'. I belong to
the 'Joyful' Wests and my mother was always known as Mrs
'Joyful' West. 'Joyful' got his name because my mother used to
tell me he used to sing a lot at sea and his hymn was 'Joyful
Canaan lies before, The spring is coming on, A few more
storms of wind and rain, And winter will be gone'. It's in the
hymn book, I think. Teddy's grandmother was one of ten, so
you got the big families spreading but I don't know much
about his grandfather's side. We've had two girls, three

164

grandchildren and six great-grandchildren, but none of them have carried the name on. West is a proper Sheringham name but they're going away like anything.

I was brought up on this road, a little further down. We both were, but we weren't mates when we were at school even though we went together. First down here to the primary school, then we used to have to walk to Upper Sheringham when we were seven. We hadn't got bikes. Left eight o'clock in the morning with dinner in a bag and got home about five. There was no early coming out in the short days like there is today. There was a real lot of snow on that Upper Sheringham road in the winter. Sometimes our fathers would clear it out. But we managed. We learned reading and writing. I got top of the class for writing but I can't write for nuts now. Top of the class for writing and spelling. We had writing and reading and arithmetic, that was your lot. Teddy was good at sketching and painting, but that he learned hi'self. I used to read a lot, he still reads, but I think television has spoiled me for reading.

I remember when the young girl at Jarrolds shop used to keep me all the new books that came in. Used to have to pay a penny or tuppence more a week, but I'd always get him seafaring books and myself love stories or adventures. My eldest girl she used to go and get the books but in the end she said, 'Well, you've had them all'. I'd work till about nine, knitting or sewing, and he'd be braiding his crab pots, and then we put our work away, had a bit of supper and an hour's read.

In time, the fishing families would have scattered but the pace has been speeded up by holiday makers searching for a coastal second home. The West's old shop has been sold to summer visitors — as always it comes down to who can pay the best price. John Henry, the mussel fisherman from Brancaster, feels vehement about it.

The pressure on this area is from holiday makers with money to throw around. I mean they can buy themselves a secluded spot. One reason there aren't young men in the village is that the houses are being taken over by holiday people. If you don't inherit a house, or your family can't help you get one, it's virtually impossible unless you save. Most of them go to the pubs and enjoy their money until they get married. Of course, then they realise they should have saved but it's too late. House prices in this village — well what can you get for ten thousand?

Fifteen years ago, before the boom set in, you could probably have bought an old cottage for three or four hundred pounds. Now it's just not on.

A local clergyman wondered, as the holiday people push inland, whether his job might become more like being chaplain to a holiday camp. Yet local people sometimes sell their family homes at the going rate and retire to council houses. You cannot blame them. It's the hard, gritty thrust of things. In each town and village the tale is the same. Most of all, Myrtle laments the splitting up of the old community.

Our house would be over eighty years. It was built from pebbles down on the beach. Teddy's family always had these four cottages, it was called Grimsby Row. There used to be Shackletons that went to the North Pole, and Ben Davies, the big singer at Sheringham. All the West End was toff's homes, and just a few fishermen. Audrey Buxton, the naturalist's wife, was a good customer. I sold her sixteen jumpers at a time for shooting parties. Teddy used to say, 'I believe the Duke of Edinburgh's got one of ours this time'. But now we're all retired and working class. These little cottages are sold directly they're empty and the visitors are often after them. The Coxes who are now at Wells used to live right opposite. Then there were all the Craskes and Coopers. The fishermen went to Whitstable, Teddy's uncle went to Felixstowe, and several went to Blakeney, Wells and Grimsby. They're all scattered now and Sheringham is different. You walk into the High Street and hardly know a soul. That's Teddy's trouble, there ain't nobody to talk to. They don't talk his language.

My mother started her little home in Gun Street, then she moved up here. Mother was the only one in her family who didn't go into service. My Aunt Lizzie and all her sisters did. She got wrong with her father ever so many times because she wouldn't, but she made up her mind she wasn't going so she did a day's washing for 9d instead. Always did have her own mind until the day she died. She used to braid nets and mend nets. I couldn't. Teddy's grandmother was a good net-mender, too, but then his mother wasn't. One or two women broke out whelks on the beach but I don't remember my mother doing it. She opened mussels at home for baiting. I've seen her get them in with ice out of the back yard, stand them infront of the fire so that they'd thaw. That was a perishing job but she opened pail after pail. I tried it but I cut them all to pieces; Teddy had to open his own!

My father was a fisherman and both my brothers were, but I never did go out to sea with them. My father wouldn't have had me, wouldn't have been troubled. I suppose he got tired sometimes but he wouldn't own it. If you'd have asked him, 'No. What have I got to be tired for?'. Nowadays if they get a hook in their hand, they come home and go to the doctor's to have it taken out, which is the right thing to do, but when they were baiting lines, if one of the fish hooks got in Father'd take his knife and cut it out. That would be out before he come home. They took some risks didn't they? Yet some of them made rare old ages. Old Mabie West died three or four months before she was one-hundred and Old 'Doker' West is eighty.

Most of the fishermen knew each other and years ago they were close. Mind Cromer and Sheringham fishermen were never very friendly. They was always hauling one another's pots. I can remember my father one day, when he went to sea, somebody'd hauled his pots and he had an idea who it was. Well he set out and said openly on the cliff that he knew who it was and so this chap come down to see him. He stood against my mother's table and he would have swore on anything that he'd never touched my father's pots. And do you know, my father wouldn't believe it? I was a girl at home and I felt ever so sorry for the man and I wished my father'd leave off. After he'd gone I said 'Do you know, that man was telling you the truth'. 'He's the biggest liar there is. That ain't no truth.' My father used to play dominoes at the coffee house. He was the best domino player. I never did see no one beat him, only one man. During the first world war we had soldiers billeted on us and they said 'We'll bring in one what can beat you'. They was all one evening playing two games. I kept hoping my father would win, hoping he'd win. They won one each. My father loved his newspaper and if there was an election on I knew all the news. He was interested in politics. I don't know what he'd say these days but he was a Liberal. He'd get the newspaper after dinner, or after tea, and he used to read to me and my mother — we'd either be knitting or sewing. He was a good reader but I've never seen him read a book.

Wives took charge of finances with good reason since their husbands might blow the lot in an evening at the pub. The

167

custom for shops to supply families on credit until the 'great boats' came in, made it vital for them to pay up debts immediately. Myrtle attests to this.

My mother looked after the money and I always have. All fishermen's wives did. They were golden sovereigns when I was a girl and when they reckoned up on Saturday night my mother would give them eighteen pence in the pound for boat money. That was if they'd been fishing during the week, because we went weeks without any money if that was rough. The men my father was partners with met and they'd put the money on the table. They'd keep the boat money separate then share the rest, each one give it to his wife. My father was given eighteen pence pocket money, he didn't smoke.

Teddy ain't a teetotaler but he never went much to a pub. His pleasures were getting his sea boots on and going to sea, reading, and years ago he'd go up into the plantains [woods] and cut sticks for his crab pots. Then this time of the year — we was only talking about it the other week — he'd come home with baskets of blackberries and I used to make it into blackberry jelly. We never had much time for hobbies. Fine weather they'd take the crab pots down and sit on the green seat down there and there'd be a yarn going on. Perhaps somebody'd be playing a concertina or he'd play the mandolin, any music. Any little child's mouth organ he'd get a tune on it. But he used to play nice on the mandolin; he played it in the sheds, indoors mostly. My father used to sing a lot but he never sung a song, all hymns.

I never went out to work but I used to do a hard day's washing because there was my mother and father as well as four of us. Afterwards I used to say, 'I've got a headache, let's go to the pictures'. We used to go four times a week. One day when we all came out of the pictures together, John Teapot was coming past. He didn't talk to me but my eldest brother said 'Hello, John' and he said 'I'm not stopping to talk because I feel condemned walking down the road with you after you've been to the pictures'. Teddy's uncle, Walter, got turned out of the Salvation Army band. He wasn't smoking because, of course, they signed articles to say they wouldn't smoke or go to football matches or anything like that: but he was always chewing tobacco.

I remember on the Cromer Road there used to be a couple

called Groom who made rope for the fishermen, I think they came from Scarborough. A little boy would be there turning the wheel for half-a-crown a week, they used to come right down the yard. I've watched them when my father used to send me up to buy a ball and they'd be stretched from the top of the garden right down to the house, pulling out the threads. The boy turned the wheel and the man had all the loose stuff hanging round his belly.

We always called a see-saw a tip-tom-tawter and after we've done cleaning the garden is full of pishameres, we haven't had any yet this year—that's ants. 'Bishy barny bee' is right for a ladybird and snails are 'dodermans'. We used to use the words all the time when we were little. I suppose if we were talking together we would now. When it's time for Teddy to change his underclothes I say to him 'You ain't shiffoned yet', I don't know how to spell it but that's a Sheringham word. Then that isn't a shed, it's a 'shud'. 'Where's your father? In the shud'. My father would call my mother 'My old woman' perhaps or 'My old lady' and he called girls 'mawthers'. I don't think they use the word much now.

At Lessingham the coast road takes one of its periodic journeys away from the sea. Just north of the village a smaller road, silver with aspen and willows, wriggles towards the coast, leaving brick farms and farm cottages straggling to left and right. Further still it carries on through fields and reed beds to a few houses nestling beneath a bank of sandhills. A white one, decorated in green and yellow paint, makes a welcoming splash of colour amidst its sombre surroundings. It is the home of Mr and Mrs Kerrison. Beryl Kerrison has much in common with Beattie, Mabel and Myrtle—dedication to her family and an absorption with life. She has been able to combine home duties with a part-time job. But only because there are not enough fish at sea to make a living from it any more.

I was born here so I've more or less been in this house all my life. It's cold in the winter, bitterly cold, but we seldom get a lot of snow and we haven't been blocked in now for three years. I like beachcombing in the winter when there aren't so many people about. I collect amber and give it to anybody likes it.

You've got the world to yourself then. We've had a lot of trouble with the hippies this year so we're glad to be left alone.

Our dads worked together. My dad had the boat and Sam's dad had the nets, so they went into partnership. When they weren't fishing they'd take loads of people to the lightships, scouts particularly. And they carried over papers, vegetables and fruit. We've been together all our lives and we both fished with our fathers, so I knew nearly as much about the sea as Sam.

When our fathers were with us seineing — drawing we called it — I used to drag the nets with a rope round myself through the breakwaters while they were rowing. I swam through the draftways where it was deep because you couldn't walk through them, and it was harder for them to pull the boat than just hold the net. We got soles and flats and perhaps the odd salmon trout. But the herring catching, well some nights you might come in with the odd one and other nights you'd come in with thousands. You just don't know, that's the interest of fishing. I used to push the three kids along in the pram and then go shrimping with a big push net. Only two or three years ago at low water there was a pool in the breakwater and that used to be full of shrimps. I'd take them home, stick them in a big boiler outside and put them on a bench to sell them. People came down to the house to buy. I'd get two big bath-fulls. I should think there was twenty pints, or something like that.

We used to go bait digging and laying lines because years ago, when we didn't have so many breakwaters, there'd be banks and in these draftways, channels leading out to the sea, and on the banks you'd get bait. But since they put in more breakwaters the beach has built up. That's made one big sea and the worms have all gone. Anyway you'd dig that bait or cut up herring and put it on the lines at low water, then bring them right up the beach and anchor them. When the sea came in, about two hours after high tide, we'd haul for cod and skate. We did that November to January time. But sometimes if Sam felt the sea was a bit dicey we'd lay what we called a pack of lines, that was three or four hundred hooks, and we'd anchor them ashore so we didn't have to go off on the sea again to pick them up.

Even in wartime, when my father was a Home Guard and Sam was in the Navy, I used to take my three children through a gap in the minefield and dig bait to lay the lines, knowing who was on Home Guard duty, mind you, because you weren't supposed to be on the beach you see. But if you knew who was on watch it was all right. I took the children along this narrow path and we used to get literally hundreds of cod. One particular time I'd caught one and when I got on my bike to take it to Manor Farm it took all my strength to hold it off the ground. We got no end of cod then.

One day Sam came home and thought he'd like to go fishing, so I popped Judith down to Mrs Cutting. But that was one of those mornings when she didn't want to stay with her. She wanted to come. The sea was a bit lumpy and we had to mind what we were doing in the big crab boat, so I was a bit angry to think she wouldn't stop, as she was only about three. However I just put her in the boat and it was the only time she was violently sick. That was rough but we knew there was some herring about and we just got full up with them. Poor little mite, she kept being sick but there was nothing we could do. Anyway, we'd just dragged the nets in when we saw Dad on the hill and signalled to him to come along and help us. But that's about the only thing I trust my husband with — knowing how to beach a boat in the sea. That didn't put Judith off, she's like me, she loves the water, though I only went with Sam in the mornings when the men couldn't go. At night I went off and rowed while he cast the nets, then he'd put me ashore and pick up the men.

Beryl's involvement with the sea began early.

I had three brothers and one sister and we all used to join in and help together. So I was more or less a proper boy. I was always down on the beach helping them because there's eight years between my youngest brother and myself. I was like a family on my own, and I stuck to my dad nearly all the while. Him and Sam's father. Even from school I used to come along the back of the hills and talk with Grandad Kerrison, ask him for pennies to go and buy some sweets, like children do. Whenever they were fishing, if I wasn't at school, I'd be there if Mother allowed me to. Of course, I had my little jobs to do at home but otherwise every moment I was there, helping them in one way or another.

Unless his wife was on the quay when the men came in, I was told, they would go straight to the pub. Very rarely did they go home first. Certainly fishing and drinking were related. Beryl had considerable experience of both.

My father used to drink a lot, of course. In those days they did. My mother had a very hard time when we were young because Father drank so much. Even when he went off fishing they'd always take some bottles on board, used to have a crate on the boat, just beer. All of them took it. Mother didn't approve, she wanted to stop him drinking, so he wasn't allowed it in the house but he'd already had his bellyful up there. The women were hard up as church mice because the men would drink. Sam realised what a waste of money that was. He likes to go for a drink perhaps on a Saturday night but he don't stay out drinking like they used to. One day I came home from school and my mother stood there crying. The baker had just come, she didn't have bread. She made her own but, she had to buy flour and yeast. This time she couldn't buy flour because she'd got no money, so she just said 'Let them go without'. But my brother laid outside ill too and that always stuck in my mind. I'd come past my father, laying asleep half way along the back of the hills, sleeping his drink off. Mother used to send me, 'Go and find Dad'. Well the obvious place was the lifeboat shed, or sometimes they'd be up at the net shed gambling, playing ha'penny nap or something like that. That's why I'm such a gambler I expect! We used to watch them. But they were good-living people, although they drank a lot, their hearts were in the right place.

The women didn't go out to work in those days—only housework. But they did have their pleasures, Women's Institute for one thing, I think that was one of the mainstays of the village life. There weren't many women who didn't go and all the villages had their own, even Palling. They were very, very helpful, especially with cooking. My mother would have gone once a month on the third Wednesday, and then the second Wednesday was the committee meeting. She used to go on her bike but I had to walk right to Palling every day to school—that's two miles. She'd also have her whist drives and socials, drama groups or perhaps a concert party. They'd make a cup of tea and it'd be a social whist drive—not as it is today, a gambling affair. Mother didn't play cards herself, so she'd do the refreshments but Dad and all of us played. It's partly because the fish are moving so therefore the community is getting less in the fishing line but I think we're getting further and further away from the real life.

On Sundays Mother was a great one for entertaining her family. She would sit out on the lawn with a great old bowl of shrimps and home-made loaves and a shortcake, that'd be your tea. You wouldn't have a lot of cake. Dad would catch the shrimps and they'd be on the lawn with tents. It was nothing for her to feed umpteen people but we were never allowed to eat in between, you had to wait for your meals. And no sitting up at the table without your clothes on; you weren't allowed to sit up in your bathing costumes, not with Mother. They were penniless sometimes but they kept these high standards. Of course, Mother was a very religious woman, too. It was a recognised thing that we all walked to church on a Sunday morning, 11 o'clock. Every family would have its individual pew. Father had to go to church, Mother made him do that and he knew he had to. They all did. Even if he went off and took people off the beach in the afternoon, he was not allowed to do anything the Sunday morning. It was church for every family. Then we'd bike to Sunday school at half-past two in the afternoon.

I think our mother was the main head of the family. I wouldn't say my father was hen-pecked but he was so dependent on her. He'd go his way to a certain degree but he'd say 'Go and ask Mother', he wouldn't give you a decision. It's the same with Sam. 'Go and ask Beryl, see what she says'. Yet I don't rule him. If he want to go out, he goes out and if I want to, I go. But mother was a fine woman, really economical always busy mending. Realising how hard up she was herself, she used to help others such a lot. There was far more intimacy in village life than there is now. There was no transport, you didn't have a car, so you didn't get out. I've never known Mother to go on the water, she didn't like swimming, and Father couldn't swim, although he got medals for life-saving. Sam can't either. I've tried to teach him time and time again but I could swim at a very young age. My brother just slung me in a draftway so I had to, and my children can do anything in the water, even the grandchildren are coming on.

When I was thirteen I was sent to Derbyshire to learn cooking. I went into the kitchens in a retreat house where the clergymen go before they're ordained. I was kitchenmaid there for just on four years, when I came back and took some summer jobs on. Did odd jobs round here, like the little summer guest house, then I went for a job as cook at Helston Hospital, well they were so short of nurses that the matron got round me to go in for nursing. And after the first month I didn't want to go in the kitchen again. I went on three or four years and got through all the exams, but we got married, Sam and I, and in wartime you either had to have your family or go back to nursing. I didn't want to be too old before we had our children so we started a family. Judith is the third, I had a boy and two girls. When Judith was three a dentist set up a practice in Stalham and I went as his receptionist. That was 1947 and I'm still there. Only part-time, unless I'm relieving for sickness or anything like that. It just give me my finance to run my car and a bit of independence. My other interest is the Women's Institute. I'm Secretary and I live and die for that. My Mother was Secretary for thirty-four years.

I still do my own bread on a Sunday — always make bread rolls for tea but I do have the baker during the week because there's only two of us now. The children usually come down on a Sunday so we're about fifteen for tea with all the grand-children. It's good to get them all together, there's a great bond between us.

Sam is sixty-one and I'm fifty-seven. On my birth certificate my name is Ruby Ruth but I'm always called Beryl. Thereby hangs a tale — Dad was drunk when he gave my name at the Christening!

8

CHIEFLY HERRING

Then up jumped the herring, the king of the sea,
Says 'Now, old skipper, you won't catch me'.
　　　　　　　　　　　—Anon. East Anglian song

This is a story of diminishing fish stocks at sea. The North
Norfolk coast is a mere microcosm of a national, even
world-wide problem. Political, economic, social, technological
and scientific. Extension of British fishing limits to 200 miles
will help counteract many years of overfishing by the fleets of
many countries but technological advances made it possible
to sweep up tremendous catches and in some cases the
damage is irreversible.

Even now the European Commission wants to reduce its
inshore fleet by an average of fourteen vessels in every
hundred. The British Inshore Fisherman's Society naturally
protests while unable fully to grasp the situation, British
fishermen feel that their rights are being swallowed up in
larger issues. For years they have meekly accepted the
assurances of successive governments that their interests will be
protected, yet time and again they have seen the government
surrender to foreign demands. While British vessels are being
driven from the fishing grounds of other countries, foreign
fishermen are being allowed to increase their activities
around British shores. Their sense of urgency is well justified.
Following a routine, waiting for the shoals to arrive, they
have held on, sometimes dependent on intermittent employment, until at last they have been driven from the sea.
Brancaster, Wells, Cromer and Sheringham are the last
bastions of a tottering industry, further south the battle is
already almost lost. Though close in their memories, the days

when men got a living wholly and solely from the sea will soon be relegated to nostalgia.

Sam Kerrison, Beryl's husband, said:

Ten years back or more there was a nice lot of longshore herrings along here. You'd go off with the boats from Cromer and Yarmouth an' it was always worth your while. You could get three or four cran a night, probably more. When I was about sixteen we went and caught them and we couldn't get rid of them. Used to come home and dump them on the beaches. But last year I went several times and the most I think I got was a box. It's the same all round. I've been to Devon for a week and the fishermen all say the same. As a matter of fact, there's only one full-time fisherman left in Clovelly. He was taking trips this time 'er year.

At the same time it is worth remembering that inshore fishermen did not often make a fat living. Coastal inhabitants generally seem to have had a strong scavenging instinct in days when it was a remunerative pastime. Daniel Defoe, visiting the region about 1722, wrote of the sparsely populated, uninviting little villages between Caister and Happisburgh where every barn, shed and stable, even the palings of yards and gardens, were built of old planks, beams and timbers from the wrecks of ships. A hundred years later Dutt described an animated scene on a lonely stretch off Happisburgh when the beach, it seems, was black with coal from a wrecked collier. Farmers came with wagons, men with donkey carts and wheelbarrows, old women with boxes and skips, and children with bags and baskets. All thronged to the beach to cart it home as if 'each lump had been a diamond'. Often the coast was strewn with cargoes: oranges, pit props and telegraph poles, sacks of wheat and even thousands of boxes of matches packed in zinc cases, apparently none the worse for wear. It was fair game for people who lived largely on their wits and the fisherman's special pickings were made from salvaging. Sam Kerrison says of his father's time:

They got half their living with the salvage that time of day. At Sea Palling they had a beach company—you've heard of these companies have you? If a boat was smashed up they didn't hardly get anything but if it came ashore, providing they got it off, they got a nice lump of money. That's what they used to rely on. There were four or five boats off Sea Palling, not too many, and we helped each other run them off the beach. If the sea was very rough, say there was a nasty swell broke on the bank, we used to lay an anchor out to sea and pull ourselves off with a rope—a hauling-off rope.

To cater for a different fishing, the type of craft also changed along the coast. The crab boat predominated as far down as Happisburgh, then at Sea Palling gave way to slimmer craft, known locally as punts. The Kerrisons had a punt.

Our boats had a cuddy forward like a hoveller. They were 18–20 foot—a nice length—and six-foot beam. You'd never hardly see a crab boat clear of Happisburgh. When I first went, we sailed. Just a lugsail, sometimes a foresail and a mizzen similar to the crab boats, because when you was drifting for mackerel the mizzen kept the boat steady. The punts were mostly built at Yarmouth but our boat, a 28-footer, was built on the Broads at Potter Heigham. I lived at Sea Palling. I went to school there and in the wintertime you'd see the old fishing smacks at Lowestoft. Winterton was one of the most important fishing villages that time of day. Every man jack from the place went fishing. There may have been a hundred if not two hundred, mostly drifting out of Yarmouth. My father and grandfather never did go drifting because they got a good living longshore fishing. Some of them used to pack up about the beginning of December and they'd earned enough to keep themselves until they started again in April. Sometimes they'd get a job on the sea defences, but I have known them not to do anything. Father-in-law went fishing with me until he was nearly eighty. My grandfather, he was a longshore fisherman and his father. It goes back. They all went off Sea Palling, off the beach. Always longshore fishing.

Drifting is a world of its own, though many longshoremen tried it before settling down. It may be remembered that George Cox also went drifting. The pattern of his journey was much the same as Sam Kerrison's.

I first went on the drifters when I was sixteen. We were ten, the skipper, mate, the oarsman and the whaleman, right down to the cook. We'd start round about April working at a place called Lerwick on Shetland Island and we'd be there a few weeks before we came down to Fraserburgh and worked this way, following the herring. About August we'd be out of Shields, then we'd start the home fishing in the middle or end of September, when the drifters worked out of Yarmouth. We'd be away five months and I must have done it ten years until the war come on and I went into the navy doing mine-sweeping. I did one more herring season after that, then came back and messed about longshore fishing. After the war there was a nice lot of fishing down here, a lot of soles and everything but I mostly concentrated on herring. I'd do as well as anybody herring catching off here and Sea Palling but since I've married I've been more or less here in Eccles.

The herring drifters were biggish boats, 80–100 foot long. When you weren't working you were generally asleep. You see, you'd have two or three on watch at a time and if you got a good catch you'd be laying fresh nets nearly every day. Say you'd caught a hundred cran, you'd come in in the morning about eight o'clock and that would take you four or five hours to get the lot out. You'd turn around, get some stores aboard and away to sea again. The skipper would probably take it out while the crew had a rest and by the time you reached the fishing grounds it would be all hands out again shooting nets. Then you'd be landing them the next morning. If you didn't get many you could box them and put a drop of ice on them to bring in the next day, but if you'd got two or three hundred crans, that took a long while to haul. Twelve hours perhaps. It was all go.

There weren't much freeboard above the deck on a drifter. You'd pull the nets over a roller so they'd come easy. There'd be two or three one side and two or three the other. You'd give them a rough shake as soon as they come — what we call 'skud' them — then you'd have two men in the hold shaking the herring down. As I said, I've been twelve hours or more hauling and if that was right bad weather, say you had a westerly wind, you'd shoot so the nets blew clear of the boat. If it fly round the opposite way you used to have to go to the other end. Because that's a rum job. It's just the same with inshore boats. If you've got an easterly wind blowing you hung on to the inside of the net and if that was sou'west, blowing offshore, you hung on to the outside. Sometimes you'd hang on for two hours and haul maybe two to see if there was any herring swimming, but I've known nets to be full within an hour. If there was a nice lot you'd haul, but if they wasn't too many you'd shoot away again and hang on.

The nets were marked with pellets. There'd be one on every net in the drifters. The modern pellets are made of some plastic material, but the old ones were canvas with all tar inside and a wooden top. They'd blow up like one of these balloons. There'd be a thin piece of wood in the top with an eye where you put your strop through to lash them on. Then there'd be a special quarter bole — that would be a mark so you knew you had a quarter of your nets in and another one for half your nets. A half-bole. The nets for the drifters would come down in lorries, or before that by horse and cart, but we'd pull the longshore ones down in net barrows. Just wooden. Make 'em yourself. No wheels, legs, and you drag 'em over the sand. I used to take about twelve nets longshoring — not too many because there'd always be plenty er herring — but in the skiff I've got now I only shoot about seven. The herring used to go in crans but now they go in tonnes.

Herring nets have a cork line along the top and then the lint goes straight down in the water. If you were shooting on the flood tide, you'd always cant your nets a bit, put them on slanting Yarmouth way, and on an ebb tide, the opposite way. I have caught tons of herring just clear of the breakwater. Marvellous. Years ago when a lot er boats come down here from Yarmouth, they'd have a dan buoy with a light on it to mark the inshore end of their nets. A hurricane lamp was tied onto the dan. I used to work one but that's very seldom because I always used to work close in against the beach. Now they have a red flasher on the dan. The Yarmouth boys'd shoot further out while I started inside of them and shot my nets more or less off the beach. I've been filled up with herring when they've hardly got any because the herrings would lay right close. A drifter would shoot about a hundred nets tied up at the top with the fid and the eye. The fid is the string you put through the eye to lash 'em together. But the longshore nets we tied them, leened them up the whole way down to the bottom, to your lowers. So it's all like one stretch.

As a rule you can make about three longshore nets out of

one deep-sea drift net because they're about twenty score deep. A score is a mesh. Along the coast here you'd start with a fleeter net which would be about six score, then you'd work up to seven and eight. Cromer, I suppose, generally fish eight, nine or ten but a mackerel net has a bigger mesh, that's the only difference. Herring would go straight through. When you're drift netting for mackerel you might haul a net or two and just get the odd one. Then all of a sudden you'd get a bunch of one or two hundred. But if you got a swim of herring they'd be regular. Sometimes when the water was clear you'd get them in your lowers. I've known them ever so thick at the bottom and up top there wouldn't hardly be any. That's when the water is sheer. We call it sheer when that's clear. But that's no good if it's too clear because the fish see your nets. If you're after herring and the water burn, that's phosphorescence, then you wouldn't get many fish either, because a herring net is lit up like fire.

When we used to pack up longshore fishing, end of November, we'd work along the sandhills, making them safe. We planted a lot of marram along here before they had the sea wall, to try and reclaim it. The wind would blow and build up a bank. But I've been on the highways fifteen or sixteen years. I don't go fishing for a living now. Yet you've fishing in your blood I think and that's that. There've been plenty of times when I couldn't get off the beach and if there's any boats up here fishing, I go down and watch them, see what they're up to. If that is rough along here we get some very big hollow seas. Big breakers. It's worse here than Cromer and Sheringham. I was always told this stretch from Mundesley to Winterton is one of the worst.

From the Kerrison's house on a clear day it is possible to see across a two-mile belt of low-lying agricultural land skirting the sea to Palling. One can even make out quite clearly a row of tiny terraced houses running down to the front. Rose, Violet, Bluebell, Pansy, Tulip, Fuschia, Daisy, Musk and Lilly Cottages. Daisy Cottage is the home of a handsome and engaging man with a rich, deep Norfolk brogue. He is Percy Feek, eighty-six, a young-old man with an air of having enjoyed life, given and taken, roughed and tumbled, and lived it to the full.

I'm really a stranger in this village. I was born in 1889 and I came here when I was a year old. My mother run away with another man and I was put out to a lady who took in washing other side er Yarmouth. She should er got five shillings a week for me, which she did. But she already had one child and then there was another baby coming on the way, so we were getting a bit of a crowd. Well her mother said to her 'I'm going to put him in the workhouse'. Only when she came to Yarmouth and she see me, she change her mind. 'He ain't going to the workhouse, I'm going to take him home'. And she brought me home. I always called her Grandmother, one of the best old ladies ever lived. Her husband went skippering out of Yarmouth on the old sailing boats and I've been connected with boats ever since I can remember. My father, he was a soldier, so that's quite a difference. It was by chance I've had the same upbringing as if I'd come from a fishing family. The fishing and the lifeboat. Her husband and all her sons, they were fishermen, lifeboatmen.

When we was boys, we passed our time away with a 'line on the beach. Go and dig the bait and lay a line for anything what come along. Then we had a big fireplace in the lifeboat shed. We used to get up there and have a game of cards for money. We usually played brag, that was really bluff you know. You could sometimes carry on if you hadn't much of a hand and your opponent, he'd chuck his hand in. The girls, they'd be out pushing the pram. That was one thing they'd had to er done. There was thirteen in some families, and there were tens, nines and eights. They were like little mothers, they had to work an' all and go into service soon as they left school, three shillings a week.

My first wife was local. She died. But my wife now was nurse to a family. She'd be down in the net shed so I got to know her. Not very well. Then when my first wife left me with two children, I spoke to her one morning, asked if she'd like to be my housekeeper and we eventually got married. That's how she come to be a London woman.

I joined the Palling beach company in 1913. There were forty-eight of us. That was a crew to each lifeboat, two lifeboats. You couldn't join until there was a vacancy, then you'd buy a share. I give £17 for mine, to share the salvage and all the other benefits what the beach company provided. But it didn't entitle me to a share of the lifeboat. That was lent by the Institution and we had the privilege of using it. When I first joined the company I went to Happisburgh Sands in the yawl. Yawls were a different class of boat altogether from the lifeboat. They had no belting round, they were long boats and they were built for speed. They had two sails, a foresail and a mizzen. That was a lugsail and every time you went about you had to lower the sail, pass it round the mast and pull it up again. The mizzen was a standing lug, that was rug up different so you didn't have to put that about, not when you went about with the foresail. They were built at Yarmouth. One was 42 foot long and one was 47 foot and seven oars a side. They had a decent beam but not a lot for the length on 'em. They were quicker sailers than what the lifeboat was, because the lifeboat had a lot of beam and was heavier. They'd fly past. There didn't have to be a lot of wind before you had to reef. But that took a good breeze before you reefed in our lifeboat. I have seen three reefs in, well, that was a gale of wind. I was just too late to race in a regatta in one of the yawls. I always used to go from here to Yarmouth to watch and once they went from here and got first prize. There was keen competition on that though. There'd be one from here, one from Winterton, one from Caister, Yarmouth and Lowestoft. All them yawls would meet at Yarmouth on this here holiday.

Say a boat came on the beach at Happisburgh Sands in bad weather, we would go for saving life first. Then when the weather calmed down, if the ship was still there, we'd lay anchors or assist tugs. If we got it off we got a pound or two, but if that was smashed up we didn't get anything. Before we had the Royal National lifeboat there were two beach companies. Then a tragedy come, 1842–43. Five were drowned when one boat capsized, then seven more lost their lives in an accident. All together fourteen drowned. Afterwards I suppose they hadn't enough men for two boats so they joined together and that's when the new company was formed.

There was a look-out pulled down 1933. You used to go up and look if that was bad weather. Of course, you couldn't always see the sands, so it wasn't so much good going up there. They'd draw lots and draw your name out and then you'd take watch, two of you, but the watching part you didn't get nothun' for. There'd be a gun rocket would fire a big bang and providing you weren't too far away you'd hear it. Well then everybody would run to get the boat off. You had rules in the beach company. If you managed to get there afore that went afloat, if you touched it you were entitled to a share. But you must touch it. That was important, so there was competition to get there. Yes, sometimes a tussle. That was the main thing, too, with the boat for salvaging. Get there first, before Caister or Winterton and Cromer. Winterton and Cromer, they were our two rivals. Each lifeboat has an area but not for salvage. There was competition there, too, I can tell you because that might ha' meant a ten-pound note for you and that was a lot of money. Get there first and get a hold as we used to say. Once you'd got a hold all the salvaging depend on you. If another boat got there first you'd try and get in along with him if she was a big boat but they wouldn't never hardly take you. Might ha' made the most of an opportunity when it came but often we'd put out in some bad gales just for saving lives.

The lifeboat was heavy — 17 ton. We shoved it down the beach on skeets. Each skeet had two rollers in it and you had three of them to keep her a-going. Took a long while sometimes, then you had a hard job to get away if that was a big swell. But we had an anchor laid out over on the outer bank with a rope to the shore to help. That pulled us off, then we could put the mast up and get the sails all ready. Soon as ever you'd done that you'd haul the rope and away you'd go. It's very exposed. We're on a point here, we get the full force of it. We've launched in some very bad weather and got away. Used to get wet through. And August bank holiday Monday we had a practice. The lifejackets made of cork were very lumbersome. You could hardly move in them. I never did put one on and I never did see nobody put one on except for the photographs. They'd keep you warm but they hindered you from work. Nobody could swim. Didn't think about it. Anyway the high boots would be like lumps of lead. The lifeboat drawed three foot of water so you had to have them on. But I can't say I ever was frightened. I had great faith in the coxswain and great faith in the boat.

I started on the drifters in 1906 and went seven year. Then the war come on so I went away in the Merchant Service. Afterwards there were forty from this village alone, fishing out of Yarmouth. All young fellers. Two or three of them got to be skippers, but I came back and bought a punt. We would start off in February with shrimping, perhaps get two or three pecks a day. We got 2s 8d a peck, that was sixteen pints. You must remember there wasn't much money about. Continue until the beginning of May and then start mackerel catching. That would last two months probably when you'd be shrimping again and seine netting. It would carry on all summer until the beginning of September when you'd start after herring. At the end of October we'd be lucky here when we packed up along with that. We'd get work on the sandhills, planting marram. And that's how the year went by.

Sam Kerrison's father used to have tents. In the summertime he made a pound or two extra so he never did go a-drifting. But what I know I learned off er him. He was a first-class fisherman. There were so many of them doing it but now they're dead and the young ones won't have it. I've been out there all night for nothing. One particular day I remember we were the last ashore and an old man on the quay said to me 'Ah well, you've got some mackerel this morning, others have'. I had two mackerel on my finger. I said 'That's the catch'. He said 'I don't believe it'. My chum says 'That's all we got for all night and we've rowed from Mundesley home'. The others had a hundred or two, which was a night's work, you see. I ain't going to tell you we didn't get a nice whack sometimes or we couldn't have lived at all. We did sometimes and then there come bad weather and you wouldn't be able to go. There was no social security. You only got what you earned. And I'll tell you we've been out some bad nights when I'd have rather been ashore but I had to go because I wanted the money. There weren't a lot of money but we jogged along and thought it was all right. Not no more.

Grandmother had seven all older'n me. Almost grown up. She died in 1921. See her in the photo with a Bible along with her. She'd read the Bible every night and say her prayers. Methodist chapel was practically full. Now religion is a thing of the past — nobody have the time. Sunday dinner-time she used to have lard to put on her head but that used to be special lard with no salt in it to keep her hair down when she put her bonnet on. That was all bonnets and long frocks and a cape. I've thought about what she must've thought of me coming home when I'd had half a pint too much! I mean we did in them days. Beer was cheap and that was good. Six pints of that would make you talk. Talk about your friends, your enemies and all! But that was good stuff. Today it's nothing but chemicals.

And when they all came home at Christmas there was more beer on the floor than they drank down in the pub. There'd be one playing the accordion and somebody dancing. One would get up and sing a sensible song. True song. Used to have some rare nights together, singing and dancing. There was one sung in The Lifeboat down there, I don't know where it originated from. All I know is the title, 'Sailor's Farewell'. That's over sixty year ago since I heard it. It was sung by a fisherman. I aren't a very good singer but it didn't have a strong tune:

It was a cold and stormy night
The snow laid on the ground,
A sailor boy stood on the quay
His ship was outward bound.

His sweetheart standing by his side,
Shed many a silent tear,
And as he pressed her to his breast,
He whispered in her ear,

Goodbye, goodbye, my own true love
This partin' gives me pain,
I'll be your own true guiding star
When I return again.

My thoughts will be of you, of you,
When the storms are raging high,
Farewell, farewell my own true love
Your faithful sailor boy.

And with the gale, the ship set sail
He bid his love goodbye,
She watched the ship 'til out of sight,
A tear be-dimmed her eye.

It was sad to say the ship returned
Without her sailor boy.
He died while on the voyage, for
The flag was half-mast high.

His comrades, when they came ashore,
Told her that he was dead
And gave to her a letter which
The last lines sadly said;

Goodbye, goodbye, my own true love
On earth we'll meet no more.
I soon shall be from storm and sea
On that eternal shore.

I hope to meet you in that land,
That land beyond the sky,
Where you will not be parted from
Your faithful sailor boy.

Years ago they used to play 'Domino Out' because they couldn't reckon up for Threes and Fives. They couldn't read, they couldn't write. Then the darts came in after the ninepins. And there was a card game we played called Euchre. You had five cards each and the jack of each pack, they were bowers. Jack of hearts was the right bower and jack of diamonds was the left bower. Jack of whatever trumps were, he was the second best card, because you always had the joker in and he was the best card of the lot. We used to play four a side. Now there ain't no village life. I mean we'd meet down there, then we had the lifeboat shed. But a lot of the young fellers got killed in the first war and I blame the television. There's only two or three of us get out and yarn these days. You can look out here after tea, you won't see a soul. We used to come out of the pub and stand there 'til eleven yarning. You know, local things.

Some things might have improved because in the village them days parish relief was very meagre. There was an old couple lived alongside me, man and wife, and the man had ailing health. Their total income was a stone of flour a week, four pound of beef or pork and two shillings. That was all they had and out of that she used to pay 6d rent. I don't know how they managed. There were only two jobs — going on the farm or drifting. That's why they went. On the farm the wages in the wintertime were only ten shillings a week and eleven in the summer. They stopped a shilling in the wintertime. I often think how I was at school singing 'Rule Britannia, we'll never be slaves' yet I was surrounded by 'em. Some of the men didn't see their children, only on Sunday. Away in the morning, late home at night, and they dussen't complain because the farmer's give them the sack and they wouldn't 've had nothing at all to do. They dussen't hardly call their souls their own. It was wrong. We never ought to've sung Rule Britannia. They had to bow to the farmer, the boys lifted their hats and the girls curtsied. If they hadn't ha' done it their father would have got the sack. At Palling Hall they employed a lot of men but I wouldn't say the master was one of them slave drivers. He was a good man and if his workers or their wives weren't well, he would look after them and send them something to eat, so I never did think we were hard done by in Palling. Not like some villages were.

One month the supply of a certain fish is abundant, the weather changes and severe north-east winds take a heavy toll of gear. Even when boats put out to sea it is too rough to haul. Reports of the Eastern Sea Fisheries as far back as the turn of the nineteenth century indicate that fluctuating and irregular rewards have always been the lot of fishermen. Skipper Woodhouse confirms it is the same today:

That have been very precarious. Some of the boats have been going out — about two mile I suppose — and they haven't got any herring. They went out of Yarmouth harbour last night for a dozen herrings and one night before that they only got three — the seals had so many out of the nets. But then we've always had hard times and good times. That's what we're in it for. This chap who works with us say he wouldn't have nothing to do with it if that was all good times. He said it wouldn't be so interesting would it?

When Sheringham's 'great boats' were away shops supplied families with goods on credit. If a boat had made a good trip, the crew might even stand in for the debts of a less fortunate one, on the principle that they were not likely to be unlucky twice running. Percy Feek remembers:

There was a shopkeeper here would let families have the groceries to a certain extent because she knew if they earned a pound they would pay her. The people were honest. So she'd let them have some on the slate. When they went herring drifting the men who were married were allowed ten shillings a week. It was sent home by the owners every Saturday, then when they finished up at Christmas or in September that would be deducted. But a single man couldn't get nothing. There wasn't much trading at Palling, only coal. I can just remember the billy boys, four old chaps used to go in one. Small craft, flat-bottomed, with a jib and a mainsail then a mizzen. They were rather bluff at the bows, they weren't good sailers, but they carried about 50–60 ton and landed coal on the beach. They'd be laid ashore at high water and at low water the farmers would come down and cart the coal out of them up over the hill into the coalyard. Then when the water came up she would soon float, being flat-bottomed and nothing in her, and away she'd go off again.

Of course, there isn't fishing now. I read in the paper a time ago the trawlers landed 7,000 ton of immature herring for poultry food and thirty-five of them would go in a matchbox. You fancy — 7,000 of them which never had a chance to live. How can there be any herring if they're all feasting and catching them? A bye-law has now been passed, so there's no fishing until a certain date in September. Well they ought to have done that fifty years ago. They caught spring herring so they never had a chance to mature and spawn. As long as they made a shilling or two a cran that was all what mattered.

A huge black lifeboat shed dominates Caister's coastal strip, otherwise her splashes of summer entertaining leave the town a trifle jaded out of season when fish and chip shops are no longer crammed with people, bakeries are boarded up and cafés are closed. In Beach Road, a food market proclaims its existence in vibrant red and white lettering while 'Chomp a Chicken Here' is smeared in white paint across the windows of a scruffy shop. But behind it the blinds are crookedly drawn. Progressing seawards there is a pert row of working men's cottages tarted up in purple and yellow, then more houses backing on to the road, their fronts overlooking a parking lot leading onto the sand dunes. Skipper Woodhouse and his brother David live here, close to the sea.

Skipper got his name from a peaked cap with SKIPPER printed across the front that he used to wear as a boy. He is sixty-two, tall, sharp-featured and high cheek-boned. He has an encyclopedic knowledge of lifeboats and speaks with a Yarmouth drawl that turns launch to 'larnch' and Caister to 'Cairster'.

Our family has been fishing for three or four generations. In my father's time there were all the drifter fishermen from Caister but there's never been all that much inshore fishing from here. I've never done anything else and my brother hasn't but there aren't many people can say that. Nearly all these others have been deep-sea fishing, then when they got on a bit they'd have a boat on the beach and go longshoring. That's how Winterton was, too. But we do other things besides fishing — I mean we've always been connected with the lifeboats. I've been mechanic in the Institution lifeboat twenty-eight years and I've been in charge of machinery on this private lifeboat since the Institution withdrew. We run a service on our own now. Entirely on our own. Raising money by all sorts of ways. Dances, collections round these holiday camps, selling souvenirs and various people have had walks for us. We had a walk by the ladies from the telephone exchange last wintertime and we're now having a launching tomorrow morning to give them a trip in the boat. They collected us £100.

The Institution withdrew because they didn't think it was any longer necessary to have a lifeboat. But we did. Mainly for the fishing boats. You see one of the arguments was that there's not so many fishing boats as there used to be, so the lifeboats haven't had to help them that amount. But as there've been so many boats, one help the other in. They were all amazed when I said there's *more* need for a lifeboat now there's less fishing. I said if there's only the odd boat or two like, if they get in trouble, there's no one to help. And that have been the case. We've had this summer about six launches with the big boat and twenty-three with the small inshore boat. The first one was given by the school children, the other we bought partly from funds and partly from trading the old one in. And this little boat has brought back about a dozen or fourteen people. Mainly from rubber beds or dinghies that sort of thing.

Since the Norfolk coast had never seen the development of sizeable industry, trade from summer visitors has been the mainstay of those who have not left to try their luck inland. Alf Large once took fishing parties to sea, 'Laddy' Lane has his boats, the Wests their shop in Sheringham, 'Shrimp' and Sam Kerrison's father hired tents. The Woodhouses, too, do their bit of summer trade. Like 'Laddy', they object to its restrictions.

Summertime we do pleasure tripping. We take about twenty-five minute trips. This year I kept in the boat all the time because I had this operation and couldn't do a lot of running and jumping in and out. Very rarely I would get round the beach after passengers but this summer there weren't the job of getting them, the weather was pretty good. So I steered and took the fares and we had another young chap with us. We can take twelve. If you go any bigger you're up against a lot of problems with the Board of Trade. We lose so much time on the beach here when the wind's coming north-east, you get the sea a bit rough. If we hire a big pleasure boat we pay for the licence and insurance, it isn't worth it. Now with these boats you don't lose anything if you don't go out. But us blokes have saved a lot of people in the course of time and we haven't drowned any.

Our people have been the same as we are now — in the lifeboats, salvage work and fishing. My grandfather was coxswain of the lifeboat, his brother took on for about a year when he gave up, and his father was in it. We are carrying on a tradition. That's the same with the fishing. And most of the people we've got in our lifeboat today, their forefathers were just the same. Actually these last three seasons we've amalgamated together with this other chap who's second coxswain of the boat. He has a fish and chip shop summertime and this time of year he fishes. We've got four or.five boats between the lot of us and we use which one would be best. We've one on the beach at Waxham, that's about ten miles along the coast, and we go up there by van. I've got my motor boat and my smaller boat on the beach here and if the herring come in a bit thicker, my brother's now anticipating working out from Yarmouth. Two years back I'd been on holiday down at Walmer in Kent and I was out in the lifeboat when the weather turned nice and fine. I said to the coxswain, 'Soon as ever you get to shore, I'm bound home'. He said, 'Won't you stop and have another night with us?' I said, 'No, there'll be herring at our place'. I came straight home, got my nets ready and went out the next night. We got sixteen boxes of herring but we ain't had anything since.

Some fish are tailing off, some aren't. There've been a big concentration of mackerel down here these last few weeks and three years back there was a lot of cod. We caught more cod than ever we've done before, but the next two years have been practically blank. We go long-lining for cod. Bait the lines in bath tins, old galvanised bath tins. The lines are about quarter inch nylon and we have the hooks about seven foot apart on three-foot snoods. That's the string what the hook is on from the line — it's a Scandinavian word. We coil the lines round in the bath tin and cover up each tier or row of hooks with the marram grass that grows on the beach. That's to protect them and keep them separate. Some people cover with paper and some with sand. We bait perhaps six or seven hundred hooks like that. Baiting with lugworm or mussels for cod, and sometimes when we go fishing for roker we bait with herring. Well, when we get off onto the fishing ground we put the anchor away with the dan-buoy on it and then, as the boat is going along either motoring slow or rowed, we shoot the hooks over with a stick. Sometimes we shoot by hand but mostly with a stick. Throw them over the side, and about every forty or fifty hooks we put another small anchor, about three pound, on. When we're working off Waxham, we put another dan on the other end and come ashore on the beach. Then we go up to the inn at Palling for a couple or three hours, and go and haul the lines back again. When the cod come to the top of the water, we put a dydle in and dydle them out. If you're going to pull them over the side like, you'll lose nine out of ten. Then someone takes the fish off as we haul.

Skate we get October and April time. Then sprats. We never used to go far enough to sea for them. One of the main reasons was that there was so much traffic about where you wanted to go — used to be all these fishing boats. Now up at Waxham you can go to sea and get a clear piece of ground to fish in. They've only had sprats the last two years. The sprats have been about but we couldn't get far enough out to sea. We go about a mile, two mile.

The nave of Palling's stubby pebble church is almost as wide as it is tall, with a ribbed wood ceiling reminiscent of the inside of a crab boat. Propped against the chancel walls are seven large boards commemorating local lifeboat rescues. Dedication to the service, team spirit, exhilaration, sometimes the glamour and sometimes the shared loss, created a tremendous feeling of loyalty in these villages. Caister, too, has a long and distinguished lifeboat record. If her days of fame are tailing out there remains considerable support and enthusiasm for the service. Skipper Woodhouse has always been wrapped up with lifeboats.

We had a lifeboat here under the Norfolk Lifeboat Association from 1841 until 1857, when the RNLI took over. When the Institution withdrew, the records stood at 1,850 lives saved. I joined the crew in 1933 and I'd only missed one service all the time. That was a medal service which I missed because I was away after a new lifeboat at the time. We actually worked here with a beach company until 1941. That was stretched out for various reasons. The last beach yawl went away in 1927 because they wouldn't look at a sailing beach yawl against a motor lifeboat, and they had motor lifeboats at other places. By 1933 there were no sailing lifeboats along east Norfolk, only us. Although they still had them at Brancaster, Wells, Blakeney, Cromer number two, Sheringham, Aldeburgh number two and at Kessingland. Well that's in Suffolk. They're were more left along the Norfolk and Suffolk coast than anywhere practically. Ours was the last lifeboat under sail to rescue from a shipwreck and that was from a minesweeper blown up in the war, 1940. We had a motor one come 1941. Anyway we still carried on the same because we maintained our own look-out and we still worked under beach company regulations. My father was coxswain when the inspector got onto him some years before this, said, 'The committee of management don't like your business of the beach company because we know there's people getting payment for saving life or going out on service and they don't have nothing to do with it'. He said, 'We're anxious to wind it up'. But my father said, 'Look, we're on about having a motor lifeboat — when we get one we'll change things then. I'm not going to get wrong with all them old men who've done this for about fifty or sixty years.' And, of course, when the war came along we got a motor lifeboat and there wasn't no question about it. We had to get soldiers to lend a hand. There were forty belonged to the beach company. I belonged to it. We only had one boat after 1929 and we used to get five shillings a day time call and ten shillings at night time, then the rest was all shared alike. For instance, if that was a day time launch and the money ran out to about a pound each, well then the seventeen crew, they'd get twenty-five shillings. And if that was night time they'd get the thirty shillings.

They were mostly inshore and deep-sea fishermen in the company in years gone by, but the mainstay of the lifeboat crew consisted of fishing-boat owners — the owners of drifters who had been to sea in their young times — and net repairers who might be inshore fishing in the season. They used to engage people who were available to come in the lifeboat just for the fishing season. They'd say, 'Now if we call you out, come down without belonging to the beach company'. Them sort of people were classed as 'outsiders'. They got three-quarters of the share and, if they went out in the boat, the five or ten shillings extra for the trip. That worked out even because there were people belonged to the beach company who hadn't got shares and they could work a widow's share. If a lifeboatman died, his widow could ask a man to work on shares for her. She'd get a quarter and he'd get a three-quarter share, same as the man who was an outsider.

Since I've been going we've had quite a bit of salvaging, on the other hand we've sometimes had some bad deals with these yachts. Most salvage is done on the basis of Lloyd's open form — no cure, no pay. The cases are settled by arbitration in London. But if a ship asks for your assistance and you can connect a tow rope or lay anchors for him, he'll engage you on a contract to get the ship afloat or into safety. Therefore it's on paper to say that you have assisted and that's settled by the solicitors and this shipping broker. Before people could write, perhaps it was done by word. But in them days if they only had one job in a year and they got a hundred pounds for it, if there were forty people involved they wouldn't all be ladies and gentlemen on it. I think it was sometimes the other way round, especially with the Palling people. On the whole, the ship-owners got a lot of valuable cargoes saved by boatmen for very little pay.

There is only one 'full-time' fisherman left between Cromer and Caister. He lives in a thatched stone cottage surrounded by a maze of new brick bungalows at Hemsby, about a mile inland. When he goes fishing he jumps into his van to cover the distance to Hemsby Beach, a pandemonium of postcards, candyfloss and taped pop, calculated to lure summer throngs to a flurry of spending. When he cannot get to sea he can usually be found in his shed standing in a vegetable plot with piles of old herring boxes, dan-buoys, beach combings, and

perhaps fifteen to twenty roughly nailed boards splashed with
white and blue paint propped against a wire fence, advertising
whatever fish he has for sale. Walter Chaney has a reputation
for individuality and for expertise as a fisherman. He is of
medium build, capped and wears, of course, a slop, rubber
boots and old trousers. His weatherbeaten open face is like his
character, outgoing and direct. Happy-go-lucky? It is his
nature, but pressures are making life difficult.

I was salmon fishing one night off Winterton and there was
a damn great splash along the net. Of course we hauled and
this great fish come up. I didn't know what the devil it was.
That looked like a big skate but I'd never seen nothing like it
before. I was just painting my boat for summertime and he
had a rough old skin chafed the paint off. Anyway I grabbed
hold er his tail and we got him aboard. That was a 55-lb
fiddler monkfish. Not an angler monkfish, they're fairly
common, but a fiddler monkfish he's a feller from the
south-west coast of Ireland. He took the wrong turning
somewhere in the Bristol Channel. He was lost. Also I got this
here sunfish, a 92-lb sunfish. Terrific thing. You don't see one
of them every day you know. He was four foot one inch wide,
thirty-nine inches deep and about eight inches through — more
like a turbot. He was in the breakers when I went down there
with my dog one morning. We see him fluttering about and of
course I thought it was a rays bream, you often got one ashore.
Don't pay much attention to them. But when I got hold of
him, it was a sunfish. That was two fish worthy to go on
television. Then there were these three skate we got on one
hook. That was unique. There was a female on the hook, one
about a stone. She was hooked all right so we weren't worried
about her because the water was sheer, you could see her
coming up. Well we're always looking out for two on a hook
because in the spring of the year they're very devoted fish, very
loving. And if the female comes on, the old man'll hang on to
her. He don't want ter lose his bit'er stuff. That's how it is.
Two on a hook has happened to me about twenty times in my
life but this time we got three, one hanging on each wing. We
gaffed one, gaffed the other. Gaffing, that's with a stick two
foot long and a hook on the end. You make sure you get him
with it. We've usually got one each and if we see anything

unusual or think we're going to lose anything we both have a go at it.

Our job is absolutely different from the Wells fishermen and the Cromer fishermen. We go in for shrimps, mackerel, herrings, skate, sea trout, sprats. If there's anything about, fishermen think there's a good living and they're after it. We listen for reports. I'm listening for herring reports at the moment. It's now September the 21st and this is the time of year they might pop out any time. I mean local reports like little boats trying here, trying at Caister, trying at Winterton, trying at Sea Palling. If you hear they've got a few boxes your ears start flapping, you rig out and go and have a look. Last night we got fifteen wonderful sea trout, the biggest weighed nine or ten pound. We got three between seven and ten pound and the rest were all over three pound. Well that's a good night's work. We do that when the weather's fine. That was a super night last night, the moon was out and there wasn't a breath of wind. That's perfect conditions. But we've been out several nights just lately and had just ones or none. Trouble is you get a few boats down there, they all get a few and salmon are such scarce fish. Obviously you thin 'em out. They come from around the river Tweed. I know because I have caught them with tabs on. I once caught two from the Tweed, they were tabbed there together—two small salmon about a foot long and I caught them still together about ten days later. That's a long way to come in ten days isn't it? I caught a spur dogfish that was tabbed on Beachy Head on the south coast. Well that's a long way, too.

We've been a fishing family I can't tell you for how long. My father and my grandfather were all connected with boats and the sea. My father had boats off the beach, longshore boats. I remember one was called *The Gladiator*, and he had one by the name of *The Pinkey*, another one *Maid of Kent*. But they couldn't get a living. I can remember hawking herring for my father after he come ashore. Hawking them at thirty a shilling, well that's a lot of herring for a shilling. My father'd get an order from two people round here who smoked herring and they'd both want about four or five hundred each, so he'd go out on a Saturday night specially to get them at three or four bob a hundred. I remember once carting two thousand herring up the beach on net barrows, helluver hard work it was. We sent them to market and when this old feller paid me out, there was only me and him, he paid me nine pence. That'll be forty or forty-five years ago when I was at school. They weren't worth catching. Even when I started, 1946, herring were two shillings a box and there was about two hundred in a box. If you get herring today they're worth two bob each. That just shows how haywire fishing has gone. The people to blame are the Ministry of Fisheries and Food. They allowed this industrial fishing, trawling for herring with a smallish size mesh, and as they trawl the mesh close up so they get the immature stuff. And they go on all the breeding grounds where the spawn is. I honestly think if they were to stop trawling on these inshore grounds in about three or four years time the sea would be alive with herring. But they just won't let them mature. All the other fish, plaice, salmon and cod, have got a size limit but you can catch a herring any size. They want them for meal and oil, for manure and that sort of thing, and they want quantity. They're not worried one bit about taking them immature. They're doing all right. They get so much a ton and there's not one of them eaten. Every fish I catch is eaten. Everything goes in food.

I've known times when as I've rowed the boat out, the herring have been coming out on the oars, there've been so many in the sea. We daren't take too many nets because if you did you'd be overloaded. You just couldn't carry them and as we've shot our nets I've seen them sinking because they've been so full of fish. I was working for Daimler at Coventry six years because you couldn't think of getting a living with herring at two bob a box and skate about thru'pence each. Nobody could. It's only recently, since the price has gone up, that you could hold your own. If the fish had kept like they were and the price was like it is now, I'd be a millionaire. Because if I could see the heap of fish I've caught in my time that'd be high as a church I should think.

All my nets today are roughly thirty yards long and about nine score deep. I mean they're nine score mesh deep, that's a hundred and eighty meshes, and a mesh is roughly a square inch. I've got three fleets, one for springers, young herring — they're a bit thin so the mesh is forty to the yard. Then when they grow a little we put in 39's to the yard. I've 36's, 38's, 39's and 40's. I usually carry about twenty-eight nets, so that's about 840 yards all leened together. We don't have a foot rope on the bottom, that's not necessary. Just plain lints. If you're in six or seven fathoms you want some good deep nets to fish properly. We fish day and night depending on the colour of the water. I've caught loads of herring during the day when you've got a nice sort of milky brown, we call it milky water. That's after a good north-west gale. North-west gales this time er year are the best thing for herring. It stirs the water up and puts the plankton, the food, in, so if there's any herring around they'll stop. If the water's sheer, well they might come in for two or three nights but there's no food in it and away they go again. You honestly want a good old northerly bust-up. Blow like hell and then you stand a chance.

When there's a lot of herring about there's always a lot of gulls. That's a good sign when you see the big old herring gulls with the big old yellow beaks and about a yard span of wing, not these little kittiwakes. You see them sitting on the beach, hundreds of them together and you think to yourself, cor blast, there's some herring about. I remember one old fisherman who's dead and gone now, poor fellow, his name was Charlie Shields. He came longshoring with me one year. He'd look over the side of the boat and he say to me, 'Walter, can you see all the oily beads near the boat?' I'd look over the side and say 'Hell if I can see anything Charlie — don't know what you mean'. Then he'd say, 'Look, look! All the oil come from the herring'. And, mind you, when we hauled we'd have a boatload. They always used to say herring oiled the sea up. We'd see slakes, we called 'em, on the sea. Instead of being dark, there'd be all light patches and we thought that was a good sign. Among a boatload of herring you might get one as red as red, as if that's bloodshot. I don't know why. I suppose he'd been damaged. There was one old fisherman who'd say, 'Look there, that's a king herring! Hull that away quick or you won't have no more'. That'd be laying in the boat as dead as a doornail but he'd say 'Hull that away' because he thought if you'd got the king herring there wouldn't be no more. Some of them had a lot of superstitions. Didn't worry me.

Inshore herring are as different from the deep-sea variety as chalk from cheese. I do a few kippers when I've got some good old October herring. You haven't tasted a kipper until you've tasted one of mine. I don't do many, I don't sell none, only a few for myself. I've got a little old smokehouse up the garden and when I get half a box I say to myself, 'Coo, lovely grub, I'll just go and smoke them'. I might do about half kippers and half bloaters. A red herring is brined — I haven't done any reds because I'd rather have bloaters and kippers — but a red herring has to be smoked for several days and salted a lot so he'll keep 'til Christmas. You need about a gallon of water at the same time when you eat a red herring, he's that sort of fish, but years ago they used to do a terrific lot of them so they'd eat them all winter. Nearly all the fishermen had big families and that was the idea, if they could live on red herring, that was cheap. But kippers and bloaters, cor they're out of this world! Years ago when you were catching a lot, you never had time to cure them, but if I could get enough today I'd make a bomb. I'd bloater 'em and kipper 'em all in lovely oak logs. There's not many people know how to salt them. You've got to salt for so many minutes. But I dussen't tell you how many. I wouldn't tell anybody, not how I do my shrimps even. Shrimps I do sell a lot, see. Hundreds of pints. I sell everything at the door unless we happen to get a lot of sprats. I skinned out seventy-three skate the other day, stood in the yard and as I skinned them people came and bought them. That's the way to buy your fish, you can't go wrong. People come and fill up their deep freeze when they've got the chance.

When my father went to sea I was only a boy but it was a fishing family and all my brothers go to sea part-time. One owns so many shops he can't keep count. Six or seven big ones, so he's the rich brother. But soon as he's finished he'll be on the beach. He loves the sea. Last night I was out with my nephew. I was on the beach and he was in the boat all night. I held the net close into the beach and I had a couple of salmon hit within a couple of yards of me. I whipped them out on the beach before the seals got them. So I was up all last night and I've been on the beach all this morning. Now it's three o'clock, look I hain't been to sleep yet but I'll be away again tonight. I've now done thirty years full time. I'm self-employed, me own boss and I haven't got a worry in the world except we get bad spells, very bad.

The hardest job today is getting a mate. You just can't get them. Anybody who want to work, they can get £30, £40, £50 a week in the Bingo, just calling out the numbers. But this fishing lark you just can't earn that sort of money unless you have a good spell.

We're just finishing the salmon up, then we shall lay some more lines and do a bit of shrimping. We tow two twelve-foot nets, one on each side, twenty-four foot span when we're doing it properly, but there's not many about now. They've been very scarce. They should come out again now the wind's got westerly a bit. After that sprats. They can be ever so good or they can be nothing. They do a lot of spratting up at Shields, put out miles and miles of nets up there and if they stop the lot, I can't see anything's going to get down this way. They're on passage, like herring. They come from the north and when they've had their time here, away they go. We're standing by now. I've got all my nets packed up ready. There's three or four thousand pounds worth of gear in here. I've got nets for everything. All nylon, the best gear you can possibly buy. I've always bought the best. I think I've got near enough gear to last me out. I'm sixty now, so there's another five years before I retire. I think the pension will be £30 a week and we can manage on that. I've got a nice little home, the little old thatched cottage, a lovely daughter and a lovely dog, a little Jack Russell. I've been in that cottage thirty years, I never want to move. I was born close by. See there's three cottages along here, I was born this end. My father had that donkey's years, then he was bombed during the war so we brought a hut off the beach, shoved it up and he lived in that until he died. No running water, no mod cons. When my father died it went up for sale, so I snapped hold of it for the gear.

I know most of the birds, I'm sure I do. I often watch them through binoculars. I know the oyster catcher, the cormorants, the guillemots, razor-bills, a cooter duck and a velvet skooter. You don't know a velvet skooter do you? I'll tell you a true story. We were going out herring catching one day when all of a sudden there was a little bird come towards me. That was a skylark . . . anyway he just couldn't make the beach and he couldn't make us. All of a sudden he dipped and went into the sea. Poor little bird he was so fatigued. I passed him about 100 yards then I turned my boat round to go and pick the poor feller up. I got hold of him and dried his little feathers. He'd just about had it. So I put him in the cupboard up the front where I thought it was a bit warmer. We went and shot our nets and do you know, that particular day we got so many herring that we had a damn job to carry them. I think we had 13 cran and that's a lot for a little boat. I always remember going to that cupboard. When I opened the door this here little bird come out with such force I had to move back. He'd revived so much that he went bre, bre, as if to say thank you and away he go. I think that the Lord up above, I think he was looking. Don't you?

When we shoot a net we say 'We shoot these in the name of the Lord'. Always. Always. When we bring them in — that's too late then. But we always thank the Lord, you know. We've been brought up in the Primitive Methodist chapel. My father weren't so much a chapel goer, but my mother was. Cor, she never missed going. When we were young we had to go three times a day and if we wouldn't go, Mother'd take us down, crying and howling, open the door and shove us in.

If the sea is fine on a Sunday we have to go. That's the best market, Monday morning. I'm fishing all the time. Either working up here on my gear or out fishing. There's always something to do because we're spoiling nets. You've got to keep them up to scratch. If you don't fish with good gear you might as well pack up. Once we caught a wreck on the bottom of the sea with our salmon nets. That was our fault, we knew there was a wreck there and we misjudged it a little, or my mate did. He should ha' hauled about fifty or sixty yards of net. Well, he only hauled about forty and of course it got a bit spoilt. That's what do happen. We don't go out more'n about five or six mile, that's all, but we know all the depths and all the best grounds for fishing.

I like my missus at home, I do. My wife has never been out to work ever since I've been married. She come and help me. If I want to go to sea tomorrow and I hain't got a mate, my missus'll come and push me out. She won't come fishing, but she might come for a trip. I dare take her anywhere, she's a good sailor. Then I'll say I might be ashore so and so time, and she'll be down there to pull me in. It's a big boat, I can't get it in on my own and sometimes you're short of a crew.

There weren't many people fishing here in my father's time. There were two or three busloads deep-sea herring fishing off Winterton in the drifters, but there would only have been about ten or a dozen longshoring. Now Winterton is a noted place for fishermen. It's built on Winterton Ness, which is a tideway. The tide is always on the churn-up so there's a nice lot of salmon and a nice lot of herring. There's none about to come now, but they would if they was about. There's no full-time fishermen at Winterton now, just three or four part-timers and two or three part-timers at Hemsby. You can go out today with an outboard on, you can take a couple of hundred worms and come back with hardly anything. Many a time I've taken out thirty nets, hauled the lot and not a fish. With the herring so scarce the seals are so numerous. My good God, when we're after herring there's always thirty or forty around all the time. I carry a .22 rifle with me, I've got a police permit and I take it every time. Have to or I wouldn't stand a chance in hell. We've got Scroby Island about two mile off Caister and there's about eight or nine hundred seals on there. When they're hungry they come down here. Imagine getting a nice eight or nine pound salmon in your nets and then a blasted seal come and whip that out. It happen all the time. It should be kept in perspective so the animal lovers have some and the fisherman is protected.

I saw a boat the other day come ashore. He was out all day for three dabs. Well I say there's no sport in catching nothing. I like fishing but if I'm catching no fish there's just nothing to it.

BIBLIOGRAPHY

Adams, W.M. *Popular History of Fisheries & Fishermen of all Countries*, 1883
Aflalo, F.G. *Sea Fishing Industry of England & Wales*, 1904
Agriculture, Fisheries & Food, Ministry of: Laboratory Leaflets, 1966–73
Bartell, E. *Cromer*, 1806
Bertram, J.G. *Harvest of the Sea*, 1865
Bertram, J.G. *Unappreciated Fisher Folk*, 1883
Buckland, F. *Report on the Fisheries of Norfolk*, 1875
Campbell Erroll, A. *A History of Sheringham and Beaston Regis*, 1970
Chamber, J. *History of Norfolk*, 1829
Clark, R. *The Longshoremen*, 1974 (Newton Abbot)
Dutt, W.A. *The Norfolk & Suffolk Coast*, 1909
Eastern Sea Fisheries. *Annual Reports*, 1890s–1975
Edinburgh, Duke of. *Notes on the Sea Fisheries & Fishing Population on the United Kingdom*, 1883
Ewart Evans, G. *Where Beards Wag All*, 1970
Fraser, R. *Review of the Domestic Fisheries of Great Britain & Ireland*, 1818
Hakluyt, R. *Principal Voyages of the English Nation*, 1589
Jolly, C. *Henry Blogg of Cromer*, 1958, reprinted 1972
Levi, L. *Economic Condition of Fishermen*, 1883
Malster, R. (ed) *East Coast Mariner/Norfolk Sailor*, 1960–70
Malster, R. *Saved from the Sea*, 1974
March, Edgar J. *Inshore Craft of Britain in the Days of Sail and Oar*, 1970 (Newton Abbot)
Piggott, E. *Recollections of —*. Ed Blanche Piggott, 1890
Purchas, A.W. 'Wells next the Sea'. *East Anglian Magazine*, 1965
Rye, W. *History of Norfolk*, 1885
Simper, R. *East Coast Sail: Working Sail 1850-1970*, 1972 (Newton Abbot)
Stibbons, J.R. *Shannocks & Crabbing*, 1975
Wenham Strugnell, K. *Sea Gates to the Saxon Shore*, 1973
Wilcocks, J.C. *Sea-Fisherman*, 1875

ACKNOWLEDGEMENTS

Besides the fishermen and their wives who have contributed, often after a long day's work, I would like to thank all those who have put up with my endless questions. Mr Stan Craske of Sheringham and Mr Laurie Jones of Brancaster for their unflagging interest and help. Mr George Death, Mr Michael Softley, Mrs. Freddy and Cyril Southerland, also of Brancaster, Mr Alf Powditch, and Mr Diddy Cooper of Wells, and Mr Teddy Craske of Sheringham. Mr H.K. Pegg, Fishery Officer, for the contacts he suggested and Mr Ned Thompson for first telling me about the whelk fishermen. I owe a debt also to Mr J. R. Aldous, Clerk and Chief Fishery Officer of the Eastern Sea Fisheries Joint Committee, for some pertinent ideas, Mr T. Upcher for the loan of a family album, Mr R. Malster for encouragement in the book's early stages and the local section of Norwich Library for supplying me with books. *The Countryman* and *Country Gentleman's Magazine* printed small parts of the manuscript before it was expanded into a book.

SALLY FESTING

INDEX